WINGED SENTINELS
Birds and climate change

*The ability of the birds to show us the consequences of our own actions is among
their most important and least appreciated attributes. Despite the free advice of
the birds, we do not pay attention.*

Marjory Stoneman Douglas, 1947

From ice-dependent penguins of Antarctica to songbirds that migrate across
the Sahara, birds' responses provide early warning signs of the impact of
climate change. *Winged Sentinels: Birds and climate change* uses colourful
examples to show how particular groups of birds face heightened threats
from climate change, and to explore how we can help birds adapt in a
warming world. Generously illustrated with colour photographs, the book
is a fascinating insight into what climate change means for birds, and the
potential consequences of ignoring these warning signs.

Janice Wormworth is a freelance science writer.

Çağan H. Şekercioğlu is Assistant Professor in the Department of Biology
at the University of Utah and the director of the non-profit environmental
organisation KuzeyDoğa (www.kuzeydoga.org).

WINGED SENTINELS

Birds and climate change

Janice Wormworth

Çağan Şekercioğlu

CAMBRIDGE UNIVERSITY PRESS

3/28/12
ww
$ 40—

CAMBRIDGE UNIVERSITY PRESS
Cambridge, New York, Melbourne, Madrid, Cape Town,
Singapore, São Paulo, Delhi, Tokyo, Mexico City

Cambridge University Press
477 Williamstown Road, Port Melbourne, VIC 3207, Australia

Published in the United States of America by Cambridge University Press, New York

www.cambridge.org
Information on this title: www.cambridge.org/9780521126823

First published 2011

Cover design by Adrian Saunders.
Typeset by Aptara Corp.
Printed in China by C&C Offset Printing Co. Ltd.

A catalogue record for this publication is available from the British Library

National Library of Australia Cataloguing in Publication data
    Wormworth, Janice
    Winged sentinels : birds and climate change / Janice
    Wormworth ; Çağan Şekercioğlu.
    9780521126823 (pbk.)
    Includes index.
    Birds – Climatic factors.
    Climatic changes – Environmental aspects.
    Sekercioglu, Cagan.
598.172

ISBN 978-0-521-12682-3 Paperback

Dedicated to Stephen Schneider: brilliant scientist, great communicator, and world birder.

CONTENTS

ACKNOWLEDGEMENTS

The authors would like to thank the many people, too numerous to list here, who provided valuable input that improved this book. We would especially like to thank Franz Bairlein for his review of the entire work, and Peter Dunn, Barend Erasmus, Lee Hannah, Esa Lehikoinen, Luke Shoo, Rob Simmons and Lochran Traill for reviewing chapters.

Çağan Şekercioğlu thanks the Christensen Fund, Conservation Leadership Programme, Mohamed bin Zayed Species Conservation Fund, National Geographic Society, United Nations Development Programme, Whitley Fund, Wildlife Conservation Society, Peter Bing and Walter Loewenstern, Kafkas University, Stanford University and the University of Utah for supporting his bird research and conservation efforts.

INTRODUCTION: THE FREE ADVICE OF BIRDS

Rockhopper numbers drop off cliff

The ability of the birds to show us the consequences of our own actions is among their most important and least appreciated attributes. Despite the free advice of the birds, we do not pay attention.

Marjory Stoneman Douglas, 1947

In the world's southern oceans, the declining fortunes of a small penguin hint at a profound and widespread change in its environment. Ocean warming is suspected but many questions remain, in part because it is not easy to study southern rockhopper penguins, *Eudyptes chrysocome*. Getting to their remote colonies, like those on Campbell Island, is costly and logistically challenging. Then there is the subantarctic weather. Storm-force winds routinely blast the island, and rain and drizzle drench it most days of the year.

Arriving at a rockhopper colony, one finds hundreds or thousands of incubating birds, packed cheek by jowl, just beyond pecking distance of each other. Others jump along steep, rocky slopes, intent on their daily commutes between nest and ocean. This penguin's reputation as one of the most aggressive penguins tallies with its appearance: red eyes, black head feathers evocative of a punk rock singer, and yellow eyebrows ending in plumes that fly in a golden halo when it shakes its head to attract a mate. When a human visitor passes amongst them, rockhoppers slowly rotate on their nests, hundreds of eyes fixed on the interloper. If one should approach too closely, an incubating bird will attack. Though standing well short of a human knee it will nip the intruder's legs with its beak and batter them with a tattoo of its sharp flippers. 'If you pick them up, they go bananas,' says marine biologist David Thompson of New Zealand's National Institute of Water and Atmospheric Research, who has studied these seabirds.

Southern rockhoppers' pugnacity and jostling, frenetic colonies belie their huge population declines over the past century. A colonial lifestyle means worsening conditions at one colony can affect tens of thousands of birds. Numbers at the Falkland Islands, for example, plummeted from 1.5 million pairs in the 1930s to 210 418 pairs in 2007, an 86 per cent decline. The global population is now estimated at between half a million and one million adults. While this may appear a large number in absolute terms, the International Union for the Conservation of Nature (IUCN) has listed the southern rockhopper as vulnerable to extinction because its long decline has apparently worsened in recent years. Threats may vary from colony to colony, but include fishing, oil exploration, introduced predators and disturbance from ecotourism. However, some other quite profound change is suspected to have happened in the wider marine environment, where penguins forage, to help southern rockhopper numbers to nosedive.

John H. Sorensen probably never expected that his off-duty passion for birdwatching would help identify a new rockhopper threat. During World War II, Sorensen was posted to Campbell Island as part of a highly secret force of New Zealanders and given the task of looking out for enemy ships that might attempt an occupation. In his spare time, he photographed and studied the island's wildlife, making meticulous notes (he went on to become a noted ornithologist).

Half a century later, Sorensen's information, along with other similar records from the island, was used to bolster more recent observations and demonstrate how Campbell Island's southern rockhopper colonies plummeted from 1.6 million to 103 000 breeding birds between 1942 and 1985.[1] With no evidence for land-based causes, warming ocean conditions were suspected. Numbers declined most during a period of substantial summer warming of the ocean's surface, and one colony's numbers temporarily increased after seas temporarily cooled.

This effect was suspected to occur via changes in rockhoppers' ocean prey, but a lack of long-term records on the seabirds' food supplies made this difficult to show. This time, researchers turned to museums to help fill in the gaps. By analysing isotopes in the feathers of rockhopper specimens, along with those of living birds, they reconstructed the seabirds' diets over time. The story advanced. Though their results were still not conclusive, what researchers found suggests insufficient food for the penguins in recent decades, in a marine ecosystem that has become less productive. In New Zealand's subantarctic, this downwards trend in marine productivity coincided with the start of the rockhopper's decline.[2]

Although climate-change effects on their marine food supplies (krill, squid, octopus and fish) are strongly suspected to contribute to this penguin's decline, the mechanisms are not yet fully understood. Apart from the penguins themselves, there is nothing obvious to measure above the ocean's surface, to which changing ocean temperatures can be linked. New research planned for Campbell Island could help fill more gaps in the southern rockhopper puzzle.

As avian instigators of scientific inquiry, southern rockhoppers are hardly unique. Birds have long prompted us to ask, and helped us to illuminate, nature's big questions. Consider Hawaiian honeycreepers. Their spectacular adaptive radiation, from a single ancestral finch to dozens of honeycreeper species that fill virtually every Hawaiian songbird niche, is a spectacular natural experiment in evolution and island biogeography. Or take bar-tailed godwits, *Limosa lapponica baueri*, whose 10 000-kilometre transoceanic journeys may entail nine-day flights completed without once stopping for food, water or rest. This feat challenges preconceptions about birds' physiological capabilities and raises new questions about animal energetics.

Birds are also sentinels, the quintessential 'canaries in the coal mine' of dangerous environmental change. Highly visible, mobile and reactive to changes in climate, they are among key indicators of global warming. Even if we were oblivious to the present changes in Earth's climate, a careful look at birds' patterns of responses over recent decades would warn us that some sort of widespread and systematic change is afoot.[3]

Prime witnesses to climate change, birds can also serve as proxies to illuminate the wider impacts of this new threat for wildlife. Migratory birds could reveal much as they travel between far-flung regions, assembling and combining information on their diverse habitats. Seabirds, like sooty shearwaters whose annual odysseys embrace the entire Pacific, provide tangible links to unfathomable ocean ecosystems. Antarctic penguins are highly responsive to changes in sea ice, and can relay information about the state of the cryosphere.[4] In essence, birds can be seen as flying (and swimming and walking) data collectors that reveal the health of diverse ecosystems they use.

Colourful, vocal and charismatic, birds hold a special place in our hearts, minds and myths. These qualities may also explain birds' status as the best-studied major group of animals. Ornithological studies of weather effects on population biology span more than 50 years, and some continuous records gathered by birdwatchers stretch back more than two centuries. Each year, birds are tracked across the globe by a multi-million-strong army of birdwatchers.

Taking the global avian pulse

Before delving into the ramifications of the relatively new climate-change threat, let us first ask how birds are weathering other, longstanding human threats. Human contact most likely led to many unrecorded bird extinctions, as species were lost before their discovery by science.[5] Polynesians' first contact with islands across the Pacific, for example, may have caused extinctions on the order of 1000 bird species. Since 1500, a total of 153 bird species are definitively known to have gone extinct.[6] Yet population levels are falling even more rapidly than this extinction rate would suggest; global bird abundance dropped by as much as a quarter over this same period.[7]

Today, roughly one in eight (1244) bird species face the threat of global extinction from wide-ranging impacts, with habitat destruction being the most serious present-day hazard. Not just rare birds, but common species – familiar due to their abundance – are declining. In fact, birds' conservation status has steadily deteriorated since the first global assessment in 1988, with birds in Oceania and seabirds declining fastest over this period. More recently, sharp declines have been driven by forest destruction in Asia. Tallies of risk to birds, however, have barely begun to account for the emerging threat of climate change.

Any new threat to birds should concern us, because their existence is very much intertwined with our own. Nearly half (46 per cent) of the world's almost 10 000 bird species are directly used by people in some way, mostly as pets or hunted for food or sport. Uses may be as esoteric as the sky burial services provided by vultures for Tibetan Buddhists or Indian Parsees (a service diminished in the Parsee case due to the recent radical decline of some vulture species), or as mundane as the use of guano for fertiliser. In Peru, where climate conditions allowed guano to accumulate over millennia at seabird colonies, 'mining' it became the greatest national revenue source for more than a century.

Birds are also critical 'mobile links', ecological actors that connect disparate habitats in time and space. From penguins pursuing ocean prey to depths of hundreds of metres to tiny hummingbirds whirring through tropical forests to pollinate bromeliads, birds possess an astonishing diversity of ecological function, unsurpassed among vertebrates. Their ecological activities benefit humans in myriad indirect but important ways. Of these so-called ecosystem services, seed dispersal is probably paramount. The seeds of more than half of Costa Rica's tree and shrub species are dispersed by birds. Birds also pollinate plants, including dozens of species of crops, and eat harmful insects.[8] In economically valuable forests, for example, birds' services may be worth US$1820 per square kilometre per year, based on the cost of replacing them with insecticides to counter western spruce budworm, *Choristoneura occidentalis*.

Scavenging birds like vultures probably do not receive enough credit for efficiently disposing of dead animals. Seabirds are increasingly appreciated as chemical and physical engineers that can shape entire ecosystems. The new volcanic island of Surtsey, Iceland erupted from the sea in 1963, but its vegetation developed best after gulls settled there in 1985. They brought seeds and organisms on their feet and in nesting materials, and ocean nutrients in their faeces, setting off a veritable explosion of plants, lichen, fungus and invertebrates around their colony.

The dawn of the 'Anthropocene' and high-velocity change

But how do these mobile ecological actors respond to changes in climate? Change has been a feature of Earth's climate over the evolutionary history of today's bird species. In what is now England, hippopotami, straight-tusked elephants and spotted hyenas roamed the landscape 130 000 years ago, when the climate was warmer than during the mid 20th century. Over the last two million years, life on Earth has repeatedly endured periods 5°C colder than the middle of last century, causing ice sheets to expand and sea levels to drop by 100 metres or more.

Yet the past 11 000 years, following the end of the last major glacial epoch and the start of the Holocene (Greek for 'entirely new') epoch, has been an unusually warm and stable period compared to the previous 400 000 years. Humans thrived under this climate stability. Our ancestors learned to domesticate animals, grow crops and transform their energy use from mainly firewood and muscle power to coal, then oil and other fossil fuels.

Burgeoning human populations have denuded and eroded continents and greatly accelerated extinctions and population declines. And as fossil fuels were burned, concentrations of carbon dioxide in the atmosphere rose from pre-industrial levels of about 280 ppm (parts per million) to 390 ppm in 2010. These and other profound changes characterising humans' influence after the Industrial Revolution, some argue, will leave a signal in geological strata so distinct it will be recognisable as a separate epoch, according to formal definition. Thus we humans have ushered in a new epoch of global environmental change of our own making, dubbed the Anthropocene (Greek for 'human' and 'new').[9]

Just as we understand the workings of gravity and tides, the heat-trapping potential of carbon dioxide[10] is also well known. Swedish physicist Svante Arrhenius predicted in 1895 that marked increases or decreases in carbon dioxide abundance would be associated with glacial retreats and advances. In fact, this greenhouse effect is what makes Earth's climate hospitable to life in the first place. Without it, the average temperature on the planet would be an estimated 34°C colder than today, an arctic −19°C. Yet to find periods with concentrations of greenhouse gases equivalent to today's, one must travel back in time two or three million, and possibly even 15 million years.[11]

Over the past century, the global average temperature rose 0.76°C,[12] with the amount of warming being greater over the past 50 years. From the 1980s onwards, each decade has been much warmer than that prior, with the 2000–2009 period being the hottest on record. The Intergovernmental Panel on Climate Change (IPCC) has found global warming to be 'unequivocal', and places an over 90 per cent probability on human activity as its primary cause. Greenhouse gas emissions, mainly from burning fossil fuels including coal, oil and gas, and from clearing of natural vegetation, are the most important drivers of global warming.

Where will the Anthropocene take our global climate? The best estimates point to further global warming of 1.8–4.0°C by 2100 unless new climate policies are put into action to curtail emissions. (This best estimate range reflects the centre point of the lowest and highest IPCC 2007 emissions scenarios, but the full range of projected temperature increase for these scenarios is 1.1–6.4°C.) Yet some climate modelling suggests that even an unimaginable 11°C of warming may be possible under a worst-case scenario.[13] Precipitation patterns are also expected to be altered by climate change. Sea levels will keep rising, sea ice will continue to diminish, and ocean acidification will continue. The warming taking place now is not without precedent in the Earth's history. However, the extent of change expected in the future will probably be beyond what most of today's fauna experienced during their evolution. What is more, the pace of climate change is extremely rapid.

Another feature of climate change is more frequent and severe episodes of extreme weather. This prospect cautions us that the journey to a warmer world may not be a smooth and gradual transition, but instead a bumpy ride punctuated by extremes and 'surprises'. We need be concerned not only about cyclones, heatwaves and droughts, but also about tipping points, for when it comes to Earth's climate, small changes can lead to large changes (chapter 7).

Examining 'fingerprints' to unmask the climate-change threat

In the chapters of this book, the 'fingerprints' of climate change reveal how the living world is responding to global warming. These fingerprints distinguish human-induced climate change from natural background variation. They are discernable not only in biological records, but in those from the oceans and atmosphere as well. Importantly, these signals reveal that birds and other wildlife are already responding to climate change. They also hint at whether birds might adapt, or lag in their responses to climate change in ways that put them at risk.

One of the clearest and most powerful fingerprints is emerging as birds and other organisms shift the timing of seasonal activities. Choosing when to breed (chapter 1) or migrate (chapter 2) can be crucial decisions, and these events are now taking place earlier among many birds. Importantly, warming may not affect plants, insects and other key elements of birds' natural communities at the same rate or to the same degree, a point with important implications for ecology.

Another key fingerprint is discernable in the shifting distributions of birds and other organisms (chapter 3). Yet as they respond to climate change, birds, plants and other constituent parts of ecosystems are likely to disperse at varying rates, distances and even different directions. Their disparate responses could also tug at the ties that bind ecological communities. Breeding seabirds provide iconic examples of the potential problems this may cause (chapter 4).

Changes in the abundance of birds and to the make-up of their communities are other fingerprints of climate change (chapter 5). In some cases, population declines driven by climate change could be severe enough to cause extinctions. This extinction threat to the birds of 'habitat islands', especially in the tropics, is the focus of chapter 6. How birds may cope with climate change, and how conservation efforts might facilitate this, is the focus of chapter 7. The repercussions for birds of humanity's own planned and unplanned responses to climate change are also explored in chapter 7.

In closing this introduction, the authors wish to clarify that this book's goal is not to exhaustively cover all positive and negative effects of climate change on birds. Although some bird species will undoubtedly thrive in a warmer world, this book is more concerned with those that may not for, as the late Stephen Schneider once quipped, 'extinction is a one-way filter'. The greater focus of this book on matters of conservation also recognises that climate indicators are tracking at or above the high end of IPCC predictions. In summary, this book's bias towards threatening processes and vulnerable species is motivated by the concern that climate change could extinguish unique forms of birdlife, a foreboding harbinger of the future that awaits humanity on a rapidly warming planet.

Chapter I

PHENOLOGY: SEASONAL TIMING AND MISMATCH

The new significance of phenology

A harmless pastime illuminates a present danger

... birds fly with song and glancing plumage, and plants spring and bloom, and winds blow, to correct this slight oscillation of the poles and preserve the equilibrium of Nature.

Henry David Thoreau, 1854

The meticulous notes of yesteryear's naturalists are helping today's scientists bolster one of the most powerful demonstrations of climate-change effects on the living world. In 1841, when Henry David Thoreau was strengthening his resolve to live alone in the woods, he wrote in his journal, 'But my friends ask what I will do when I get there.' Thoreau answered with his own question, 'Will it not be employment enough to watch the progress of the seasons?'

Observations echoing this simple and timeless desire are found in his book, *Walden*, a record of life in his one-room cabin at Walden Pond near Concord, Massachusetts. 'I was startled by the loud honking of a goose,' he wrote of one early winter night, 'and, stepping to the door, heard the sound of their wings like a tempest in the woods as they flew low over my house.' Yet Thoreau's observations on seasonal change went beyond mere poetic musings. 'I take infinite pains to know all of the phenomena of the spring,' he wrote in his journal in 1856. His detailed records, jotted down in tables drawn on large sheets of surveyor's paper, are now proving invaluable to efforts to document the biological response to climate change.

Thoreau's observations follow a long tradition known as phenology (from the Greek *phainomai*, 'to appear'), perhaps as ancient as the origins of farming. Today, a renaissance in phenology is being driven by the imperative to understand the effects of climate change on the living world.

Broadly speaking, phenology is the study of the timing of plant and animal life-cycle events or phases in relation to climate: the budburst and flowering of plants, the emergence of insects, and the arrival, nesting, egg laying and departure of birds.[1] The timing of these seasonal events is critical, affecting many aspects of ecology including competition between species and their interactions with prey, pests and diseases. The phenology of plants may even feed back and influence climate, via changes to the temperature and humidity of land surfaces, and less directly through plants' uptake of carbon.

The term 'phenology' was coined by the Belgian botanist Charles Morren in 1853, but the earliest signs of phenological accounts stretch back to the great Mediterranean civilisations and Asia. Records for cherry tree flowering in Japan have continued unbroken since the ninth century AD. More of an art until medieval times, the study of phenology was truly galvanised as a science in the 18th century, when Swedish naturalist Carl Linnaeus created the first reported international phenological network.[2]

Like Thoreau, who was a poet and slavery abolitionist, many intriguing characters have embraced phenology over time. Robert Marsham, another passionate naturalist, began meticulous recordings of 27 'Indications of Spring' on his Norfolk estate in 1736. His descendants continued this tradition until 1958, creating the United Kingdom's longest phenological record. For Parisian academic René-Antoine Ferchault de Réaumur, phenology helped unlock nature's mysterious workings. In the 1730s he discovered that plants flower when summed temperatures from over previous months reach a certain value. Phenological forecasts based on weather trends, and phenological maps indicating the expected beginning of spring, had agricultural and economic utility in past centuries. In modern times, however, scientific interest in phenology waned.

A powerful indicator of climate change

With climate change, 'the scientific community's view of phenology as a harmless pastime of natural historians has changed dramatically ...'.[3] Phenology is believed to be the most responsive aspect of nature to climate change. Global warming, by driving changes in phenology, could produce wide-ranging consequences, not just for birds but also for agriculture, forestry, human health and even the global economy.[4] Yet phenology is also important because it provides powerful evidence for the living world's response to global warming. (Other climate-change impacts, such as population effects or changes in community composition, are more difficult and costly to detect.)

This new era of phenological research explores the importance of time as a constraint on wildlife; how species cope with this constraint under climate change may indicate their ability to survive and persist. Birds hold a prominent place in this inquiry because they are highly visible and relatively easy to observe. Despite its important and evolving role in climate-change research, phenology is still not a well-understood ecological science. The considerable attention now devoted to this field could remedy that, and birds' responses are expected to help illuminate the mechanisms driving changes in phenology.[5]

At the same time, the scarcity of long-term records on seasonal timing lends new importance to the meticulous notes of yesteryear's naturalists. Thoreau's writings have allowed Boston University researchers, led by Richard Primack, to show that plants around the site of his famous cabin now flower a week earlier than during the mid-19th century.[6] And Marsham's phenological records have allowed UK scientists to demonstrate birds' earlier arrival in warmer springs, showing their responsiveness to temperature change. 'I believe these old records are invaluable,' says environmental scientist Tim Sparks of Poznań University of Life Sciences, 'We simply don't have the luxury of starting to collect data from now to see what effects the changing climate has.'

This phenological renaissance is also being bolstered by modern-day Thoreaus in their thousands. Observing seasonal change is popular with the public and easily communicated by the media, making 'citizen scientists' an indispensable and fast-growing source of data for the vast phenological networks now used to monitor global warming and other environmental change (chapter 7).

Understanding the annual cycles of birds

Timing is everything

Ultimately, the constraints imposed by the changing seasons – long and short days, heat and frost, monsoon and drought – orchestrate the ebb and flow of life over the year. Optimal conditions to breed and raise young may prevail only briefly, as in temperate regions during summer. It is important to have an understanding of the mechanisms that drive birds' annual programs and synchronise these with seasonal changes, because this could help reveal whether or not birds' seasonal timing will keep pace with climate change. These control mechanisms may also suggest whether birds will cope if they fall out of step with conditions in their environment.

The key activities in birds' annual cycles – breeding, moulting and (for some) migration – all impose energetic demands and constraints. These stages have evolved to take place at an optimum point in the year, synchronised with cycles of food, warmth and precipitation, to help birds endure and benefit from seasonal change. Each major activity is generally best separated from another in time, or occurs with minimal overlap.[7] However, overlap in breeding and moult is hard to avoid for some birds such as Arctic-nesting species with a short breeding season. Birds may also differ greatly in the extent to which they can flexibly sequence events, such as breeding, in their annual cycles. Depending on the species, breeding may be predictable, variable or opportunistic. Because these differences between species are substantial, it is impossible to generalise about birds' annual cycles.

Birds' capacity to cope with changing environmental conditions is shaped by phenotypic plasticity, which is the ability of an individual to change its physiology, morphology or behaviour (its phenotype) in response to environmental conditions. One demonstration of this plasticity is the ability of many birds to adjust the seasonal timing of life-cycle stages to cope with short-term changes, such as natural year-to-year variation in spring temperatures.

Rhythms and cues

How are birds able to prepare themselves for seasonal changes? Even when kept captive under controlled and constant conditions, devoid of external cues such as daylight changes and other seasonal variation, many birds display persistent natural rhythms. They moult, progress through the gonadal development that accompanies breeding condition, and undergo the weight changes and restlessness that typify migratory condition. Remarkably, in some species these cycles can apparently run for an entire life span with no influence at all from the outside environment. One male African stonechat, *Saxicola torquata auxillaris*, completed 12 such free-running natural cycles over a span of 10 years when kept under these constant conditions.[8]

Demonstrated experimentally in more than 20 bird species, these self-sustaining rhythms are thought to be under genetic influence. Such circ-annual rhythms (from Latin, *circa* meaning 'about' and *annus* meaning 'year') are thought to be strongest in long-distance migratory birds. Along their migratory routes, many such birds would experience different patterns of photoperiod; they would therefore be expected to be among those species most in need of endogenous control. Spontaneous endogenous rhythms are also seen in some resident birds of equatorial regions, where day length varies little over the course of the year. Among temperate resident and short-distance migratory birds, experiments suggest that these cycles are less persistent and rigid.[7,8]

Experiments show these free-running internal clocks, despite being persistent in many birds, drift out of synchronicity with the seasons in the absence of an environmental time-keeper, or *zeitgeber*.[9] In birds, photoperiod is thought to be the principal time keeper that resets their internal clock and synchronises it with their environment. Day length and changes in day length are fixed for a given calendar date and latitude, making photoperiod a fairly reliable cue. With their annual cycles entrained to photoperiod, birds can adapt physiologically and prepare for predictable environmental change. Photoperiod, for example, controls the timing and length of the period over which many birds' gonads mature.[10]

Photoperiod is not the only cue used by birds. Because weather and food supplies can vary somewhat from year to year for a given calendar date, additional cues are needed to fine-tune birds' timing so they can cope with this short-term variability. These additional cues, which may include temperature, rainfall, breeding density and food availability, fine-tune the timing for maturation or regression of gonads, or of egg laying.

So whereas photoperiod brackets the window for reproduction, ambient temperature is probably an important supplementary cue for many birds. This would explain why most birds that breed in north temperate zones begin to lay their eggs earlier in warmer springs. Studies of great tits, *Parus major*, suggest this effect of temperature on timing of breeding may be a direct one, rather than acting indirectly through temperature effects on food abundance, for example.[11]

Predictive cues like temperature can be vital, because when birds must make the decision to breed, many can have no direct way to assess how much food will be available for hungry chicks, or to gauge other important aspects of their ecology. Their gonads must develop and eggs be laid well before the arrival of weather and food conditions that will prevail when their offspring hatch. Natural selection favours the most reliable cues, because timing mistakes can have severe ramifications for birds' breeding success and fitness.

Some environments are highly unpredictable but opportunistic birds may still be able to capitalise on favourable conditions, however fleeting. In the Central Australian desert, zebra finches, *Taeniopygia guttata*, are the archetypal opportunists, capable of breeding in different months in different years. Hatching of their first clutches typically coincides with the first flush of grass seeds in this zone of highly unpredictable and irregular rainfall. Precisely what mixture of cues these finches use is not understood, but maximum supplies of ripening grass seeds are thought to be critical determinants of when breeding occurs.[12]

As well as their internal clocks and the external cues already mentioned, birds' timing of breeding may be influenced by their physical condition. Some birds also have a refractory period in their annual cycle. After their spring breeding season, many resident birds of temperate zones become unresponsive to long days as a cue that would otherwise keep their gonads active. This prevents reproduction from occurring at disadvantageous times of the year, and allows birds to complete post-breeding activities in time. Short winter day lengths end this refractory period.

Plant and insect phenology

Birds and mammals are endothermic (warm-blooded) animals that internally regulate their body temperature, but the plants and insects that critically underpin their ecology are not. The rate of these latter organisms' biochemical and physiological processes may rise by two or three times for every 10°C temperature increase.[13]

For many plants, accumulated heat is a significant driver for the timing of budding, leafing and flowering in temperate climates. In general, budding begins earlier and speeds up, in a linear fashion, as temperatures rise. As well, photoperiod may influence the start and end of plants' rest phase. In insects too, temperature is a driver of phenology. With climate warming, insects are expected to pass through juvenile stages more quickly, emerge as adults sooner, and have a longer flight phase. Some insects have a rest phase, or diapause, with photoperiod being the most important cue for its start and end, although temperature and other factors may play a role.

In temperate zones, temperature strongly influences the phenology of many birds, and the plants and insects upon which they depend. However, in the tropics temperatures vary less, and wet and dry seasons are the norm. This rainfall seasonality drives phenology, strongly affecting fruiting, flowering and leaf emergence. Insect abundance varies in parallel with plant resources, peaking during the wet season and bottoming out during the dry season. Because these seasonal variations can create bottlenecks of nectar, fruit, insects and other resources, many tropical birds breed during periods of high food availability, like the start of the wet season. Despite the importance of rainfall variation for the phenology of tropical birds and their communities, little is known about how climate change may affect rainfall and the resource cycles that depend on it.[14]

Climate and time constrain breeding

The most demanding stage of the annual cycle for many birds, breeding is energy-intensive and can be very time-sensitive. However, as we shall soon see, climate change could affect when birds breed and when critical food sources are available during the breeding period.

The other phases of birds' life cycles tend to be arranged around reproduction, to allow this to happen at the optimum time and place. To acquire enough protein to form eggs, females must eat considerable quantities of food. In some waterfowl, producing a single egg requires twice as much energy as these birds would normally use to maintain their basal metabolic rate for a day. Incubation costs some birds even more energy than egg formation. Some female waterfowl spend up to 90 per cent of their time attending the nest, and this drastically limits their time to forage. Next comes the crucial requirement of feeding the young, and this is the most energy-costly stage of the annual cycle for most birds (some birds expend even more energy during migration).

The choices of when to reproduce and how many eggs to lay have profound ramifications for offspring survival. In many species, breeding as early as possible gives individuals a better chance to secure the best breeding territories and mates. In some species, early-breeding birds tend to lay more eggs, and this is considered especially important for species that raise only a single brood in a season. On the other hand, among young hatched progressively later in the breeding season, offspring survival generally declines. This is also true for some raptors, even though their prey may become more abundant as the season progresses.

Just how early a bird can actually breed runs up against limits. Severe weather such as spring snowstorms can directly threaten birds' survival, force them to spend energy to stay warm, and reduce food supplies such as insects or seeds. Thus in many birds the opposing constraints of hostile weather and the disadvantages of late breeding bracket a time period for optimal egg laying. In the Arctic, this period may be as short as a single week per year, with sharp cut-offs for the survival of offspring born either too early or too late. However, this imperative to breed within a narrow, optimal time window does not hold for all birds. Species reliant on food sources that are not temperature-dependent may be less restricted.

Another important constraint for some birds is the relatively fixed nature of the period from the start of laying through to chick rearing. Once they begin to lay, birds can produce at most one egg per day. Nonetheless, some bird species can strategically vary the number of eggs in their clutch, the time interval between laying each egg, and the overall incubation period (by shifting when they commence full incubation or by pausing incubation). Great tits in the United Kingdom, for example, strategically synchronise their chicks' hatch date by varying clutch size and the start of full incubation.[15] However, there may be costs; extending incubation could give predators more opportunity to attack the nest.

During breeding, high energy needs and time constraints compel many birds to synchronise periods of high food requirements with times of abundant supplies. Some birds may even rely on different food sources across the breeding period. Emperor geese, *Chen canagica*, for example, eat shellfish and other marine food prior to their arrival at breeding grounds, then switch to land-based food. Great tits are among the well-studied group of birds reliant on peaks in insect abundance to feed their young. In the Netherlands, great tits are thought to eat insects from larch trees, *Larix deciduas*, and birch trees, *Betula pubescens*, during egg formation, but provision nestlings with caterpillars that feed on oak, *Quercus robur*, budbursts. Whereas budburst in birch and larch trees is not temperature-sensitive, in oaks it is highly sensitive. Some bird species produce young as food supplies are at their peak, while others do so as food availability is increasing or declining.

Shifting seasonal timing

One of the most divisive topics to face the Intergovernmental Panel on Climate Change was that of the biological response to recent global warming.

The journal *Nature*, 2003

'Season creep.' So widespread and conspicuous is the effect of global warming on seasonal timing, it has spawned this neologism. Shifts in the timing of seasonal events are cause for concern because, as we have already emphasised, time is of the essence when it comes to many birds' breeding success. Phenological shifts are also important in climate science because they provide one of the most thoroughly documented fingerprints of global warming on the living world.[16]

Because temperature is a primary driver of life, considerable attention has focused on the response of plant and animal phenology to the 0.76°C of global warming over the past century (although warming has been more pronounced in some regions than others). Other aspects of climate change, such as altered patterns of precipitation or wind, may affect phenology, too. Mounting concentrations of carbon dioxide are also expected to have direct but complex effects on plants, possibly delaying or speeding up budburst, flowering and senescence.

Phenological shifts in plants and animals: a global snapshot

Because plants, birds and other organisms respond to interannual variations in climate, their phenology naturally varies somewhat from year to year. However, there is now powerful evidence that climate change is altering these seasonal rhythms, with changes in both temperature and phenology being most pronounced since the 1970s. Warming is affecting the phenology of a wide spectrum of life. In some cases, insects are emerging earlier and progressing more rapidly through their life cycles, the timing of zooplankton abundance is shifting, frogs are chorusing earlier, and fungi are fruiting earlier and longer in autumn. In Western Canada, poplar trees, *Populus tremuloides*, advanced their bloom date by 26 days over the course of the 20th century.

Presented with a patchwork of studies showing hundreds of such changes worldwide, most biologists became convinced that climate change is influencing living systems. Nonetheless, stronger evidence was needed to convince policy makers and the general public that climate change, and not just natural year-to-year variability, is the driver of these widespread yet often subtle phenological trends.

The answer was to combine these myriad studies on phenology into 'meta-analyses' that would expose the underlying coherent shift in seasonal timing, and confirm the fingerprint of climate change on the living world. One key effort, by Stanford University biologist Terry Root, climatologist Stephen Schneider and their colleagues, incorporated 64 studies on the phenology of almost 700 species or groups of species, spanning the period 1951–2001.[17] Spring phenology, they found, had advanced (become earlier) by an average of 5.3 days per decade.

Another important meta-analysis by University of Texas biologist Camille Parmesan and Wesleyan University economist Gary Yohe revealed that, among 172 species of birds, butterflies, amphibians and plants, spring phenology advanced by 2.3 days per decade. A broader look at 677 species showed that 62 per cent had advanced their phenology, and 87 per cent of those that had responded did so in the direction expected given climate change. This gave 'very high confidence' that climate change is already affecting life on Earth.[18]

Yet questions persisted. Could the many studies that led to these results, some wondered, reflect a publishing bias towards positive evidence of climate-change impacts? Data that might yield contradictory results could be overlooked if this were true. These concerns were put to rest with the world's largest phenology study, encompassing 561 plant and animal species from 21 countries across Europe. This enormous and systematic pool of data confirmed that spring or summer phenology had advanced by an average of 2.5 days per decade in Europe from 1971 to 2000, and that previous such findings were not the result of bias.[19] 'We are not selecting records because they show what we want them to show. We're looking at everything we can get hold of,' says Sparks, one of the study's authors, 'There's a hugely strong message there that ecosystems are changing. And the evidence is racking up.'

This general pattern of earlier spring phenology continues to be seen in most temperate land regions in the Northern Hemisphere. However, autumn responses have been less clear-cut. Some evidence suggests a general delay in autumn events, such as leaf colour and leaf fall, and an extension of the growing or greening season, but the picture emerging from different studies is still somewhat ambiguous.[19]

Birds' breeding timing is shifting

Because the choice of when to breed is such a critical decision for birds, their reproductive timing is the focus of considerable research that aims to gauge their response to climate change. (For the billions of birds that migrate each year, the scheduling of these journeys is also likely to influence their ability to cope; chapter 2).

In fact, earlier laying in birds provides some of the strongest evidence for the effects of climate change on wildlife. University of Wisconsin-Milwaukee ecologist Peter Dunn and Cornell University ecologist David Winkler combined the results of numerous long-term studies (with one set of records stretching back to 1897) on 68 bird species of Europe, North America and Australia, and found that 59 per cent of species are laying significantly earlier. They estimate that for every degree Celsius of warming birds are laying an average of 2.4 days earlier.[20,21]

Interestingly, one of the earliest studies to reveal the fingerprint of climate change on birds was made possible by volunteer ornithologists in the UK. Their observations since 1939 have amassed probably the largest record of the timing of birds' breeding, the British Trust for Ornithology's Nest Record Scheme. This showed that changes in climate were affecting seasonal timing across a wide range of bird groups. More than half (19 out of 36) of species studied were breeding earlier in the 1980s and '90s than during the prior two decades. There was a tendency for earlier breeding to be associated with warmer spring temperature.[22]

In Europe, analysis of 40 000 nest records for *Ficedula* flycatchers (small, insect-eating passerines) provided powerful results. Nine out of 25 populations from diverse locations are laying earlier across Europe. Importantly, where spring temperatures increased most, the birds advanced their schedules most but, in areas that cooled, laying was delayed. These findings, demonstrated across a wide geographic area and incorporating different climate patterns, helped show that birds are responding in a direction expected with climate change, ruling out publication bias.[23]

Far to the south, in east Antarctica, a very different pattern of response has emerged among some seabirds. Together, Adélie penguins, *Pygoscelis adeliae*, emperor penguins, *Aptenodytes forsteri*, and six species of petrel now arrive more than nine days later at their colonies in Adélie Land, and lay eggs more than two days later, on average, than in the early 1950s.[24] Only one species, the south polar skua, *Catharacta maccormicki*, laid its eggs earlier over this period. East Antarctica's average annual climate has warmed less than the continental average since the early 1950s. Interestingly, however, the seabirds' seasonal timing generally fails to correspond with air temperatures in the months before arrival and laying. Instead, the delays are linked to decreased sea-ice extent, and may reflect declines in their food supplies. Among seabirds breeding in the rapidly warming North Sea and the high Arctic, contrasting trends are also seen, with some species breeding earlier and others later.

Mismatch: global warming tugs at trophic ties

Individualistic responses

These contrasting results hint at the idiosyncratic responses possible as climate change affects birds and the other organisms in their ecological communities. This raises an important question: will climate change pull apart the links of the food web?

In fact, the individualistic nature of different species' responses to climate change is well documented. Take the food web of Eurasian sparrowhawks, *Accipiter nisus*. These raptors specialise in preying upon woodland birds, and tend to single out young birds lacking in experience and therefore easier to catch. In a Dutch study population, a picture of disparate timing shifts has emerged for breeding sparrowhawks and organisms from three successive trophic levels of their food chain: passerine birds (coal tits, *Parus ater*; blue tits, *Cyanistes caeruleus*; great tits; and pied flycatchers, *Ficedula hypoleuca*), caterpillars (largely *Operophtera brumata* and *Tortrix viridana*), and oak trees.

The avian predators' phenological responses, though they varied from year to year between 1985 and 2005, tended to be weaker than the next level down the food web. The weakest response was at the top. Sparrowhawks did not advance their hatching date at all, even though matching the peak demands of their young with peak food abundance is considered important.[25] Sparrowhawks studied in Denmark have also failed to advance their laying date, despite an advance in the breeding date for five bird species they prey upon.

Why might climate-change-induced timing shifts differ among species, populations and regions? This is an important but still largely open question, and the reasons may be many. The magnitude of climate change in different regions may vary, being insufficient to trigger a response in some localities. Even if temperatures are changing locally, organisms may not respond if their phenology is instead influenced by other climate variables like precipitation, or by non-climate variables like photoperiod. Alternatively, organisms may be responding but in ways too difficult to detect.

Physiology may also have a role. Some evidence suggests smaller-bodied birds are advancing their laying date more for each degree Celsius of warming. With their higher thermoregulatory costs per gram of body mass, smaller birds tend to be more sensitive to temperature, a possible reason for this finding. Birds' ecology and diet may also come into play. Generalist birds have a greater choice of food sources, and may be less responsive to climate change. European sparrowhawks, for example, may switch to other prey; the four prey species in the above Dutch example made up only about one-fifth of the sparrowhawks' diet. Alternatively, birds' responses might be constrained if the food used during their laying period is different, and has advanced less with climate change, than that used during the period they feed their nestlings.

Another hypothesis is that the stronger response seen in a prey species as opposed to its consumer (as in the passerine–sparrowhawk example) could be a strategy that allows a prey species to avoid predation. Differences in life-history characteristics, such as whether birds are migratory or sedentary, single-brooding or multiple-brooding, may also determine if and by how much they modify events in their schedules under climate change.

The mismatch hypothesis

Regardless of their cause, these individualistic responses to global warming raise the concern that even relatively small changes in climate could alter finely calibrated ecological relationships. Critically, birds' reproduction could become mismatched or mistimed relative to their food species.

This mismatch hypothesis is not a new concept. Its origins can be traced back to 1914, when fisheries biologist Johan Hjort attempted to explain why the numbers of new recruits to cod stocks varied from year to year. Newly hatched cod larvae's survival, he believed, hinged on a 'critical period' for feeding. Numbers of new recruits are thought to be greatly affected by how well this critical period matches or synchronises with sufficient plankton food supplies. The food delivery potential of breeding great tits and blue tits also underscores the importance of synchrony. In the UK's Wytham Woods, the 'flow rate' of energy to their nestlings was up to five times greater when the abundance and size of their caterpillar prey peaked, compared to the periods before and after this peak.[26]

The mismatch hypothesis has still greater relevance today because, with climate change, mismatches[27] in phenology may become widespread. Predator–prey relationships could become uncoupled or otherwise altered, as could those among mutualists, and between parasites and their hosts. In fact, mismatch could cause powerful disruptions in living communities by fundamentally changing the way different trophic levels interact, thereby affecting the structure and functioning of ecosystems.[4] Birds provide model examples of mismatch under climate change. Some of the potential consequences, they reveal, include fewer and lighter offspring, population declines and, in the most extreme cases, the potential loss of unique populations (chapter 5).

Caterpillar eaters expose mismatch mechanisms

In the Netherlands, long-term studies on insect-eating birds have helped throw some light on the mechanisms behind climate-change-induced mismatch. Like a great deal of such research, this work focuses on the reproductive stage, when many birds have high energy demands but face time constraints for food availability. Because they must prepare to breed well before caterpillars or other key food sources emerge or peak, these birds must rely on cues besides food abundance to guide this decision.

Great tits in the Hoge Veluwe, an area of oak and pine woodland in one of the Netherlands' largest national parks, exploit a food web typical to a broad group of small, insect-eating forest birds. Great tits eat winter moth caterpillars, which in turn feed on the leaves of oak trees. To breed successfully, these birds must synchronise offsprings' peak food demands with caterpillar peaks (figure 1).

Winter moth caterpillars emerge in the spring after oak tree buds burst open. However, the caterpillars are available for only a short period because, once fully grown, they pupate in soil. If these caterpillars hatch too early, before oak buds are available, half may perish within five days. But hatching too late also creates problems for caterpillars.

As leaves mature they become tougher, decrease in nutritive value, and increasingly contain tannins and other defensive compounds. Caterpillars that hatch too late and eat increasingly inedible foliage may die, or pupate into lighter moths that produce fewer eggs. By placing nets beneath oak trees to collect caterpillar droppings, researchers were able to estimate when caterpillar biomass was highest in the Hoge Veluwe. This peak typically lasted for three weeks, although its start date might vary by as much as three weeks from year to year.

As for great tits, four weeks typically elapse between egg laying and the period of the nestlings' greatest food demands. Ideally, caterpillar biomass should be highest when offspring are 11 or 12 days old. If parents time their breeding too early or too late to match chicks' peak demands with the caterpillar peak, they raise fewer or lighter offspring that are less likely to survive.

How do rising temperatures affect this web of relationships? The estimated caterpillar peak is taking place earlier, but the laying date of great tits has not kept up. And whereas in 1985 the interval between the birds' laying and their food peak was 37.5 days, by 2004 it shortened to just 26.6 days.[28] Now, when the chicks reach their critical period, many great tits are unable to profit from a caterpillar peak that has already passed; by 2005 there was a mismatch of about five days.

Even if birds, and the insects and plants they rely on, all respond to temperature as a cue, they may vary in their sensitivity. Different organisms may also use different or unrelated mechanisms and cues. These differential responses are critical concerns where climate warming accelerates the budburst of trees and the growth stages of insects. Insect numbers and biomass may peak earlier, and the duration of their peaks could be truncated.

Temperature, a cue many birds use to fine-tune their breeding timing, is affected by climate change, whereas day length is obviously not. But photoperiod is the primary cue many birds use to set the window for their reproductive efforts. And whereas for birds the period from the start of egg laying through to chick rearing is relatively fixed, warming has been shown to halve the development time of winter moths, from about 40 to just 20 days. In essence, climate change appears to be reducing the reliability of photoperiod, temperature and other cues as accurate predictors of future food supply.

One way to conceptualise mismatch is to view it as a problem caused by the lag in time between birds' decision-making period (about when to breed) and the time at which natural selection actually operates on their decision (the period of peak food demands during chick rearing). In sparrowhawks, 53 days typically elapse between egg laying and peak food demands of young, compared with roughly 30 days for passerine birds (although sparrowhawks have a wider food peak than passerines). The longer lag time may explain the sparrowhawk's incomplete response to the earlier availability of young passerine prey, described above. One hypothesis is that larger animals that experience a longer lag time between the 'environment of decision making' and the 'environment of selection' will be most vulnerable to climate change because they would be least able to respond to climate change in a flexible manner.

Other factors that could prevent breeding birds from keeping up with earlier food-supply peaks include the energy and time constraints imposed by spring moult and migration schedules, or the need to avoid severe weather.

How much is enough? The climate-change yardstick

Unlike the population at the Hoge Veluwe, some great tits are taking climate change in stride – so far at least. In southern England, a population in Wytham Woods is tracking its fast-changing environment closely.[29] Compared to 1961, these great tits are laying their eggs about two weeks earlier, and mismatch occurs only in springs of rapid warming. These birds have also strategically varied clutch size and the start of their incubation period in ways that help synchronise their nestlings' demands with the food peaks of winter moth caterpillars. Why this population is tracking climate change while some great tit populations elsewhere may become mismatched is not understood.

With climate change, the crucial question is, 'can birds keep up?' Changing phenology may be interpreted as a positive sign if it helps birds adapt to climate change; conversely, a timing shift may be inadequate to track prey or other requirements, revealing that climate change is negatively affecting birds. As the different circumstances of great tit populations in the Netherlands and the UK demonstrate, a 'yardstick' is needed to gauge whether birds are shifting their schedules sufficiently to track the changes in their environment driven by global warming.

The yardstick, argue Marcel Visser of the Netherlands Institute of Ecology and Christiaan Both of the University of Groningen, should be applied to the most demanding and important activity in a bird's annual cycle: the breeding stage.[30] As the key determinant of a bird's fitness, this stage should occur under optimal conditions, such as during high availability of food supplies. By evaluating the conditions surrounding this stage, it should be possible to shed light on whether shifts in phenology are adaptive and sufficient.

However, it will also be important to consider these effects within the wider context of birds' ecology, because many other aspects of their environments may be shifting with climate change. If food abundance were to increase overall, for example, this might counter any minor mismatch between food demands and supply peaks. Parent birds might be able to compensate for mismatch by having more broods, or investing more care in their offspring. Of course, climate change may alter the timing of migration and other key stages in birds' annual cycles (chapter 2). And it could affect important aspects of birds' ecology besides their prey, further influencing their ability to cope.

Despite a burgeoning scientific literature on phenology, few studies have actually sought to apply this yardstick approach, or otherwise assess how organisms' fitness is affected by climate change. Among the small number that have, the results are cause for concern. Visser and Both reviewed 11 examples, among birds and other taxa, that gauged whether a species's phenology was keeping up with the abundance of its food supply. In five cases a species's phenology advanced too little, and in three cases too much, compared to the food supply, leading Visser and Both suggest that mismatch could be a problem for many species. They caution that it remains difficult to assess the extent of this problem; not only have very few studies used the yardstick approach, but examples of species with adequate responses may be overlooked by the scientific literature.

Inflexible responses in a changing climate

Mosquito shift plagues Arctic seabirds

The problem of mismatch with food abundance is clearly important. But the case of Brünnich's guillemots, *Uria lomvia*, shows how warming can detrimentally affect other time-sensitive aspects of birds' breeding ecology. With the demise of the great auk, *Pinguinus impennis*, the Brünnich's guillemot and closely related common guillemot, *Uria aalge*, became the largest living members of the auk family, the Alcidae. Unlike its extinct, flightless relative, the Brünnich's guillemot is a strong flier, commuting up to 100 kilometres from its high Arctic colonies to catch prey. Also an excellent diver, it uses its wings to 'fly' underwater. However, this bird's remarkable versatility does not appear to extend to an ability to cope with warming at Coats Island in Canada's Hudson Bay.

This breeding site is unusual among Canadian Arctic colonies of Brünnich's guillemots in being located in an area of abundant mosquitoes, including *Aedes nigripes*, a species that excels at preying on some incubating birds. The mosquitoes make their appearance after most snow has melted, and are especially prevalent on hot, still days. Since the mid-1980s, mosquitoes have been appearing and peaking in abundance earlier, in the first half of July rather than the second half, possibly due to climate change. This creates a problem for guillemots, because mosquitoes now greatly overlap in time with their incubation period, from the last half of June through to late July.

In the past, the rare deaths of adult Brünnich's guillemots at this colony usually resulted from aggression between the birds. However, after mosquitoes became more abundant during their breeding period, observers recorded deaths of birds as they were incubating their eggs. These deaths tended to occur on hotter days, when clouds of mosquitoes were dense enough to obscure visibility. The single foot of a guillemot might be covered by more than 50 feeding mosquitoes. When exposed to full sun, incubating birds were often seen spreading their wings, laying their heads on the ground, lolling from side to side and panting heavily. Deaths of birds took place only at the colony's edge, where mosquito attacks were most severe, and in areas exposed to afternoon sun. Egg losses were also highest on hotter days at these peripheral sites. However, prior to the period when mosquitoes emerge, high temperatures and low winds are not linked to egg desertion or deaths of adults. A combination of heat and mosquito attacks most likely explains these fatalities, posing a threat to guillemots that could intensify as warming increases.[31] As we shall see, diminishing sea ice is also challenging the ability of these seabirds to provision their young (chapter 4).

Although other seabirds are known to abandon their nests when attacked by parasites or suffering from dehydration, some Brünnich's guillemots evidently do not. These birds seem unable to adapt their behaviour to the earlier mosquito peak, perhaps because conditions like these were not a common feature of their evolutionary history. Unlike the great tits of Wytham Woods, they seem to lack the flexibility to track this kind of change in their environment. The ability to modify activities in the annual cycle can vary, not just between species but within them as well, depending on the population, sex and even individual.

Past experience may influence the flexibility with which individuals of some species can adjust their breeding schedules to climate variations. Among red-cockaded woodpeckers, *Picoides borealis*, in North America, younger females are less likely to shift their laying dates than experienced birds, which laid their eggs increasingly earlier in conjunction with climate change.[32] Prior experience of abnormal climate conditions could also influence birds' responses to such events in future, even in short-lived species like the song sparrow, *Melospiza melodia*. In western Canada, some song sparrows were more likely to shift their breeding dates if they had previously experienced warmer El Niño spring conditions in their second or third breeding season.[33]

Does having more broods relax time constraints?

Birds' ability to adapt to climate change may also depend, in part, on whether they produce just one brood per breeding season, or multiple broods. Single-brooded birds may be constrained by the need to synchronise feeding with a single peak in food availability. Single-brooding species have advanced their laying dates at four times the rate of birds that produce two or more broods.[20]

Multi-brooding birds may be less time-limited by their food sources, which may be more varied, or be abundant for longer or peak multiple times during the breeding season.

A greater sensitivity to shifts in food peaks, and greater risk of mistiming, may help explain why, in France, single-brooding species had more nega-tive population trends than multi-brooding species from 1989 to 2005.[34] Climate warming in western Europe, particularly marked since 1990, may be behind the different responses of these two groups.

Opportunist breeders may use the immediate presence of food as a cue to breed. The directness of the relationship between their decision and food availability provides a level of predictability. Such birds may adapt more readily to climate-change-driven shifts in the timing of food supplies. Birds that rely mainly on temperature or rainfall cues may also cope better than those reliant on photoperiod or other fixed cues unlikely to be affected by climate change.

Mistiming across the seasons

Asymmetric climate change: old rules no longer apply

There is no reason to expect warming, or other aspects of climate change, to occur uniformly across all seasons of the year. In fact, asymmetries in climate change across months or seasons could be common. This may cause problems for some birds, such as the black grouse, *Tetrao tetrix*, a forest-dweller undergoing strong decline in Finland since at least the 1960s. Polygamous black grouse males, with their glossy dark plumage, strut their stuff in elaborate mating displays. They flaunt lyre-shaped tail feathers and startling white rumps, squaring off against each other while emitting an ethereal quavering, hissing mating call in a bid to attract females. In Finland, female black grouse lay their eggs in early May in nests on the ground. Their precocial chicks leave the nest the same day they hatch. Though fed by the female on their first day, the chicks fend for themselves thereafter, at first foraging for insects, then slowly shifting to a plant-based diet. They can fly after about four or five days, but require about three weeks to fully develop their capacity to thermoregulate.

Temperatures affect when black grouse breed, and in Finland the weather they experience during the last three weeks of April most strongly influences when they mate. During this calendar period, temperatures in Finland have warmed, and black grouse now lay eggs and hatch their young earlier than they did during the 1960s.[35] In contrast to this April warming, temperatures during the period after the chicks hatch, in June, have not increased in Finland. In fact, years of adverse, cold weather during this post-hatching period have become worse still and more frequent, while good years have become scarcer. An earlier breeding schedule has effectively shifted the black grouse chicks' critical post-hatching phase to a time in the year when they are now more likely to confront low temperatures.

During their first 10 days, particularly their flightless post-hatching period, the chicks are more vulnerable to heat loss and hypothermia than when they are older. Colder weather also places greater demands on their energy budget. Insects become less active and harder to find and chicks may need to move around more to forage, possibly increasing their vulnerability to both hypothermia and predators. Advancing hatching by even a couple of days increases the chicks' likelihood of being exposed to colder and more variable weather during this sensitive period.

These changes may explain why early hatching among black grouse is tied to lower reproductive output in Finland when, to better adapt themselves, the birds should actually delay, not advance, mating or hatching. If these climate trends continue, as predicted, this mismatch between chicks' critical period and suitable weather for rearing them may worsen, imperilling the black grouse's recovery in Finland.

A natural refrigerator breaks down

In Canada, a population of grey jays, *Perisoreus canadensis*, illustrates how warming outside the breeding season can disrupt parents' ability to feed young. These jays prepare for cold winter and spring months by hoarding formidable quantities of food, sometimes stealing from humans (hence their popular name 'whiskey-jack', derived from an Algonquian word for a troublesome forest spirit). A single grey jay collects thousands of berries, insects, fungi and even flesh from carcasses, impregnating each finding with sticky saliva before caching it in a tree crevice. A bird may cache more than 1000 pieces during a 17-hour day. Much of this food is perishable, and grey jays are unusual among hoarding birds in their reliance on cold weather to preserve it. These resident birds breed unusually early in the year, sometimes starting clutches in February when temperatures are still well below freezing and snow cover is likely to be near its maximum. To survive through winter and breed, grey jays depend on their cached food.

It might be tempting to assume these substantial hoards could buffer grey jays against climate-change-induced mistiming. However, this strategy of 'storing food in the refrigerator' no longer seems to be working for an Algonquin Provincial Park population, at the extreme southern edge of their range in this part of eastern Canada. After observing this population decline, ecologist Thomas Waite and naturalist Dan Strickland sought to test whether significant autumn warming since 1975 might be a factor.[36]

Although they found temperatures varied considerably from year to year, following warmer autumns the birds' breeding success was very likely to be poor. (In areas where birds could supplement their diet through constant access to bird feeders, breeding attempts were equally likely to succeed regardless of autumn weather.) Over time, clutches of their pale green, speckled eggs grew smaller, numbers of nestlings declined, reproductive performance generally worsened, and the study population shrank.

Waite and Strickland hypothesise that the crucial link between the warmer weather and the declining population is 'hoard-rot'. They suggest that this population's decline may be linked to climate change that has effectively broken the birds' natural refrigerator. Although warmer autumns may improve the survival prospects for some resident birds in temperate climes, they create conditions hostile to these grey jays at the southern edge of their range.

Challenges and unknowns

It is clear that climate change is driving shifts in the timing of seasonal events, but how this will affect birds' ability to cope with climate change is still not well understood. Even basic questions about climate and phenology remain unanswered. For example, how do different aspects of weather – temperature, precipitation and extremes such as drought and hard freezes – interact to influence phenology? The effects of asymmetric climate change on phenology constitute another important research gap.

To adequately detect the living world's response to climate-change signals, data sets of at least 20 years' duration are needed. Unfortunately, these long-term records are scarce. This complicates efforts to understand birds' responses, and makes it difficult to tease apart natural year-to-year climate variations from longer-term climate-change signals. Care must also be taken to rule out other potential causes of shifts in phenology, such as pollution and land-use changes.

Most of what is known about phenological shifts comes from European and North American records, and vast gaps remain in the understanding of birds' responses on other continents. In the tropics, changes to precipitation patterns are likely to be critical for the ecology of many bird species, yet most research has focused on how birds' phenology responds to warming temperatures.

Their phenology may be shifting, but for individual species the all-important question 'how much is enough?' requires an understanding of how different trophic levels respond to climate change. So far this question has barely been addressed. Knowledge of how prey abundance varies with time, and how birds should modify their schedules to track this, is still rudimentary. In fact, when it comes to the various mechanisms that could allow birds to flexibly cope with climate change, very little is yet known.

Studies of mistiming or mismatch have mainly focused on the breeding phase, and in particular on the timing of food supplies and nestlings' peak demands. However, the duration of food availability, not just peaks, may be critical. Other stages of birds' annual cycles are also likely to be affected by climate change. As the next chapter illustrates, considering annual cycles in their entirety is important if birds' responses to climate change are to be understood. The all-important implications of these phenological changes for avian population dynamics are still largely unclear (chapter 5).

Conclusion

Phenology is a sensitive and easy-to-observe indicator of climate change. Because it explores the importance of time as a constraint on wildlife, it may also help reveal whether bird populations can adapt or persist under climate change. This explains the resurgence of scientific interest in phenology over the past two decades, and the mushrooming phenological networks that provide an important opportunity for the public to participate in climate-change research.

Important and energetically demanding events in birds' annual cycles are timed, with the help of endogenous and external cues, to coincide with optimal environmental conditions, such as abundant food for raising young. Many birds are already shifting the timing of their breeding in association with climate change, a response likely to intensify as warming gathers pace. Phenological changes in plants and animals provide some of the strongest evidence for climate-change impacts on the living world and could have wide-ranging implications for biodiversity.

The timing of seasonal activities is changing, but it is also critical to learn whether birds and the species they interact with are keeping up with global warming. Individualistic responses to climate change could cause the different trophic levels of food webs to become uncoupled, disrupting ecological communities. In birds, inquiry has focused mainly on insect-eating species breeding in seasonal environments. For these birds, a limited period of optimal weather and a critical need to synchronise energy demands with food sources may impose constraints on their ability to adapt to climate change.

Some birds appear to be shifting their seasonal activities in ways that allow them to track climate change. Others, however, are mistimed or mismatched with prey or other key aspects of their ecological communities. This has potential consequences for reproduction, including fewer and lighter offspring, and reduced fledgling and adult survival. However, it is still too early to know which species will suffer or prosper from shifts in phenology driven by climate change.

To understand whether birds are mismatched, their wider ecological communities, including symbionts as well as predators and prey, must be considered. Climate change may have important effects on phenology during the breeding season, but is also likely to influence events during other phases of their annual cycles. Where phenology has already revealed the clear signal of climate change, understanding why bird species and populations vary in their response is vital if we are to understand and predict whether they can adapt.

Chapter 2

MIGRATORY BIRDS FACE CLIMATE TURBULENCE

Synchronised odysseys in a changing world

The extreme lifestyles of bar-tailed godwits suggest how demanding, time-sensitive schedules could make some migratory birds vulnerable to climate change. Each September in Christchurch, New Zealand, the cathedral's bells have traditionally rung for 30 minutes to welcome the first of these large wading shorebirds. A bit of celebration is called for, because some bar-tailed godwits migrate from Alaska in a single hop of more than 10 000 kilometres – the longest non-stop flight recorded for a land bird. These avian endurance champions owe this feat to extraordinarily efficient physiology, abundant food and favourable southward winds.

After spending long Arctic summer days breeding, bar-tailed godwits gorge on worms and shellfish on the food-rich Yukon-Kuskokwim Delta mudflats. By departure time their hearts and flight muscles have enlarged, their blood has thickened to carry more oxygen, and their weight has doubled until roughly 55 per cent of their mass is fat, which is even more energy-efficient than high-octane automobile fuel. Their transformation from breeding machines to fat-fuelled flying machines complete, these godwits await favourable winds to boost them towards New Zealand.

From 2006 to 2008, satellite transmitters allowed a captivated human audience to follow their formerly unverifiable movements, confirming suspicions that some of these marathon migrants complete their journey without resting, to cover at least 1000 kilometres a day. Exactly how these godwits fly continuously without food or water for about nine days is a question that challenges our understanding of vertebrate physiology.[1]

Small wonder that godwits excite the public's imagination. But in 2008 their arrival in Christchurch drew attention for another reason. They were almost two weeks earlier than normal, and climate change was immediately speculated to be one possible cause. In fact, shifts in the timing of bird migrations are becoming widespread, a fingerprint of climate change that commands increasing scientific scrutiny. As it turns out, migratory birds have much to reveal when it comes to climate change, and perhaps much to lose.

Birds are key mobile links (see the introduction to this book) and, as the most mobile of them all, migratory birds contribute to the functions of diverse ecosystems. This makes migratory birds prime witnesses to global climate change. Monitoring the migration timing, physical condition and numbers of these globe-trotting data collectors can provide clues about the stability and integrity of their environments, and reveal how wider ecosystems are affected. The six subspecies of red knot, *Calidris canutus*, for example, each wing their way along a separate migratory route, and could testify about the state of Arctic tundra, African desert coasts, European estuaries and Australian beaches. It also helps that, when it comes to climate-change effects, more is known about migratory birds than any other migratory animal group.

An ancient and important ecological pulse

Despite humanity's fascination with bird migration, much about this phenomenon still eludes us. Rooted deep in evolutionary time and, of all the animal groups, best developed in birds, migration is thought to have emerged independently a number of times across diverse lines of birds. Natural selection continues to shape bird migration as environmental conditions change, and can be expected to do so under global warming.

Although up to half of the world's almost 10 000 known bird species have been speculated to be migrants, the first systematic assessment revealed that about one-fifth of bird species make regular long-distance migrations.[2] Many journeys are remarkable feats in terms of physiology and energetics. Some birds that cross the hostile Sahara desert may weigh as little as about 10 grams and could fit into the palm of one's hand. Others, like great bustards, *Otis tarda*, weigh up to 20 kilograms. Over their pole-to-pole journeys, Arctic terns, *Sterna paradisaea*, experience more daylight hours than any other animal. They also clock up to 80 000 kilometres per year, and the equivalent of three return trips to the moon over a possible 30-year life span. Other migrants regularly fly over the Himalayas at altitudes of up to 9.6 kilometres. Some penguins swim hundreds of kilometres every year to migrate, and there are land birds that undertake migrations by walking.

To navigate, birds use celestial (sun, stars and skylight polarisation) and geomagnetic (intensity and inclination of force line) information, as well as landmarks. Yet how birds such as bar-tailed godwits find their way across featureless expanses of ocean and the equator, where they cannot use magnetic compasses, is still a mystery.

Travelling has its perks – and pitfalls

Migration is thought to allow birds to capitalise on seasonal environments and to provision themselves with rich food supplies, shelter and space. Migrants can also avoid harsh climate conditions that would sap their energy. A red knot wintering in the Netherlands during January, for example, must spend almost twice as much energy to maintain its metabolism as it would wintering on the West African coast (2.9 watts as opposed to 1.5 watts).

However, migrations are also time-consuming, and in some birds constitute the biggest source of mortality over the year. Mortality rates for black-throated blue warblers, *Dendroica caerulescens*, appear to be 15 times higher during migration than during the non-migratory phases of their annual cycle. Migrants may encounter adverse weather and avoid predators. Running out of fuel, succumbing to exhaustion and contracting disease are other risks. Nonetheless, migration's very persistence implies that its benefits generally outweigh its costs.

Currently, migratory birds are much less threatened or near threatened with extinction than sedentary birds.[2] Nonetheless, complex threats are probably behind declines in many of the world's major flyways. Some shorebirds from around the Pacific Basin, for example, including the critically endangered spoon-billed sandpiper, *Eurynorhynchus pygmeus*, are affected by loss of important tidal flats in Saemangeum, Korea due to a massive reclamation project. Migrants from Africa to the Palaearctic have shown 'sustained, often severe decline' from 1970 to 2000, with long-distance (intercontinental) migrants doing worse than short-distance migrants or residents.[3] Among the waders of Africa, West Asia and Europe, more than half of populations are undergoing accelerating decline. In eastern Australia, populations of migratory shorebirds declined by 73 per cent from 1983 to 2006.[4]

A migratory paradox? Mobile but vulnerable

As highly mobile animals that can traverse oceans, mountain ranges and deserts, will migratory birds be able to take climate change in stride? Paradoxically, a dependence on multiple habitats could actually make things worse for some. Because climate change may affect any or all the diverse habitats the birds depend on throughout the year, some researchers argue, this greatly increases the chance that migrants will be negatively affected at some stage of the annual cycle.[5] In particular, many migratory birds depend on reliable, high-quality refuelling sites. Changes to just one crucial site can adversely affect entire populations. If climate-induced changes were also to compromise breeding, overwintering and stopover habitats, the total effect could be catastrophic for some.

Suggesting the magnitude of this threat, the British Trust for Ornithology estimated that climate change could significantly affect the abundance of 84 per cent of 298 migratory birds listed with the Convention on the Conservation of Migratory Species of Wild Animals (CMS).[6] This is roughly the same proportion as the sum of all other major human threats to these birds (80 per cent). Climate change also looks likely to compound the problems of many at-risk birds among these migrants, since 73 per cent of species expected to be at risk from climate change also face other human threats.

New tool to solve migration's lingering mysteries

Swallows certainly sleep all the winter. A number of them conglobulate together, by flying round and round, and then all in a heap throw themselves under water, and lye in the bed of a river.

Samuel Johnson, 1768

Gauging this climate-change threat is difficult because the routes and destinations of so many migratory birds are unknown. Until the 19th century, many Europeans thought migratory birds survived winter by living at the bottom of ponds or beneath the sea, or by turning into mice. Returning explorers began to recognise the African arrows found on storks that, having somehow survived impalement, continued their migration to Europe.

These *pfeilstorchs* (German for 'arrow storks') provided some of the first clear evidence from Europe of long-distance migration.

Fortunately, today more sophisticated tools are on hand to trace birds' movements, and help reveal how they may be threatened by climate change where they breed, refuel and overwinter. This is a particular challenge when it comes to migrants overwintering in tropical or equatorial regions, where a dearth of research means that the ecological conditions many birds face may only be guessed. In 2007, a European–African team was guided to the first known African wintering site of globally threatened aquatic warblers, *Acrocephalus paludicola*, by isotope analysis of feathers gathered from birds in Europe. This analysis revealed where in Africa the feathers might have been grown, leading the conservationists to north-west Senegal. This technique is increasingly used to establish bird migration routes.

The satellite technology used to follow the bar-tailed godwit's record-breaking flight is extremely helpful for revealing flight routes and ranges, like those of critically endangered northern bald ibis, *Geronticus eremita*. Three of these birds received satellite tags in the Syrian desert in 2006, after researchers discovered a breeding population of seven individuals there in 2002. (Prior to that, the only known remaining populations of this ibis were non-migratory ones in Morocco and Turkey.)

The three satellite-tagged birds from Syria headed down the Rift Valley to Yemen, then across the Red Sea before settling down for the winter in the Ethiopian highlands. Çağan Şekercioğlu joined Mengistu Wondafrash and other researchers from the Ethiopian Wildlife and Natural History Society to search for the birds in an area indicated by their GPS coordinates. After driving and hiking for days on rugged roads in the Ethiopian hinterlands, they found four birds in a lush, cultivated valley with a stream and small lakes. These birds, considered extinct for decades in Ethiopia, may have constituted the world's entire migrating northern bald ibis population.

One disadvantage of satellite and GPS technologies is that they require receivers or tags too large to place on small songbirds. Now, thanks to tiny light-detecting, geolocator backpacks, even small birds' migratory routes can be traced. These devices log the time of sunrise and sunset, revealing a bird's latitude and longitude. Placing the 1.5-gram devices on songbirds for the first time (purple martins, *Progne subis*, and wood thrushes, *Hylocichla mustelina*) in 2007 revealed that their springtime migrations from Central America to Pennsylvania, USA were three times as rapid as previously believed, as the birds sometimes covered more than 500 kilometres in a day.[7] This technique could prove revolutionary, although it requires birds to be recaptured after they return from their migrations.

The 'greenness' of the habitats birds experience in far-flung parts of the globe can now also be revealed, thanks to satellite data on Earth's radiation. Known as the normalised difference vegetation index (NDVI), it indicates the greenness of vegetation, a sign of plant growth and vigour also assumed to indicate the availability of insects and other invertebrate food. But because NDVI data only became available in 1982, it is not possible to compare current conditions with those further in the past.

The control of migratory birds' annual cycles

Birds need to optimise every aspect of their lifecycle to the resources available. It's a very complex game, one you wouldn't want to convert into a board game because the rules would be too complicated.

Tim Sparks, 2010

A concern with climate change is its potential to cause timing conflicts in migratory birds. This threat makes it important to know what governs their decisions to migrate and undertake other activities in their annual cycles. Control over the timing of life-cycle events is especially relevant for birds that must exploit seasonal abundance in multiple habitats at precise times of the year.

Among obligate migrants,[8] the main aspects of control over timing, including migration initiation and direction, are thought to be under genetic control, governed by the type of endogenous circannual rhythms described in the last chapter.[9,10] These rhythms prepare birds physiologically for migration, by controlling migratory fattening and the urge to migrate. In some migrants, innate and very rigid control tends deliver them to their destinations on almost the same date each calendar year, even if the weather conditions vary.

Here again photoperiod, which varies reliably for a given latitude and date, is an important cue or *zeitgeber* to synchronise birds' circannual rhythms to the calendar year.[11] Photoperiod also plays a role in accelerating or inhibiting birds' migrations, for example, by speeding up pre-migratory physiological preparations. Other cues for migration are not known with certainty, but may include temperature, food supplies, precipitation and social bonds between birds.

The rhythms of many migratory birds can therefore be seen as free-running, self-sustaining and innate templates, synchronised reliably to annual calendar dates by photoperiod. Some bird species, however, are facultative rather than obligate migrants. For these birds environmental conditions, and especially food resources, are thought to influence decisions to migrate. This group includes many nomadic and irruptive species that can undertake once-in-a-lifetime journeys over hundreds or thousands of kilometres, in response to cold temperatures, drought, or lack of water or food. Preparation for migration may entail among nature's most extreme changes in weight, physiology and body structure and behaviour. Red knots are even known to markedly shrink the size of their guts before migrating.

Like other birds, migrants must cope with year-to-year variation in weather and other environmental conditions. By fine-tuning their migration schedules, many are better able to arrive at the optimal time. Birds may also adjust their migratory behaviour by learning from their own experience or from experienced flock members, and these behavioural changes can be made within days. Some researchers hypothesise that birds whose migration is under strong endogenous control will respond slowly to changes in their environment, over the course of generations, if these responses require them to evolve genetically.

Demands and constraints of migratory schedules

Tightly choreographed lives

Strictly scheduled and demanding migrations could prove a liability under rapid climate change. Long-distance migrations can be energy- and time-consuming, taking weeks to complete. En route, migrants must cope with unfavourable weather and stay on course. They must avoid predators and disease, and survive in diverse habitats and sometimes unfamiliar terrain. They may also face time pressures imposed by short-lived but vital food sources. The various demands of migration may conflict with one another, creating bottlenecks in terms of nutrition and energy as well as time, especially for long-distance migrants.[12]

These various demands are thought to leave some long-distance migrants like the red knot with very limited scope for flexibility in their annual schedules. Each year the *rufa* subspecies completes a round trip of more than 30 000 kilometres from South America's Tierra del Fuego to the Canadian Arctic. Its northbound trip includes a crucial refuelling stop in Delaware Bay on the US mid-Atlantic coast, timed to capitalise on the spawning of horseshoe crabs, *Limulus polyphemus*. Arriving at this site, the fatigued birds look like long-legged bundles of feathers and bones, but they may double their weight in just two weeks by feasting on energy-rich crab eggs. By departure time for their long flight to the Arctic they carry so much breast fat that their legs seem short and they appear to almost waddle. Commercial overharvesting of Delaware Bay's horseshoe crabs has been blamed for this bird's recent, alarming decline. Finally arriving in the Arctic, the red knots' epic exertions are rewarded by long Arctic summer days, good feeding opportunities and fewer diseases – but in an extreme seasonal environment where suitable breeding conditions and food supplies expire abruptly after two or three months.

Speed, stopover and refuelling

The dilemma of the red knot's declining crab-egg supplies shows how refuelling sites can act as springboards, but also as bottlenecks if food is limited. Any climate-change effects that alter the quality and predictability of food resources at sites like these could be critical. Although declines in migratory birds are often attributed to changes to their breeding and non-breeding grounds, changes to stopover and refuelling sites may be equally important. Being able to take sufficient fuel on board is vital for birds to complete their journeys, especially for those crossing deserts, oceans and other large barriers.

The fat stores accumulated by feeding at stopover sites may also nourish developing egg follicles, as in some goose species. Among the largest Arctic-breeding birds, geese take considerable time to build up fat stores by eating plants. For some, successful migration is thought to entail riding the crest of a 'green wave' of new, nutrient-rich plant growth up a climate gradient to their breeding grounds.[13] These birds feed on the flush of fresh spring vegetation until its nutritional value tapers off, then travel to the next staging point to repeat this process. Fattening at the last stopover before breeding sites can be especially crucial for fuelling both flights and egg production.

This is because these geese may arrive ahead of the green wave on their breeding grounds, and cannot adequately refuel at that time. Instead their arrival is thought to be timed to allow hatchlings to benefit from local peaks in new spring vegetation. The importance of en route supplies is shown by Arctic-breeding barnacle geese, *Branta leucopsis*, where almost 40 per cent of the fat stores females rely on during the laying period may have been laid down thousands of kilometres way, in the Wadden Sea.[13] As we shall see, however, climate change could test the ability of some geese to ride the green wave.

Breeding and incubation

Climate change, by affecting the fortunes of birds during migration, could also have an influence on their breeding period. One important strand of effects stems from the power of weather to influence how many birds perish or survive during migration (a topic we will return to shortly). Even if a bird survives migration, arriving in poor condition may compromise its ability to reproduce or even stay alive in the breeding grounds.

Climate change could also influence birds' reproductive period by affecting their arrival time in their breeding grounds. An early start optimises breeding success for many birds (chapter 1). In temperate regions, arriving early at breeding sites gives migrants the opportunity to capture the best breeding territories, select high-quality mates, increase their offspring's chances for survival and possibly produce more clutches. Yet in some cases, even though advancing their arrival time would benefit birds, their migration schedules prevent them from doing so. Birds that arrive too early, on the other hand, may encounter greater risk of death from sudden cold snaps or delays in sufficient food supplies. The time constraints imposed by climate and food supplies conspire to create a very narrow window of opportunity for Arctic-breeding birds such as geese. They may have just a single week in the year to lay eggs with good chances for their young. The effect of climate change on the timing of this suitable period, and on the birds' ability to track it, could be critical.

Interrelated: good plumage, timely flights and successful breeding

Just as conditions during migration can influence when, and indeed if, an individual may breed, moult also demonstrates the interdependence of birds' life-cycle stages. The quality of a bird's plumage affects its flight performance, but also its ability to attract mates and stay warm. This shedding and replacing of feathers is another important activity birds must fit into their annual cycle, one that also demands extra energy. Exceptions notwithstanding, moult generally does not overlap with migration, because an incomplete plumage would make these journeys more difficult.[14] In fact, moult timing can even affect the start of migration.

Climate-change effects during birds' non-breeding period could also influence their other life-cycle stages. Because birds should not take off until they achieve suitable physical condition, food-supply problems at their wintering grounds can draw out migratory preparations, and affect their arrival date on breeding grounds. Taken together, these various interdependencies suggest that birds may not be able to adjust one life-cycle stage without modifying the others. These constraints could limit or delay their ability to adapt to new conditions,[15] like those imposed by climate change.

Migratory bird phenology is shifting

Heralds of spring

Given the critical importance of timing for many long-distance travellers, how has climate change affected their migratory schedules? A long tradition of noting migratory birds as harbingers of spring has proven invaluable to answering this question. Because of migratory birds' usefulness to people, and especially farmers, records of their arrival and departure timing date back three centuries in Europe, with some continuous sets of observations spanning more than 250 years. Importantly, these records demonstrate the strong relationship between temperature at a given locality and the date a migrant makes its spring appearance. However, these temperature fluctuations in their breeding grounds cannot explain all the year-to-year differences in arrival time, and this suggests other factors, including conditions along migration routes, also play a role.

The complete migratory pathways of birds are unknown in many cases, one factor that makes it impossible to study their progression over entire routes. Instead other methods are used to gauge how migration timing is affected by climate change. Most studies use birds' first arrival date (the first spring record of an individual of a given species) and median arrival date, measures that correlate well with each other. First arrival dates are an easy, less-costly way to gather data, but may be misleading if early birds' behaviour is atypical (the same could be said for date of last departure in autumn).

Earlier arrival on breeding grounds

One reason that arriving migratory birds make excellent indicators is because they are easy to observe. This is an understatement when it comes to the large and highly conspicuous white stork, *Ciconia ciconia*, a migrant that provides an model example of how migration phenology is shifting with climate change. In Poland, white storks are considered good-luck omens, and their bulky and virtually permanent nests are welcomed in villages and farms, where the birds construct them on roofs, electricity poles and trees.

The arrival of one of these migrants is hard to miss. 'It's a huge bird that flies like a pterodactyl,' says Tim Sparks. 'The data are incredibly good on white storks because people know exactly when a six-foot wing span bird returns from Africa.' This unique situation has allowed Sparks and his colleagues to accumulate accurate data on the storks' arrival timing. 'By and large these huge birds are getting earlier,' says Sparks, 'And we've definitely got evidence that the birds that return early and breed early are actually producing more chicks than those that come later.'[16] By arriving earlier, white storks increase their chances of occupying a good nest, and start egg laying earlier.

Migratory birds breeding in Australia and in North America have also shown a trend towards earlier arrival. In fact, the 'overwhelming balance of evidence'[15] suggests a widespread shift in migratory bird phenology in recent decades, and the consensus is that climate change is likely to be responsible. Birds would be expected to arrive earlier in their breeding grounds as the climate generally warms – and this is indeed the case. One analysis of records from 19 countries in Europe, covering the period 1950 to 2009, revealed that birds' first arrival dates have become, on average, 2.8 days earlier per decade (based on 440 species). The mean or median arrival dates advanced somewhat less, by an average of 1.8 days earlier per decade (based on 214 species).[15]

This substantiates an earlier analysis of Eurasian birds that revealed a similar pattern for 'early birds'. Earlier-arriving individuals advanced their migrations at a greater average rate (0.37 days per year) than the rest of their populations (0.1 days per year).[17] Whether this is because earlier migrants are responding more strongly to climate change, or simply reflects methods used to collect data, is still unknown. The strength of the advance in arrival time also varies greatly between species, and among different populations of the same species. Furthermore, some migrants have not changed their spring arrival timing, and others have even delayed it, highlighting the individualistic nature of birds' responses.

The trend towards earlier arrival may actually be stronger than data suggest. Where overall numbers of birds are declining, this would reduce the chance to spot early birds. In this way, falling numbers could mask phenological shifts, distorting the results of studies using first arrival date (rather than average arrival date). In the USA, the use of first arrival date indicated that just 11 out of 32 passerine bird species arrived earlier. But when mean arrival date was used, 26 species were revealed to have arrived earlier. Nineteen of the species underwent marked populations declines over the study period, and this explained most of the difference between these two sets of findings.[18]

This problem, whereby declining bird populations may mask the true extent of timing shifts, may be widespread. The number of human observers may also play a role. Whereas a century ago migratory birds' arrival was keenly anticipated and noted by a greater portion of a then-more-rural population, now, despite higher numbers of professional ornithologists, there may be fewer observers assiduously noting first arrivals.

Mixed messages and furtive exits: autumn departure

In contrast to arrivals, climate-change effects on birds' timing of departure from their breeding grounds are less well understood, and the trends more ambiguous. In Europe, responses may reflect the fact that autumn, unlike the other three seasons, is not warming. These mixed messages may also signal the differences in species' annual cycles or ecology. The relative importance of a given bird's breeding and non-breeding season, for example, may determine whether earlier spring arrival translates into earlier or later autumn departure.

In theory, long-distance migrants should time departure to allow them to take advantage of any beneficial conditions in their passage and wintering areas during late summer or autumn. Some long-distance migrants breeding in Europe and crossing the Sahara to winter in Africa may have advanced their entire breeding phase. Arriving earlier, breeding earlier and departing earlier, it is thought, allows them to cross this desert barrier in time to capitalise on benign conditions in the Sahel region as its rainy season ends in September.[19]

Short-distance migrants may face different constraints, and some that winter in the Mediterranean are showing a tendency to delay autumn migration. If they departed earlier, this could deliver them to poor end-of-summer resources in the Mediterranean basin. Because rainfall normally takes place in autumn and winter in this region, its ecological conditions tend to improve as autumn progresses.[20] In North America as well, over the past four and a half decades, autumn departure has been taking place later in some short-distance migratory songbirds and earlier among some (long-distance) Neotropical migratory songbirds.[21] Yet other research that compares these two broad groups of migrants has produced results that contrast with these findings.

The vague picture of migrants' autumn phenology likely reflects a smaller number of studies and fewer data on this phenomenon. Any trends may also be masked by the greater difficulty of detecting birds during autumn. After all, departure is a furtive affair compared to spring arrival, when birds tend to sing more and establish breeding territories; and some bird species, such as North American warblers, have less distinct plumages compared to their easily identifiable spring breeding plumages.

Length of stay on breeding grounds

Their comings and goings may shift in time, but how does this affect the overall period migrants spend on their breeding grounds? Evidence from the field in Europe suggests that whereas some migratory bird species may be lingering longer, others are not. And in North America, various breeding songbird species lengthened or shortened the period spent between their migrations, in some cases by more than 15 days, from 1961 to 2006.[21] Climate-change effects on the length of stay on breeding grounds seem to be another area of contrasting results.

What could explain the differing responses? Where climate warming provides long-distance migrants with a longer season of appropriate breeding weather this could, in theory, improve fledgling survival or allow more time for second broods. Single-brooding species might be expected to shift their entire annual cycle, including advancing autumn departure. Multi-brooding species, on the other hand, may be expected delay departure if they can produce more broods. In Denmark, multi-brooding species extended their breeding season by 0.43 days per year, whereas single-brooding species shortened their breeding season by just slightly more, 0.44 days per year, over the period 1970–2007.[22] For any given bird species, however, responses are likely to depend on much, including the latitude and climate trends of their breeding site. Where mid-summer droughts worsen, for example, any migratory bird might find it advantageous to advance its entire summer schedule and depart early.

Possible mechanisms for shifts in migration timing

Climate warming is apparently driving many birds to arrive earlier in their breeding grounds, but how do they achieve these timing shifts? They may do so by beginning their migration earlier, migrating faster or shortening the distance they migrate (by shifting where they spend their non-breeding season, for example; chapter 3). Exactly how and why they may arrive earlier is likely to be complex and varied. Certain birds, such as some geese, swans and shorebirds, may be unable to speed up migration if they already operate close to their physiological limit. However, in other birds, such as small passerines, faster migrations have already been observed.

A look at global-warming effects on weather patterns en route could be enlightening. Weather can affect birds' departure times, migration speed and stopover duration. It can introduce major risks, such as extreme weather that can kill thousands of travelling birds in a single event. Despite its importance, establishing the effect of weather along bird migration routes is still very much a work in progress.

Blowing in the wind

Wind is one aspect of weather that can be critical for successful migrations. Wind speed and direction influence birds' migrations by affecting their flight costs, their need to refuel, and ultimately the duration of their journeys. However, the effects of wind on arrival timing, and how these relationships may be affected by climate change, are largely unexplored.

Migrating birds are thought to be aware of wind conditions, and demonstrate the importance of wind direction and clear skies by generally beginning their migrations under fine, anti-cyclonic conditions that provide tailwinds or light winds. Tailwinds save energy and time. Trade and anti-trade winds allow some birds to achieve impressive ground speeds, as much as 180 kilometres per hour. Headwinds, on the other hand, impede progress. Radio-tagged barnacle geese migrated from Svalbard to Scotland in 5–15 days during favourable winds in 1994, but took 9–36 days to make the same journey in 1995 during mostly unfavourable winds. Unhelpful winds may force birds to land and wait – if they can. Over sea, if birds become exhausted or are simply blown off course, high mortalities can follow. Some migratory journeys demand quite specific wind conditions, such as the following winds that boost long-haul, non-stop fliers. Soaring birds such as raptors migrate with the help of thermal updrafts, and take advantage of the warm weather that produces these conditions.

If climate change alters wind currents, some birds may benefit and others may suffer. Song thrushes, *Turdus philomelos,* sped up their April passage from France to the Baltic region in association with more frequent favourable tailwinds over the last 40 years (an earlier start to benign temperatures also enhanced their migrations).[23] According to one theory, bird populations accustomed to variable conditions during migration may be able to adapt, while those whose migrations have been characterised by stable and reliable winds may be more adversely affected if conditions change.[24]

Heat, cold and bad weather

There is still only poor understanding of climate-change effects on other aspects of weather that influence the success of bird migrations. Temperature has long been recognised as an important factor in birds' arrival timing, but when it comes to its direct effect on bird migrations, it is hard to separate from other weather conditions favourable for flight. By and large, birds depart during clear nights with good visibility.[10]

As for adverse weather, migrating birds are more vulnerable to extreme cold and snow than better-adapted, year-round residents. Migrants seek to avoid these potentially fatal conditions, both en route and in their breeding areas. Rain and cloud also interfere with migration, including birds' ability to navigate by celestial or ground-based cues; these conditions may force them to land, possibly delaying arrival. At sea, land birds flying into clouds or mist become disoriented, mill about and often turn downwind, a strategy that may deliver them to clearer weather.[10] If the most intense tropical cyclones become more frequent under climate change as some climate models suggest (even as they project cyclones may become less frequent overall), this could affect birds that migrate through areas that experience these storms (chapter 5).

Indirect effects of weather

Climate change could also have important but indirect influences on migration timing via its effects on birds' food supplies, even exerting opposite effects at the different sites birds use over the course of their annual cycles. Where climate warming brings more favourable weather during spring, this may advance plant and insect development in birds' passage and breeding areas. These improved conditions for both foraging and migration may allow birds to speed up the latter phases of their spring migration through Europe or North America.[20]

In arid zones, climate-change effects on rainfall are likely to be important. Rainfall declines could reduce birds' food supplies and delay their departure, potentially constraining migrants' ability to adapt to climate change (chapter 5). On the other hand, if changes in climate lead to improved food supplies for birds in their non-breeding grounds, their fat reserves may be bolstered and their plumage quality enhanced. Among barn swallows, *Hirundo rustica*, overwintering in Africa, moult rate was higher during years of higher winter rainfall. This may allow birds to arrive earlier in their breeding grounds.[20]

Myriad strategies, individual responses

Although many birds are clearly arriving on their breeding grounds earlier with global warming, these changes to migration phenology are likely to be species-specific (as are changes to breeding phenology; chapter 1). This is unsurprising given the multitude of migratory strategies: diverse routes, flight speeds, stopover sites and non-breeding areas. Indeed, different strategies are seen among even among closely related species.

Further contributing to their individualistic responses, the temperature changes that birds experience with global warming may vary across both regions and seasons. Where migrants pass through different zones with partially independent climates, they may even face unequal rates of climate change in different stages of their annual cycle, and this could affect their ability to adapt. Species that migrate earlier in the spring, when weather tends to be more variable, may be expected to show a greater degree of response than late-migrating species.

Idiosyncratic responses like these challenge efforts to predict how climate change will affect migratory birds. Yet it may be speculated that some large birds have less scope to vary migration timing if they face relatively tight time constraints to complete breeding, moult and migratory journeys. Regardless, migratory birds' widely differing strategies and ecology could explain why some species have not changed, or have even delayed their spring arrival in recent decades, despite favourable changes in spring conditions in their breeding areas.

When males must be ready to contend: protandry

In many cases special circumstances tend to make the struggle between the males particularly severe. Thus the males of our migratory birds generally arrive at their places of breeding before the females, so that many males are ready to contend for each female.

Charles Darwin, 1871

Studying protandry could help indicate how different migratory bird populations might shift their timing, and even whether they can adapt to climate change. Protandry, the earlier arrival of males at breeding sites relative to females, is thought to occur in species whose males are under competitive pressure to stake a claim on limited resources such as breeding territory. Among barn swallows, males arrive first, select a nesting site and, when females eventually arrive, attract their attention to the site through circling flight and song, while showing off their long tail feathers. In general, males in prime condition are most able to arrive earliest and capture the best 'real estate'.

There is concern that climate change could differently affect the arrival times of males and females in these protandrous birds. This is because the two sexes migrate at different times of year, or may even use different wintering areas. If the weather at their breeding grounds becomes more benign, protandry could become more pronounced. In fact, this has already been observed among some barn swallows that migrate from Africa across the Sahara to breed in Denmark. Males arrived earlier on their breeding grounds as April temperatures warmed over the period 1971 to 2003. However, the egg-laying date for the birds has not changed; unlike the males, female barn swallows have not shifted their arrival time.[25]

In contrast to these barn swallows, the degree of protandry among some other European-breeding songbird species has not changed with warming. In the birds that display protandry, sex differences in the onset of migration timing are thought to be controlled by disparities in their response to circannual rhythms or daylight changes. Because these mechanisms are 'hardwired', changes to them would theoretically require genetic evolution. This could make adapting to climate change in their breeding grounds a slow process for protandrous birds.[26]

Mismatch in migratory birds

In a rapidly warming world, these individual responses of birds, and the animals and plants upon which they depend, could prove problematic for migrants with finely tuned annual cycles. In 1990, Finnish zoologist Lars von Haartman hinted at the problem after observing pied flycatchers, *Ficedula hypoleuca*, come and go at his country estate for half a century, writing, 'It would be a surprise if a small songbird was the first herald of an unknown change in climate, a matter which concerns us so deeply'. Sixteen years later, other Finnish biologists declared, 'The pied flycatcher has indeed become a herald of climate change . . .'[27]

This small black and white bird has become a textbook case of mismatch in migratory birds. An insectivore, it is appreciated for its ability to suppress harmful insects, and is often provided with nest boxes in plantations and important stands of oak trees in Europe. It breeds in Europe and western Asia and winters in western Africa, mainly in the Sahel. In these wintering grounds, cues about spring conditions along its migratory path or breeding areas may be unavailable.

In the Netherlands, some of these pied flycatchers have not advanced their arrival at their breeding grounds over the years (despite showing some weak tendency to arrive a little earlier in warmer years). Their breeding timing is failing to keep up with earlier abundance peaks of caterpillars, an important food for their chicks. They have been breeding sooner after their arrival, but not soon enough to track earlier food peaks. Adding to their problems, in warm years the food peak is not just early, but also shorter because caterpillars grow and pupate more rapidly, after which time they are no longer available as food.

Among nine populations studied around the Netherlands over the 1987–2003 period, the greatest declines were seen where food peaks were earliest,[28] and where the birds' laying dates responded most weakly to temperature. Some pied flycatcher populations declined by about 90 per cent. In the areas where food peaks are latest, and early breeders are still able to lay and hatch their clutches in time, population declines are far less severe, around 10 per cent.[29]

For migratory birds, the ability to respond to changes in food peak timing is critical. Yet their responses may also reflect other time-sensitive events in their environments, like the need to avoid adverse early-season weather on their breeding grounds. This is why, some theorise, birds' arrival dates should ideally advance somewhat less than the advance of their food peak. Nonetheless, if birds fail to advance their timing sufficiently, many will fall behind the phenology of their breeding grounds, and the relationship between their arrival timing and local temperature will no longer be the same. 'Mistiming as a result of climate change is probably a widespread phenomenon'[29] and, as the case of the Dutch pied flycatcher suggests, it may lead to population declines in migratory birds (chapter 5).

It is not just migrants' arrival timing that is affected by warming. A closer look at events in and around pied flycatcher nests reveals complex responses across a whole range of traits that impinge on their breeding success. In years with an earlier food peak, some pied flycatchers are breeding earlier and are also producing more eggs. But these larger clutches can actually exacerbate the birds' mismatch problem. Because they can lay only one egg per day, a larger clutch prolongs the pre-hatching phase. The birds may compensate somewhat by speeding up the incubation process, but not enough to track the advancing food supply; in years with an early food peak, chicks hatch an average 10 days after it passes.[30] Larger broods also sap parents' energy, taking a toll on their survival, experiments suggest.

These complex responses highlight the interrelatedness of different events in a bird's life history. They also show that to successfully track climate variations, birds must optimise not just their migration timing, but also their laying date, clutch size and incubation. These responses are not just complex – they are also individualistic, making it difficult to generalise about climate-change-induced mismatch in migratory birds. For example, in contrast to some declining Dutch study populations, pied flycatchers in northern Germany bred earlier, laid more eggs and fledged more young over the 1970–1995 period. But in south-western Finland, although many pied flycatchers are arriving steadily earlier, they are breeding later relative to the phenology of their environment. For unknown reasons they are delaying breeding after their arrival and laying smaller clutches.

Habitat matters: forests, marshes and mountains

Migrants' varied responses may also reflect the different habitats they use. In the Netherlands, populations of pied flycatchers and other long-distance migratory insect-eaters declined strongly in forests from 1984 to 2004 – but not in marsh habitats.[31] Whereas forest birds must contend with a brief spring food peak, marsh birds experience a more drawn-out period of insect abundance, supported by the continuous growth of reedy vegetation through spring and summer. This wider food peak may explain the better fortunes of marsh-dwelling long-distance migrants. Resident and short-distance migrants, on the other hand, declined neither in forests nor in marshes. First, this indicates that the problems experienced by forest-dwelling long-distance migrants did not stem from a general decline in their habitat quality. Second, it suggests that resident and short-distance migrant birds may better track food supply changes, a topic we will return to shortly.

Altitudinal migrants, those that migrate upslope and downslope along mountainous terrain across the seasons, may also become mismatched. As their climate warmed, American robins, *Turdus migratorius*, advanced their spring arrival at their high altitude breeding grounds in the Colorado Rocky Mountains, over the 1974–1999 period. Yet the snow-melt date at high altitude has changed little, possibly due to increased winter precipitation (as predicted by climate models). Arriving birds must wait an additional 18 days until bare ground is exposed before they can hunt for earthworms, their prey.[32]

Warming puts more predators across migrants' paths

Climate change could also influence the seasonal timing of predators that hunt migratory birds. When waves of migrating peregrine falcons, *Falco peregrinus*, encounter Western sandpipers, *Calidris mauri*, migrating south-wards along Canada's West Coast, their effect on these shorebirds is like a 'raptor tsunami'. A single peregrine falcon can capture two to four birds daily, and shorebird communities demonstrate fear as they take evasive action to avoid this threat.

Climate warming could make sandpiper migrations more perilous still. The sandpipers' arrival time in their Arctic and subarctic breeding grounds, from tropical wintering areas, is fairly fixed. Moreover, the timing of their dangerous southward, post-breeding migration along the coast also varies little. Falcons, on the other hand, are likely to strongly advance their arrival at their breeding grounds in years when early snow melt makes this possible. They can then move to coastal areas sooner with their young, ready to intercept the southbound sandpipers. These early snow-melt years may increase the sandpipers' chances of encountering falcons.[33]

Climate change affects migratory readiness

The rigid programs of some long-distance migrants notwithstanding, many birds have scope to alter their migratory strategies under climate change, even without evolving genetically. Migratory behaviour is actually a con-tinuum, and most migratory populations typically have a small number of individuals with very weak or even no migratory activity. Partial migrants are able to monitor local conditions and migrate (or not) to capitalise on food availability and weather.[34] Diminishing seasonality is one climate-change effect that could result in reduced migratory readiness, and may occur where winter temperatures increase more than those of summer.

Breeding greenfinches, *Carduelis chloris*, in Finland exemplify migrants in a state of flux. A formerly largely migratory population is becoming increasingly sedentary, as more birds remain in Finland instead of migrating to northern Germany for the winter. Similar trends have been seen in a range of different European and North American birds, including red kites, *Milvus milvus*, Eurasian chiffchaffs, *Phylloscopus collybita*, and great crested grebes, *Podiceps cristatus*. In each case, more individuals are opting to stay on their breeding grounds, effectively increasing the bird fauna overwintering at some higher latitude regions. This trend would be expected to continue with warming. However, access to bird feeders during winter may also be playing a role. Examples of birds staying on at their non-breeding (wintering) grounds are scarcer.

These flexible responses notwithstanding, ornithologist Ian Newton warns that, '[t]he persistence of long, roundabout migration routes provides a cautionary reminder against the notion that birds invariably behave optimally'.[10] Most examples seen so far entail gradual, incremental change that is advantageous. Yet for some birds, viable change would require a great departure from their current strategy, such as a change in migration direction; intermediate changes might prove lethal. It would therefore be a mistake to assume that all birds can alter their migratory behaviour if the conditions of their environment rapidly change under global warming.

Long-distance migrants' unique vulnerabilities

Unfortunately, the potentially conflicting pressures of optimal timing of migration and breeding may make long-distance migrants such as godwits particularly vulnerable to the effects of climate change.

Jesse Conklin et al., 2010

Turning to migrants that may lack the capacity to alter their migratory behaviour, one of the most apparent patterns has been the tendency for long-distance migrants to advance their spring arrival more weakly than short-distance migrants under climate change. Exceptions exist,[35] but the majority of studies comparing these two groups have found this effect for birds breeding in Europe and North America.[15] In fact, some long-distance migrants have even delayed their arrival on breeding grounds, despite warming and earlier plant and insect phenology in these locations.

Interestingly, among bar-tailed godwits, an individual's departure date at its New Zealand non-breeding area is strongly related to where it breeds in Alaska.[36] Individuals breeding in northerly Alaskan locations depart New Zealand later. This may reflect the delay in the start of snow-free periods in Alaska's far north – two to four weeks later than in this state's south-west. These birds also return to New Zealand in the same order they depart. These strictly scheduled migrations suggest endogenous control, since the godwits are unlikely to be aware of conditions in Alaska – far across the world – while staying in New Zealand.

These godwits' rigid schedules may have evolved to help them exploit favourable winds and predictable peaks in fuelling resources. But a lack of flexibility could make them especially vulnerable to climate change, if their arrival timing in Alaska no longer matches suitable spring breeding conditions, or if their migration schedules fall out of step with en-route fuelling resources or favourable weather for travel.

Cued or clueless?

One possible constraint on flexible responses may be a lack of cues. Spring conditions on their breeding grounds may be advancing, but how do long-distance migrants, possibly thousands of kilometres away, obtain reliable information to schedule their time-sensitive passages? A lack of cues, some researchers theorise, could explain the weaker advance of long-distance migrants' phenology with climate warming. The greater the distance between breeding and non-breeding ranges, the less likely these areas will be to share common changes in climate conditions. Under global warming, the strongest average temperature increases are taking place at higher northern latitudes. In the tropics, seasonality is more influenced by precipitation than temperature, which varies less than in the temperate zone.

It is possible that birds decide to depart from their wintering grounds independently of weather conditions in their breeding grounds. They might then adjust their migration speed accordingly, as they encounter the influence of large-scale climate systems like the North Atlantic Oscillation. Interestingly though, evidence suggests some long-distance migrants might actually have clues about their far-flung destinations. In sub-Saharan Africa, where many European-breeding long-distance migrants overwinter and stop over, February temperature anomalies correlate with those in Europe. However, the strength of this relationship has declined over the past 25 years; this could detract from birds' ability to adjust their migrations to climate conditions, and adapt.[37]

But there might be a much simpler explanation for the different level of response seen in short- and long-distance migrants. Their migration phenology could merely reflect different weather conditions during the periods they travel. Many long-distance migrants to Europe travel through this continent only for the latter part of their journeys, relatively late in spring when weather is less variable than earlier in the season. European short-distance migrants, on the other hand, are on the continent

year-round, and may be expected to respond more rapidly and appropri-
ately to the changes there. Another explanation for the stronger advance
in short-distance migrants may be shortened migration distances (chapter 3). If birds use wintering areas still closer to their breeding grounds, this
could improve their ability to predict spring conditions and adjust their
schedules.

Tight scheduling may be another constraint on flexible responses. Long-
distance migrations can be time-consuming, taking weeks to complete; pied
flycatchers' ability to adjust to climate change may be limited by their top
migration speed, and by when they can leave their sub-Saharan wintering
grounds. Birds migrating in long stages with few stops for refuelling, rather
than short hops, may also be more vulnerable if critical stopover sites are
affected by climate change. Climate conditions in their non-breeding areas
may affect their flexibility too, via effects on their habitat quality, food
supplies, and the time needed to build up fat stores (which ultimately
influences their departure timing).

As suggested by New Zealand bar-tailed godwits' strictly scheduled
migrations, timing in some long-distance migrants is more likely to be
under endogenous control. Some researchers hypothesise that this could be
another constraint to flexible responses to climate warming. If the mechanisms controlling the timing of such birds' migration onset needed to
evolve genetically, their adaptive responses to climate change would probably occur only slowly, over generations. Others point out that little is yet
known about which bird species' migrations are or are not under strict
endogenous control. Moreover, they argue, past variations in climate are
likely to have promoted variation in the genetic make-up among birds in
any given population, and this implies that some birds would 'fit' new conditions (if these conditions were within the bounds of those experienced by
their populations in the past).[15]

When it comes to a lack of flexibility to respond to climate change,
Arctic-breeding shorebirds may be especially vulnerable. Genetic diversity
is the raw material for natural selection, and some question whether the
generally low genetic variability seen in Arctic-breeding shorebirds species
will hinder their ability to adapt, now and in the future. The red knot is
emblematic in this sense. Its genetic make-up indicates that its numbers
probably dropped in the past, possibly when climatic charges limited the
extent of high-Arctic breeding areas and forced the birds through population

bottlenecks.[38] Even if all six red knot subspecies are considered, this species still ranks as among the least genetically diverse of a range of bird species studied.

Likewise, the very conservative migratory behaviour seen in shorebirds augurs ill for flexible responses. Among 43 documented cases of altered bird migration routes, not a single one of them involved a species of wader. As another example, Neotropical songbirds have retained circuitous migratory routes that are artefacts of climate conditions that have long since passed – another testament to the conservative nature of genetically controlled migratory behaviour.

Nonetheless, the behaviour of many long-distance migrants may be more flexible than supposed. Pied flycatchers, for example, advanced their spring migration through Northern Africa by 10 days between 1980 and 2002. One explanation put forward for this advance was improved rainfall in the Sahel, indicating how factors apart from photoperiod – in this case, habitat quality – can influence migration timing.[39] Yet these flycatchers were still unable to arrive earlier in their breeding grounds, probably due to other environmental constraints they face during their journey.

Trans-Saharan migrants: crossing a formidable barrier, greeted by drought

With their time-sensitive passages and climate-sensitive African wintering areas, trans-Saharan migrants like pied flycatchers are considered key indicators of the climate-change effects on migratory species.[40] From 1970 to 2000, this group of long-distance migrants from Africa fared much worse than related short-distance migrants or residents of Europe. Many (though not all) of the declines were in the populations of birds using dry, open habitats in Africa during their non-breeding season.

Unknowns remain as to where, south of the Sahara, many of these migrants spend their non-breeding season, or the habitats they use there. Complicating this picture further, birds may vary their location, migrating within Africa over the non-breeding season to track favourable conditions. Nonetheless, many are thought to overwinter in the Sahel, one of the planet's most sensitive climate zones. A belt of semi-arid grasslands, thorn shrublands, savannas and steppes, the Sahel spans the African continent, sandwiched between the more arid Sahara to the north and somewhat less arid savannah to the south (known as the Sudanian savannah). Life-giving July–September rains drive the Sahel's single yearly pulse in the growth of grass, seeds, and insects and other invertebrates. Even in normal years, this flush of productivity quickly fades after the passing of the rainy season and migratory birds' autumn arrival.

The Sahel's history is punctuated by periods of crippling drought. The last severe event (1972–84), from which there has been partial recovery, was one of its worst droughts on record. How will climate change affect the Sahel in future? This is still a matter of debate. Although some climate models suggest both the Sahel and the Sahara could receive more moisture, others predict increased drought for the region. The latter scenario would be expected have a harmful effect on some birds overwintering in Africa.

The Sahara already presents migrating birds with a formidable ecological barrier – a desert crossing of roughly 1700 kilometres that some accomplish in a single flight, others in stages. Many migrants rely on helpful tailwinds to successfully traverse it and reach the Sahel, and changes in tailwind dependability and speed affect their safety margins. In dry years, birds without sufficient fat loads may starve during migration.[41] It is not known how climate change could affect stopover areas, including refuelling sites critical to migrants' successful desert passages. The important role of energy reserves for successful desert crossings has some researchers asking whether these migrants' physiological limits will be exceeded, and which species are likely to cope best and worst under future climate change.

The already lengthy overall journeys of these migrants may grow still longer if climate change affects their European ranges. Nine out of 17 species of *Sylvia* warblers studied may experience northward shifts in their European breeding distributions by this century's final decades.[42] For example, the 4800 kilometre journey of barred warblers, *Sylvia nisoria*, from Central Europe to sub-Saharan Africa, could in future extend to more than 5600 kilometres. Longer overall migration distances may exacerbate any mismatch problems. They would also require these trans-Saharan migrants to increase their fuel loads by about nine per cent of lean body mass, on average. If taking more fuel on board were possible, birds would need more time to feed prior to migration, or additional time in stopovers.

Given the new challenges posed by climate change, will some trans-Saharan migrants choose to simply overwinter in Europe instead of migrating to Africa? This possibility is suggested by the first winter records of pied flycatchers around the Mediterranean.[15]

Asymmetric climate change: green waves get choppy

A separate set of climate-change challenges face geese that ride the crest of a green wave to their Arctic breeding sites, challenges that potentially affect their ability to stay well-fuelled and make timely arrivals. For these geese, favourable conditions at both refuelling sites and destinations are crucial for breeding success in the highly seasonal Arctic environment. The need to exploit these resources creates considerable timing challenges, partly because vegetation growth hinges on local climate.

In Europe, the timing of spring has advanced more than that of other seasons, making climate change somewhat uneven over time. This advance is greatest at intermediate latitudes. Modelling suggests that, in future, climate change will also be uneven across the different zones birds migrate through. This asymmetric climate change is already taking place along the north-east Atlantic flyway of geese. North-west Europe is warming, but spring weather conditions at their Russian Arctic breeding grounds are unchanged. Yet even if temperature increases were a *uniform* 1°C, plant growth in the Wadden Sea and Baltic flyways of barnacle geese would advance by eight days, whereas breeding site vegetation in Russia would advance by a mere four. This is because, in the Arctic, vegetation growth cannot occur until temperatures rise above the freezing threshold.

Global warming that is uneven in time and space could disrupt the climatic gradient of the green wave and cause problems for geese. Local cues that prompt the birds to leave, namely particular growth thresholds in plants, are useful only as long as local and distant sites keep the same relationship. Geese that heed the earlier 'spring bite' in their staging areas would arrive on breeding grounds to find colder conditions than in the past, and longer delays until plant growth starts. The speed and magnitude of climate change along their flyways are very likely to push traditional migratory schedules out of synchrony with food sources, and affect the way geese build up the fat stores so crucial to breeding success.[13]

Can geese adapt? On top of climate change, many goose populations are being squeezed out of their natural habitats by agriculture or other land-use change. Since the early 1990s, for example, growing numbers of barnacle geese bound for Russian Arctic breeding areas have delayed their winter departure from the Wadden Sea by four weeks, despite the earlier arrival of spring there. This subset of birds then virtually skips traditional spring stopovers in the Baltic region. The suspected reason for avoiding this area is the increasing numbers of predators like eagles and greater competition for food on shrinking agricultural land.[43] Although the cultural traditions and flexible responses of these long-lived birds are expected to help them adapt, some experts question whether geese will be able to track the increasing velocity of change predicted in coming decades.[44]

Knowledge gaps and challenges

More than once an entire flock, distinct by the unity of their calls, came into range and passed out of hearing, keeping up their regular formation with the precision of a swiftly moving but orderly body of horsemen … It was a marvel and a mystery enacted under the cover of night, and of which only fugitive tidings reached the listeners below.

Orin Libby, 1899

The extreme and enigmatic lifestyles of bar-tailed godwits, red knots and other endurance champions of the bird world provoke fascinating questions that defy easy answers. Unravelling the effects of global warming on these globe-trotting bird species will necessitate studying their entire annual cycles. However, the current lopsided concentration of scientists and research funding in the North Temperate Zone fails to reflect this need. The ease of and far more funding for conducting research in relative comfort in developed countries means far less is known about migrants' movements to and from their non-breeding (wintering) grounds and passage areas in the tropics and southern latitudes. Climate change is a global problem, but as long as relevant research remains narrowly focused, mainly on passerine birds at their European and North American breeding grounds, answers and solutions will remain elusive.

Innovative use of tracking, imaging and molecular marking technology has confirmed the epic nature of some long-distance odysseys. These technologies could also help reveal whether birds use climate-sensitive habitats like the Sahel, and even shed light on the ecological conditions encountered there. Building on this work, a network of bird ringing (or banding) stations in the developing world be a cost-effective way to monitor climate-change effects (chapter 7).

Studies of migration phenology overwhelmingly focus on temperature effects, with little information to be had on the influence of other climate variables. Changes to precipitation, wind, snow-melt date, plant growth, atmospheric pressure and sea-ice extent could also reveal much about migratory birds' responses to global warming. Another oft-overlooked aspect is the potential unevenness, across seasons and regions, of changes in climate. Yet this asymmetric climate change could have a bearing on whether migratory birds become mismatched or adapt.

Conclusion

Migratory birds, especially long-distance migrants, provide powerful examples of the climate-change effects on wildlife. Despite surviving past turbulent climates and glacial periods, many migratory birds now face a combination of climate change and other escalating human threats – an uncertain future. Migratory birds are important components of wetlands and the Arctic tundra and other high-latitude ecosystems, where future climate-change impacts are expected to be profound (chapter 3).

Their wide-ranging annual travels, active metabolisms and sensitivity to change make migratory birds integrative sentinels that could allow us to monitor climate change and ecosystem health perhaps better than could any other network of observations. These same characteristics also make some migratory birds vulnerable to climate change. The alarming decline among many migratory groups in the face of a wide spectrum of human threats adds urgency to research efforts.

The greater bulk of studies suggest that many migratory birds are arriving earlier on their breeding grounds in recent decades, in association with climate warming. Yet some birds are not advancing their spring migrations enough to keep up with climate change. Where they fail to track climate-driven changes in their breeding grounds, mismatch between peak demands of the nestlings and food supplies can occur. Among pied fly-catchers in the Netherlands, mismatch has been implicated in population declines. Climate change that is uneven across seasons or migratory flyways may also decrease the predictability of their food supplies en route to their destinations, increasing the likelihood of mismatch.

Although many migratory birds are displaying a degree of flexible response to global warming, it would be a mistake to assume all birds can alter their migratory behaviour. Most (but not all) studies indicate that long-distance migrants are advancing their spring arrival less than short-distance migrants. The reasons for this may be many and varied, including conflicts between optimal migration and breeding times, or strict endoge-nous control. Long-distance migrants with less scope to shift their migration timing may be more vulnerable to climate change.

Chapter 3

RANGE SHIFTS AND RESHUFFLED COMMUNITIES

Climate's role in bird distributions

Dwindling ecological capital at the world's biggest duck factory

In North America, changes to the climate of the world's most productive waterfowl habitat could put this 'duck factory' on a path towards an even greater conflict with human development. Both the origins and the future fate of the Prairie Pothole Region are inextricably linked to changes in climate. When ice sheets moved across North America more than ten thousand years ago, they scoured depressions and left uneven deposits of sediment. This glacial sculpting laid the groundwork for a roughly 700 000 square kilometre swathe of millions of wetland ponds, dotted across the grasslands of the Northern Great Plains. Frigid winters lock the region in ice and snow but in spring, melting snow and rain fill the ponds. The rapidly greening landscape comes alive and its ponds harbour a veritable explosion of aquatic life. Beyond the bulrushes of pond margins, concealed in long grasses on nearby land, millions of nests produce the majority of the continent's ducks in most years. The region also provides crucial breeding and stopover habitat for migratory birds.

The Prairie Pothole Region's suitability for farming, however, has led at least half of its ponds to be drained or altered – a classic case of human land use in conflict with internationally important wildlife habitat. On top of this habitat-loss threat, climate trends over the last century have made this region's eastern wetlands too wet and its western ones too dry. In both cases this has reduced wetland productivity.

What does the future hold for the duck factory? Climate modelling[1] for the north-central USA portion of this region suggests pond numbers could decline by about half, and the numbers of breeding ducks they could support would also drop by roughly half, from five million to 2.1–2.7 million birds.[2] A more recent and fine-grained climate analysis, by South Dakota State University biologist Carter Johnson and his colleagues, details the potential problems in store for the region's dabbling ducks, such as mallards and teal.[3] To raise their young, most such birds require that ponds retain surface water for a minimum of 100 days, on average. Yet with future climate change, water volume will drop and wetland ponds will dry out more quickly. With 2°C of warming, the number of years with this 100-day 'hydroperiod' would drop by two-thirds; with 4°C of warming, such years would be virtually eliminated. The western wetlands of this region would dry still further, becoming too parched to support the numbers of waterfowl they have in the past.

The region's best future climate for this habitat would shift east – where 90 per cent of pothole wetlands are already drained for agriculture. 'Unless these wetlands, and nesting habitat in the adjoining uplands, are protected and restored,' warns Johnson, 'there is little insurance for waterfowl against future climate warming.'

The duck factory dilemma arises because climate affects where birds and other organisms may be found. The changing climate is expected to impose a 'forced march' on many wildlife species as they seek to adapt. Plants and animals have responded to dramatic changes in climate over history, but today landscapes radically altered by humans, like the wetlands-turned-farmland just described, impose new obstacles.

Birds' well-known sensitivity to weather means their distributions or ranges[4] (range being the geographic area where a given species or population is found) are often climate-limited. Birds are also sensitive to changes in climate. Like other 'warm-blooded' animals they are predisposed to live in a particular thermal environment or climate. Each species has a specific thermoneutral zone, the range of ambient temperatures that permits it to maintain constant body temperature and carry out normal body functions at rest, without resorting to special mechanisms to heat or cool itself.

The precise climate factors that determine the distribution of any given species may be varied and complex. Climate, moreover, is not the only determinant of ranges. Birds must find food, compete with other birds, avoid predators and cope with disease. This explains why more emphasis is placed on these biotic interactions for animals, whereas climate is widely seen as the paramount controller of the distributions of plants. Biogeographical history, including past extinction episodes and major disturbances such as fires and cyclones, may also influence species' distributions. The distribution patterns of some birds and other wildlife have also, for centuries and even millennia, responded to hunting and other human activity. Nevertheless, climate is often assumed to be the ultimate, albeit indirect, underlying determinant of bird distributions.

Big pieces missing from the bird-distribution puzzle

It may surprise some readers to learn that, for 98 per cent of bird species, precise distributions are still unknown. Most maps of bird distributions are based on sites species are known to occupy, supplemented by information about where they are inferred to be. But very few species are actually found throughout this entire mapped geographical range, or *extent of occurrence* (EOO); ecological constraints imposed by vegetation, elevation and micro-climate make this unlikely. Birds' *area of occupancy* (AOO), the portion of the EOO they actually occupy, may be much smaller, by even an order of magnitude.

This means that some of the most specialised and threatened birds are not actually found where presumed,[5] and many threatened birds with narrow ranges may be even rarer than their range maps suggest. What is more, for 1500 bird species, most of them near threatened, even the coarser EOO information is lacking.[6]

Possible climate-change effects on birds' ranges

The importance of climate as a determinant of ranges begs the question, 'how might bird distributions respond to global warming?' In theory, to persist in a changing climate, populations of birds and other wildlife may rely on two fundamental types of response. They can either adapt to the new climate within their current ranges (chapter 7); or shift to an area that matches their climate tolerances (and otherwise meets their needs), known as niche-tracking. These two types of responses are not exclusive, and species may rely on both to varying degrees.

But if a population neither adapts nor tracks its niche, it could effectively find itself outside the conditions that make up this niche. Cold-adapted species, for example, are those considered most likely to face the most thermal stress in a warming world. In France, the response of birds to the extreme six-month European heatwave of 2003 hints at the possible consequences of exceeding climate tolerances. In areas experiencing the greatest temperature extremes, species with the narrowest thermal ranges suffered the largest annual declines in population growth over 2003–2004.[7] Once climate change exceeds the tolerances of a species, if it neither shifs nor adapts it is considered likely to be at risk of extinction, regionally or globally. Fossil evidence supports this theory, revealing that past extinctions occurred among species unable to adapt or shift in concert with changing climates.

It may not be known which of the many aspects of climate – from rainfall and humidity to daytime summer heat – most strongly influence the distribution of a species. Yet some generalisations are possible. Upper and lower temperature and precipitation thresholds are often crucial determinants of ranges. In North America, winter night-time temperature (cold) is thought to define songbird species' northernmost boundaries, most likely a reflection of limits on the energy they need to spend to stay warm.

As the climate of most world regions warms, birds and other wildlife would be expected to track suitable climate conditions. Because climates are relatively cooler towards the poles and at higher elevations, species are expected to respond to climate warming by tracking their niches polewards or upslope (though exceptions exist). These range shifts are considered less likely to be realised by the progressive movement of individuals, and more likely to occur as juvenile birds settle in new areas. If unable to disperse or adapt, bird populations at the low latitude or low elevation (warm) edges of their ranges are generally thought to be at greatest risk of dying out.

Changes to precipitation, including not just overall quantity but also the frequency and intensity of rainfall events across the year, may be even more important than temperature change for some birds. Towards the equator, and generally in more arid or high-temperature regions, water-related aspects of climate may strongly influence birds' ranges (chapter 6). At Namibia's Etosha Pan, flamingos start to breed only when annual mean precipitation exceeds 419 millimetres, and reproduce successfully only at levels between 510 and about 700 millimetres. Water must flood the pan and remain for three months. Too little and the pan dries up, predators invade and flamingos abandon their attempt. Too much water and nests may flood, bringing the breeding event to ruin.[8] Precipitation may also determine distributions by influencing the availability of water for birds to drink and via the constraints it imposes on food abundance.

Therefore, in dry tropical and subtropical regions and those elsewhere with generally arid conditions, declining precipitation and rising temperatures may be expected to cause ranges to contract from low-latitude or lower-elevation boundaries. In humid regions, effects are likely to be more unpredictable because complex interactions between species may be the overriding factor in animal distributions.[9,10]

Climate change is not uniform across the globe and varies from region to region, even at the scale of local areas. Within a single species, it could also have divergent effects on individuals in different parts of their range. In Spain, European dippers, *Cinclus cinclus*, face negative effects with warming as supplies of aquatic insects decline in tandem with reduced water flow to creeks. Yet in Norway, warmer winters have increased the dippers' winter survival.

As birds come and go, species richness may change

Where species shift their ranges under global warming, the character of a region's bird fauna could change, as could its species richness: the total number of species found in a given area or community. Generally speaking, species richness is higher in tropical regions around the equator than in temperate or polar regions. In low-latitude, high-temperature regions, precipitation best predicts species richness. At high latitudes, temperature tends to be the most important factor. Today, many centres of high species richness for birds are protected as conservation areas.

Species richness will depend on the net effect of bird species colonising or remaining in a given area, balanced against those lost as populations shift out. Climate warming is generally expected to increase species richness in temperate, boreal and Arctic regions, and at high-elevation sites. In arid tropical and subtropical regions, however, species richness would be expected to decrease where precipitation declines and temperatures rise.

Climate change will transform birds' habitats

Loss and deterioration of habitat seem to be the most likely impacts of climate change on vertebrates.

Rob Robinson et al., 2009

The distributions of birds may be expected to move if the climate tolerances of their populations are pushed, but their ranges may also respond as climate change exerts numerous other effects on their habitats. Rising sea levels, melting sea ice (chapter 4), and altered fire regimes are some of the obvious ways birds' habitats could be transformed. Climate change may also affect vegetation and other vital ecological underpinnings of birds' habitats. In the Arctic, for example, pronounced warming is expected to increasingly allow shrubs to invade the treeless tundra. In the mountains of Switzerland and the Canadian Rockies, plant zones are migrating towards summits. Forests are crucial habitats for many birds, but climate change could cause some to die back and transform others (chapter 6).

The burgeoning atmospheric carbon dioxide emissions that drive global warming also affect ecosystems in direct ways. Rising carbon dioxide levels are affecting ocean chemistry (chapter 4), and have a stimulating effect on most plants' growth. This gas also affects the proportion of growth devoted to leaves, stems or roots. In some Australian habitats, for example, rising carbon dioxide levels are likely to result in trees with thicker canopies, yet how this might affect birds' ability to forage is unknown.

Elevated carbon dioxide levels can also cause plants to grow tougher and less nutritious leaves (leaves containing less nitrogen, and therefore protein, a key nutrient for leaf-eating insects). This may affect the abundance of some insects birds rely on for food. Weedy plants, if they respond more strongly to higher carbon dioxide levels, may expand their ranges. The myriad effects of carbon dioxide on plants are complex, and their potential effects, in combination with those of climate change, remain far from clear.

Evidence for range shifts driven by climate change

The marching begins: plant and animal responses

This is an unexpectedly strong response, suggesting that current warming trends are swamping other, potentially counteractive, global change forces.

Camille Parmesan, 2005

Range shifts are expected with climate change, but are they already underway? First, there is clear evidence of warming likely to have been caused by human activity. In 2007, the IPCC reported that average warming had occurred since about mid-century on all continents except Antarctica. More recently, it was revealed that even Antarctica has warmed, on average, since 1957 – although the effect is rather uneven across this continent.[11]

Second, there is powerful evidence that species are shifting their distributions in concert with this climate warming, another key fingerprint of global warming on the living world. From the Arctic to the Antarctic, on land and in oceans, diverse forms of life are on the move, from plankton and dragonflies to penguins. The distances entailed may be large, including 680-kilometre shifts of some butterflies or the 1000-kilometre shifts for some marine copepods (a type of crustacean; chapter 4).

Yet measuring range shifts poses challenges. Many species are found across entire continents and beyond, and this makes collecting data on their entire distributions difficult and costly. Most investigators therefore infer range shifts rather than measure them directly. They might measure population movement at a range boundary, such as the poleward shift of the northern (cold) boundary of a Northern Hemisphere species. Range shifts may also be signalled by a change in the make-up of local ecological communities, such as an increase in the abundance of a species normally found at lower latitudes (those living under warmer conditions).

By combining hundreds of studies like these to create meta-analyses, researchers have established firm evidence of climate-driven distributional changes. One such meta-analysis, encompassing data for 99 birds, butterflies and alpine plants, revealed significant range shifts, averaging 6.1 kilometres per decade polewards or 6.1 metres per decade upslope.[12] Among species that shifted their distributions, 81 per cent did so in the direction expected given climate-change predictions. Evidence for range shifts in a broad range of wildlife species continues to mount.[13,14]

This spatial signal of climate change has emerged strongly from a noisy background of yearly climate and weather fluctuations. It is also detectable despite the influence of habitat destruction and other human impacts that might drive disparate and even opposing range shifts. These findings provide high confidence that climate change is already affecting biodiversity, and also unmask it as one of the most important drivers of changes to species' distributions today.

Expanding or contracting with warming?

The distributions of many species are shifting, but what does this imply about their overall range size? The possibility that climate change may drive range contractions has important conservation implications, since small and shrinking ranges are considered key criteria for gauging extinction threats (chapter 5). Initially, most examples of range shifts entailed the extension of species' (cold) high-latitude boundaries towards the poles or of their high-elevation boundaries upslope. Examples of expected contractions of species' ranges from their (warm) low-latitude or low-elevation boundaries were scarcer.

It may be that some organisms at their warm-range margins are less responsive to climate change, or that current levels of warming are insufficient to cause populations to abandon these locations. Whereas high-latitude limits of species' ranges may be more constrained by cold, at lower-latitude range boundaries water scarcity (in arid regions) may play a greater role, as might interactions with other species (in humid regions). In some areas range shifts may be occurring, but are still too subtle to measure. Finally, local extinction may occur more slowly and be harder to detect than colonisation. Studies that measure only the presence or absence of a bird species cannot detect large shifts in population density until the very last individual disappears. If adult survival is high, this could take a long time – another factor that could mask range contractions.[15]

Despite the greater difficulty of detection, evidence of range contractions has begun to mount. The changing climate has been linked to the extinctions of dozens of harlequin frog species (chapter 5) and of butterfly populations. In fact, by 2006, University of York conservation biologist Chris Thomas

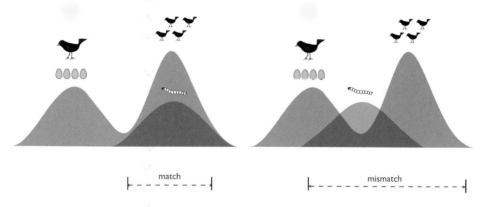

|———— match ————| |———————— mismatch ————————|

(**Top**) A rockhopper penguin living up to its name. Climate change effects on ocean food supplies are one suspected cause of rockhoppers' serious decline. Image: Çağan Şekercioğlu

Figure 1 Match versus mismatch. Cued by environmental stimuli (like day length), some birds lay eggs at a time that will permit peak availability of prey (like caterpillars) to match the peak food demands of their chicks. Under climate change, environmental cues may no longer accurately predict food peaks that are taking place earlier. If birds' laying does not keep up, a mismatch between food supplies and chicks' demands can result. Based on: Stenseth N.C. & Mysterud S. (2002) Climate, changing phenology, and other life history traits: Nonlinearity and match-mismatch to the environment. Proceedings of the National Academy of Sciences 99(21):13379–13381. Copyright (2002) National Academy of Sciences, USA.

(**Top**) A winter moth caterpillar feeding on oak leaves. Pied flycatchers (right) are among the well-studied group of birds reliant on peaks in the abundance of such insects to feed their young. Image: Christiaan Both

(**Above**) Hunch-backed bundles of fat and muscle, bar-tailed godwits are endurance champions of the bird world. Long-distance migrants' demanding schedules could leave some vulnerable to timing conflicts under climate change. Image: Phil Battley

(**Below**) The pied herald of climate change. In the Netherlands, where some pied flycatchers' breeding timing has become mismatched with peaks in their insect prey's abundance, population declines of up to 90 per cent have been seen. Image: Christiaan Both

(**Bottom**) Pied flycatcher nestlings at 12 days of age, around the time of their peak food demands. Image: Christiaan Both

(**Above**) Male barn swallows arrive before females in their breeding grounds, and compete with other males for prime territories. In Denmark, some male barn swallows are arriving still earlier, but female arrival timing is unchanged. Image: Çağan Şekercioğlu

(**Top**) Africa's Sahel during the wet season. Trans-Saharan migrants from Europe cross a desert barrier of some 1700 kilometres to reach the Sahel. Some (but not all) climate models predict increased drought for the Sahel region. Image: John Newby/Sahara Conservation Fund

(**Above**) Indega Bindia, senior ornithologist at Senegal's Djoudj National Park, holds an aquatic warbler. Europe's most threatened migratory songbird, this warbler now faces a new threat from climate change. Image: Martin Flade, Aquatic Warbler Conservation Team, BirdLife International

(**Above**) Solving a migration mystery. Five years of investigation led an international team to the first-known African wintering area for European-breeding aquatic warblers, in Djoudj National Park, south of the Sahara. Conservationists prepare nets in the birds' wetland habitat to carry out ringing. Image: Wolfgang Maedlow, Naturschutzbund Deutschland

(**Left**) This bald ibis was satellite tagged in Syria in 2006, then traced to a valley in the Ethiopian highlands, where they have been presumed extinct for decades. Monitoring migratory birds' movements will be vital to conservation efforts under climate change. Image: Çağan Şekercioğlu

(**Top**) North America's duck factory: the Prairie Pothole Region is the world's most productive waterfowl habitat. Yet climate warming is expected to reduce pond numbers and cause many to dry up more quickly. Image: Jim Ringelman/Ducks Unlimited

(**Above**) Climate models suggest the Prairie Pothole Region's best climate conditions for breeding birds will shift eastward in future, where 90 per cent of pothole wetlands have already been drained for agriculture. Image: Jim Ringelman/Ducks Unlimited

(**Above**) A capercaillie lek. The world's largest grouse, the capercaillie is adapted to open mature pine woods. In the UK, its core range is found in ancient Caledonian forests and conifer plantations of north east Scotland. Climate change and other threats could drive a second capercaillie extinction in the UK. Image: Desmond Dugan

(**Below**) Brünnich's guillemots at Coats Island in Canada's Arctic. Incubating birds face attacks from mosquitoes that now appear earlier in warm years. Image: Jennifer Provencher

and his colleagues asserted that, 'The new evidence suggests that climate-driven extinctions and range retractions are already widespread.'[16]

Bird distributions are changing, too

Now we turn from general biodiversity to the question of range shifts in birds. As mobile animals that are reactive to change in their environments, many birds are considered capable of dispersing to new areas relatively quickly. Birds, like other organisms, are expected to shift their distributions polewards or upslope, where local and regional climates accord with global warming. Evidence from Europe, the Americas, Asia, Antarctica and Australia suggests this is taking place in many species. Although global warming is a strong candidate as a driver of these changes, in many cases it is not the only candidate.

A warming climate is the most likely explanation for range shifts in British birds from 1968 to 1991. The northern (cool) boundaries of 59 southerly bird species shifted northwards by almost 19 kilometres, on average.[17] In Finland birds are also on the move, in concert with very rapid global warming after 1976. In just 12 years, 116 southerly breeding bird species apparently shifted their distributions polewards by almost 19 kilometres. Smaller-bodied species, it turned out, tended to shift further than larger-bodied species.[18] In a more dramatic example, some breeding birds of continental Europe, including black redstarts, *Phoenicurus ochruros*, Cetti's warblers, *Cettia cetti*, and possibly little egrets, *Egretta garzetta*, have begun to breed in the UK in recent decades, with climate change named a plausible, but not definitive, cause.

From Poland comes evidence of upslope shifts. Traditionally wetland birds, white storks shifted their nesting ranges at least 500 metres upslope in a region of the Tatra mountains during 1974–2003, in areas with small bodies of water. Climate warming is a possible cause, although the availability of new habitat on former farmlands, abandoned after the collapse of communism, could also play a role.[19] In Italy's Alps, a weak upslope shift was also noted for the majority of bird species during 1994–2005. Again, this happened during a period of climate warming, but other explanations are possible.[20]

Turning to the Americas, birds are also shifting upslope at tropical Monteverde, Costa Rica. Fifteen lowland bird species colonised higher-elevation cloud forest habitat and established breeding populations in these zones, from 1979 to 1998 (chapter 6). As for latitudinal shifts, in North America, the northern boundaries of 254 overwintering birds shifted northwards by an average of 1.48 kilometres per year over the 1975–2004 period. Their centres of abundance also shifted polewards, by 1.03 kilometres per year. Interestingly, although the bird populations sporadically colonised then retreated from their northern boundaries, colonisations predominated to drive overall poleward shifts. Climate change, along with other human factors, is likely to be driving these trends.[21] A separate study by the Audubon Society found similar results for North American birds' centre of abundance: over the 1966–2005 period, northward shifts among 305 species averaged 56 kilometres (about 1.4 kilometres per year), with 60 species moving as much as 160 kilometres. From New York State comes scarcer evidence that some northerly breeding birds have also shifted their southern (warm) range boundaries polewards, by 11.4 kilometres between 1980 and 2005.[22]

From Asia, reports are much scarcer. In China most crane species have apparently expanded their winter distributions to higher latitudes since the 1970s, and climate change is a reasonable explanation.[23] The upslope range shifts of some tropical South-East Asian birds also suggest a response to climate warming. Comparisons of two field guides suggest 94 species shifted their upper, lower or both boundaries upslope during 1971–1999, a period of climate warming.[24]

Turning to the Southern Hemisphere, dramatic changes at some tropical seabird colonies on islands off Australia' south-west coast suggest poleward (southward) expansions are underway (chapter 4). Further south still, on Antarctica or its associated islands, ice-dependent emperor, *Aptenodytes forsteri*, and Adélie penguins, *Pygoscelis adeliae*, have undergone marked populations declines at some lower-latitude colonies (chapters 4 and 5).

Flight distances and destinations change

Range shifts can also be viewed through the lens of changes to migration distance. Among 73 bird species breeding in Britain and 30 breeding in Germany, roughly one-third changed the length of their migratory journeys in recent decades. Although most alterations entailed shorter migrations, some birds lengthened their journeys or made other changes.[25] Some individuals are even effectively ceasing to migrate at all (chapter 2). Although a warming climate is an oft-cited reason, changing migration patterns may also reflect changes in food availability (such as more bird feeders) and hunting practices.

As might be expected with climate warming, many migrants are wintering at higher latitudes or in other zones that were formerly too cold. Where this shortens their journeys to breeding grounds, the energy demands and risks of migration may be reduced, and birds may be better able to predict spring onset in their breeding grounds (chapter 2). Among 24 birds breeding in the Netherlands, half significantly shortened the length of their migrations to their wintering sites over 1932–2004, probably due to climate change.[26] Small but growing numbers of European-breeding birds that formerly wintered in Africa are now wintering in the Mediterranean region, including house martins, *Delichon urbica*, yellow wagtails, *Motacilla flava*, and lesser kestrels, *Falco naumanni*. As warmer winters tend to leave more ice-free waters near breeding areas, increasing numbers of white-fronted geese, *Anser albifrons*, and other waterfowl are also cutting their migrations short, to stay in north and east Europe rather than travel further south and west. Their use of new staging and wintering sites has prompted urgent calls for new protected areas.[27]

Some migratory birds' breeding distributions are also shifting. On Norway's coast, barnacle geese, *Branta leucopsis*, have shifted their spring ranges north since the early 1980s, in conjunction with spring warming and changes to agriculture. Some brightly coloured European bee-eaters, *Merops apiaster*, have expanded their breeding range northwards, as have black-winged stilts, *Himantopus himantopus*. In some cases migrants have increased their travel distance within Europe by up to 1000 kilometres.[25]

Future range shifts under climate change

The most frightening result of all approaches to model range changes are the large movements of ranges expected to occur within the next 50–100 years . . .
Katrin Böhning-Gaese & Nicole Lemoine, 2004

If birds' distributions are already shifting with current levels of warming, how might they respond in future as global warming escalates? In fact, this task of predicting wildlife distributions' response to climate change is expected to be critical to conservation efforts and, some argue, one of the greatest scientific challenges this century (chapter 7).

Towards this goal, climate-envelope modelling is an important tool. It uses a species' present-day distribution to first provide an idea of the climate conditions that suit it. This 'climate envelope' is then used to infer where it might be distributed in future, under climate-change scenarios. Climate-envelope models are not without their criticisms, however.[28] They omit important factors that may determine species' distributions, such as competitors, predators and disease, not to mention human activity. Because of these shortcomings, it is important to bear in mind that results of these models are essentially hypotheses, not predictions or guaranteed outcomes.

Nevertheless, climate-envelope models can indicate the direction and magnitude of potential range shifts under climate change. And despite their limitations, the IPCC stated in 2007 that when it comes to assessing extinction risk, climate envelope models still appear to offer more realistic results than other options. Their estimates provide an idea of the nature and extent of possible changes, giving conservation authorities the chance to avert some of the most serious effects on threatened species.

An emerging picture for European birds

The task of estimating future range shifts has only just begun, but evidence so far suggests that many bird species will need to disperse considerable distances to keep up with climate change. The most comprehensive modelling effort to date is *A Climatic Atlas of European Breeding Birds*.[29] University of Durham palaeoecologist Brian Huntley and his colleagues used the climate of European bird species' breeding ranges during the 1980s to estimate their climate envelopes. They then connected these to a 'middle-of-the road' climate-change scenario (projecting European temperature will increase by more than 2°C, but as much as 6°C in some Arctic regions, by 2090[30]) to infer future ranges, all on a continent-wide scale.

This modelling suggests considerable change is in store for European-breeding birds. The centre of the average bird's future potential range of suitable climate would shift 545 kilometres north-east, and range boundaries for large numbers of species could be displaced by about 1000 kilometres. Annual warming is expected to be the main driver for these northward range shifts; however, the southern boundaries of birds' ranges are also likely to respond to drying, particularly in southern Europe.

Crucially for conservation efforts, this modelling suggests the average bird's breeding distribution would shrink by about a fifth (assuming it will not adapt and persist outside its climate envelope). Although the future ranges of some species could be larger, most are likely to be smaller, with Arctic, subarctic and some Iberian Peninsula birds suffering the most severe reductions. Across the continent, average species richness could decline by 8.6 per cent if birds can fully disperse to populate areas of suitable climate in future; but if they are unable to disperse at all, average species richness could decline by 40 per cent. For six species, suitable climate conditions could entirely vanish from Europe. Moreover, modelling suggests individualistic responses will prevail: no two bird species would be expected to undergo identical range shifts, even if they have similar distribution patterns today and live in zones with similar prevailing climate, plants and animals.

Other modelling highlights the particular vulnerability of Europe's boreal and Arctic land birds. All 27 species studied could face range contractions in Finland and adjoining parts of Sweden, Norway and Russia. In fact, if unable to adapt in their current ranges, 70 per cent of these bird species of forests, heaths and mires could lose more than 60 per cent of their climate space by 2080, even under a less severe climate scenario (2°C global average warming by 2100). The climate envelope of the bar-tailed godwit, for example, would shrink by a drastic 98 per cent in this region. For many of these northern birds, the Arctic Ocean would present an absolute barrier to poleward range shifts.[31] This prospect of shrinking climate space demonstrates why the long-term effects of climate change at high latitudes are cause for concern.

An incomplete sketch in vulnerable Africa

Information on birds' possible range responses to climate change is still scarce in many parts of Africa, with the region south of the Sahara being the focus of most research. This lack of knowledge is a concern because, of all continents, Africa is generally considered most at risk from global warming, partly because much of its territory outside the tropics experiences an arid or semi-arid climate.

A study on 34 bird species of South Africa, as well as mammals, reptiles and insects, suggested that more than three-quarters (78 per cent) of these animals were likely to experience range contractions with expected warming of 2°C.[32] Again, modelling indicated idiosyncratic responses were likely, although species' distributions would generally shift eastwards and to higher elevations. These shifts would tend to concentrate biodiversity in South Africa's eastern and south-eastern highlands, roughly reflecting the country's east–west gradient in dryness (the west being generally more arid). Overall, the species richness of South African wildlife would most likely decline under climate change, losses being highest in the arid west. The flagship Kruger National Park could lose up to two-thirds of species studied, creating new conservation challenges.

Other research on the broader region south of the Sahara also suggests that range contractions are in store for many breeding birds.[33] Some species may need to shift more than 500 kilometres to track suitable climate conditions. Where many African semi-arid zones expand, bird habitat could contract. On the Horn of Africa, the restricted ranges of species could contract further. The distributions of birds found in moist tropical forests, and those along the equator, however, may be displaced very little, as long as their forest habitats remain relatively unaffected.

At Africa's southern tip, two remarkable biodiversity hotspots for plants are considered at high risk from climate change: the Succulent Karoo; and the Cape Floral Kingdom, a zone rich in proteas, an ancient and diverse group of plants with spectacular flowers. Within these two hotspots, bird species with small ranges[34] in the southern and western extremes are thought to be most at risk from climate change, as are those restricted to mountain slopes and tops, and to islands. Estimates of future range shifts for six of these at-risk birds revealed some would lose more than half their available climate space, and birds unable to adapt or shift would be under threat.[35] Notably, of the climate-change-susceptible species identified, many are not currently considered threatened.

Range shifts in the Americas

Birds of the Americas could also experience large range changes under global warming. Modelling for species of the north-eastern USA suggests that a warmer, wetter and more variable climate over the course of this century could drive large distribution shifts. Among 150 resident and migratory birds, 22 per cent of species would lose more than a quarter of their ranges, while 38 per cent would see their ranges expand by a quarter or more. Even minimal warming of 1°C could cause suitable habitat for high-elevation species to shrink by more than half. Some iconic and abundant species in this region would probably decline significantly, even under milder climate-change scenarios.[36]

In southern and central USA, modelling suggests species richness would probably decline (except at high elevations) as temperatures rise. On the other hand, in relatively cool regions and at high elevations, such as some portions of western and north-eastern USA, bird species richness could increase.[37] One study specifically focused on Neotropical migratory birds[38] indicated that climate change is likely to bring about an overall decrease in the numbers of species in every US region. In the Great Lakes region, for example, although an influx of birds would partly offset a 53 per cent loss of species, overall numbers of Neotropical species would still fall by 29 per cent.[39]

Further south, in Mexico, 'severe ecological perturbations' are possible, according to A. Townsend Peterson of the University of Kansas Natural History Museum and his colleagues.[40] When they modelled range shifts for a whole community of Mexican fauna, including 1179 bird species, they found climate change would probably drive species to colonise the major mountain ranges, and to disappear from the country's broad Chihuahuan Desert and north-western coastal plain. By 2055, as dozens disappear or are displaced by colonisers, species turnover could exceed 40 per cent in many areas. 'Although only limited numbers of species will face entirely unsuitable conditions for persistence,' Peterson and his colleagues note, 'others will experience drastic reductions and fragmentation of distributional areas, or extend their distributions, creating new natural communities with unknown properties.' This threat of novel, reshuffled communities is an important topic we shall return to later in this chapter.

Turning to South America, modelling also suggests problems are in store for birds of the cerrado, the world's largest expanse of tropical savannah, mostly located within Brazil. A study of 26 widespread cerrado birds revealed that range contractions of up to 80 per cent are possible for some under climate change, if they do not disperse or adapt in their current ranges.[41] Their ranges could also shift, by an average 175–200 kilometres, mainly towards south-eastern Brazil. Cerrado habitat is already highly fragmented by farms, but such a shift would shunt the birds' distributions towards the most populous and developed part of the country. Species with smaller ranges would moreover experience the greatest reduction in range size, suggesting rare species could become rarer still.

Shifts on tropical mountains in Australia

Turning to Australia, research has revealed cause for concern in a zone of high biodiversity and endemism in the country's north-east, the Wet Tropics of Queensland. As the climate now found at low to mid altitudes shifts towards mountaintops, the current climate space of some Wet Tropics birds could contract dramatically. Altered precipitation patterns could also have a critical effect on this ecosystem. These and other climate-change threats to tropical birds are explored in more detail in chapter 6.

Shrinking ranges and natural 'dead ends'

Rapid movement of climatic zones is going to be another stress on wildlife . . . In effect we are pushing them off the planet.

James Hansen, 2006

Here we turn to threats posed by range contractions, a recurrent theme in many of the modelling results just described. The prospect of declining range size is a concern because this may be expected to lead to smaller populations and thereby elevate extinction risk. Heightening this concern is the possibility that bird populations may decline even faster than the comparable loss of their range extent suggests. Where their ranges both contract and shift, birds could be under increased threat from climate change. For some species, shrinking, shifting ranges could even lead to extinction under global warming (chapter 5).

Where populations track climate change polewards or upslope with global warming, birds may face significant natural barriers to their dispersal, including oceans, mountain ranges or mountaintops, the Earth's poles, and deserts. In tropical sub-Saharan Africa (the Afrotropics), a study of approximately 1900 birds revealed that, for a large number of species, their current ranges end at natural barriers. These are places where terrain, vegetation and topography alter abruptly and dramatically.[42] In Central Africa, for example, the tropical rainforest range of the violet-tailed sunbird, *Anthreptes aurantium*, terminates where savannah begins. Generally speaking, if birds' ranges come up against the edges of habitats where they are not well adapted to survive, these hostile habitats could effectively block their escape routes under climate change.

Another challenge populations may face as they attempt to track global warming is the prospect of disappearing climates: those that simply cease to exist in a warmer world. Disappearing climates pose an extinction threat, and are expected to be concentrated in tropical mountain regions (chapter 6) and the poleward regions of continents, as the above case of Finnish Arctic and boreal birds suggests.

Wetlands too often fall beneath the radar

These dispersal challenges created by natural barriers are particularly relevant to some ecosystems deemed especially vulnerable under climate change: those of coasts and wetlands, tundras and mountains.

Highlighting the role of oceans as a barrier, sea-level rise poses a major threat to wildlife of coastal intertidal areas and wetlands. In the USA, sea-level rise could bring about 20–70 per cent reductions in the coastal intertidal habitat for internationally important numbers of shorebirds at four out of five sites studied, under warming of 2°C this century.[43] In fact, sea-level rise is already affecting both the quality and extent of intertidal habitats, like those of the USA's Delaware Bay, an important stopover and refuelling site for red knots (chapter 2). If this area loses 57 per cent of its intertidal habitat by 2100, as is considered plausible, its tidal flats 'could not possibly support shorebird numbers that are even only fractions of their current sizes'.[43]

Across the world in northern Australia, vast coastal swamps are also at risk. This includes those of Kakadu, a birdwatchers' mecca that harbours more than 280 species. Barely above sea level, its wetlands are vulnerable to saltwater incursion with even slight sea-level rise – yet the rate of sea-level rise across northern Australia is currently four times the global average. Its effects, compounded by those of possibly higher numbers of intense tropical storms, could inundate these highly productive freshwater wetlands, profoundly affecting their bird populations.[44] The spectre of storms in combination with sea level rise is expected to be a threat to other coastal wetland habitats as well.

Loss of coastal wetlands and intertidal areas could be especially severe where coastal defences, such as dams and dykes, prevent the natural inland retreat of these habitats as sea-levels rise. Steep shorelines may also present a natural barrier to wetland retreat. In this way, bird habitats in estuaries and deltas could be inundated from their seaward boundaries, yet blocked from their natural landward movement (chapter 7).

Efforts to replace coastal wetlands lost to rising seas could conflict with human development, because many low-lying areas are already inhabited by large populations of people or used for agriculture. Salt marshes, habitat for many coastal breeding and wintering birds, could also be affected by climate change.

As for inland wetlands, the duck-factory dilemma at the start of this chapter epitomises the threat to such habitats around the world. Wetland ecosystems are especially vulnerable to changes in water level, rainfall and evaporation, but these critical changes are harder to predict under global warming. Nonetheless, the hydrological cycle is expected to become more variable with climate change. This could cause wetlands to flood at times, directly threatening some nesting birds and possibly damaging wetland vegetation. At other times wetlands could dry out, reducing birds' food supplies and eliminating the water barriers that protect them from predators. In the Arctic, melting permafrost will cause lakes and wetlands to drain in some areas and new wetlands to be created in others. The balance of these effects is unknown, but significant shifts to species' ranges and migration routes are likely to follow, and some species are likely to be threatened with extinction.

The prospect of increasingly deteriorating wetlands is a critical concern for bird conservation, since these habitats are crucial breeding and stopover areas. Changes in water regimes are considered the most widespread climate-change threat to 298 migratory birds listed under the CMS, affecting 53 per cent of these species, including the aquatic warbler (chapter 2). Another threat is intensifying human demand for fresh water. Where temperatures rise, human populations grow and water tables fall, the freshwater needs of people are likely to conflict with wetland birds' habitat requirements.

The slow-motion threat to tundra breeders

The Siberian crane, *Grus leucogeranus*, highlights the climate-change threat to birds breeding on the Arctic tundra. This crane is one of the most highly specialised members of its family, including its unique and complex courtship ritual of dance and song. Mated birds, standing as tall as a small human adult (140 centimetres), throw their heads back and point their beaks skywards in an extended display known as unison calling. Because they may mate for life and, according to unconfirmed reports, have reached up to 83 years of age in captivity, Siberian cranes symbolise good marriages and long life. Despite being an auspicious symbol, this critically endangered crane is in peril and faces a range of immediate human threats, which would only be compounded by global warming.

The most aquatic of cranes, it has quite specific habitat requirements. A dependence on wetlands makes the roughly 3700 surviving individuals vulnerable to many of the climate-change risks described above, in both its Arctic breeding areas and non-breeding areas in China (a separate, very small population breeds in Russia and overwinters in Iran). Siberian cranes breed in wide-open tundra and taiga wetland, in landscape that provides good visibility. This makes an absence of trees important. Yet long-term climate warming is expected to allow trees to colonise the crane's habitat and reduce tundra and taiga by up to 70 per cent.

Most of the several hundred million migratory birds that breed in the Arctic nest on the vast, treeless plains that characterise tundra landscapes. Found between polar deserts to the north and the tree line to the south, the tundra's low-scrub vegetation is kept tree-free by permafrost, permanently frozen subsoil. The pronounced climate-change impacts expected on the tundra would greatly reduce not only Siberian crane habitat, but also important breeding areas for many birds. Subarctic scrub, then forest, would invade, causing suitable breeding habitat for shorebirds to halve over this century as tundra area contracts to its lowest extent for the past 21 000 years. But it is also apparent that the growth, phenology and reproduction of Arctic vegetation will show complex responses to warming and increasing levels of carbon dioxide in the atmosphere.[45] High-Arctic shorebird species appear to be at special risk, facing a squeeze between advancing low-Arctic vegetation and the Arctic Ocean. Bird species from the south are expected to move in, competing with and possibly displacing tundra birds. New pathogens, predators and parasites may also colonise the tundra. With the Arctic region now warming at almost twice the global rate, some of these changes are already underway.

Among Arctic tundra breeders, those using coastal habitats outside the breeding season have combined requirements that could expose them to some of the most severe long-term climate-change threats. Take the red knot, a high-Arctic breeder with a demanding migratory schedule and low genetic diversity (chapter 2). Although warming may at first increase the abundance of its arthropod prey, providing more food for chicks, unabated warming is expected to gradually put the squeeze on this tundra breeder.

In a pessimistic scenario, habitat could be reduced by up to 70 per cent in Europe if carbon dioxide levels triple over the next century or two.[46] The loss of summer Arctic Ocean sea ice would also mean the loss of its cooling effect on land nearby. Changes in vegetation, food, predators and disease would also impose a toll, possibly taking breeding success as low as near zero. Outside the Arctic, the type of coastal threats discussed above may affect the red knot's intertidal staging areas, crucial for rapid refuelling.

Some birds may prosper in a rapidly changing Arctic, if global warming improves their short-term and medium-term survival prospects by tempering harsh Arctic environments and improving plant productivity. Yet over the long-term, the transformative power of global warming could alter the climate conditions that now underpin Arctic breeders' ranges. By eliminating specific types of habitats, it could push some close to extinction. In this way, climate change may not only compound the risks to endangered species like the Siberian crane, but it could also threaten sharp declines in species now widespread.

Shrinking climate space for temperate mountain birds

In the United Kingdom, the prospect of shrinking climate space for the capercaillie, *Tetrao urogallus*, highlights the global warming threat to wildlife of some mountain regions. The capercaillie is the world's largest grouse, and males may weigh in at almost seven kilograms. Resplendent in black plumage and breast feathers lit with a green metallic sheen, males spend the greater portion of their drawn-out courting season intimidating the competition. Posturing begins at the crack of dawn, as the male fans his tail feathers, holds his neck erect and points his beak skywards to let forth a peculiar clicking, popping and grunting call, much of it thought to be outside the range of human hearing.

Adapted to open forest habitat, capercaillies in the UK are confined to Caledonian pinewoods and conifer plantations, mainly in the eastern Highlands of Scotland. Caledonian forests are among the last remaining wild places in the British Isles. Once widespread throughout the Highlands, they have been radically reduced in extent, to just 180 square kilometres. Capercaillies were reintroduced to Scotland during the 1830s (they are also found in forests elsewhere in Europe), and this UK population now hovers at around 2000 individuals, down from an estimated 20 000 birds in the

1970s. Habitat loss and fragmentation, collision with forest fences, and other human threats already make it one of the UK's most at-risk birds, but this upland bird also faces a growing threat from climate change.

Climate change may already be associated with poor breeding success in capercaillies. Spring warming has become more drawn out and delayed during April. Yet this is a period when warmer temperatures would improve hens' nutrition: the hens need cold winters followed by warm temperatures when they are fattening up to lay eggs. Modelling also suggests a long-term threat: the area of climate suitable for capercaillies could shrink by up to 99 per cent in the UK by mid-century, if a worst-case global warming scenario eventuates.[47]

Mountain ecosystems worldwide tend to be species rich and harbour relatively high numbers of endemic species, but their upland populations could face a severe threat where their climate space contracts or even disappears (chapter 6). Nonetheless, many mountains are expected to continue to be crucial for biodiversity conservation; climate warming could drive lowland species to shift upslope into cooler mountain refuges, making these zones ever-more important as bird conservation priorities (chapter 7).

Range expansions also expected

The above paragraphs focused on shrinking ranges and the resulting conservation threat. Models suggest that range contractions will predominate in at least some regions. Nonetheless, some birds may be expected to expand their ranges under global warming. Pink-footed geese, *Anser brachyrhynchus*, breed in Svalbard, an Arctic archipelago north of mainland Norway. Today, their productivity is thought to be limited by the availability of suitable nesting sites, and possibly by spring feeding habitat in staging areas, crucial for building up their body reserves for breeding.

With warming of 1°C, the suitable nesting distribution for pink-footed geese could markedly expand northwards and eastwards, increasing by 84 per cent.[48] With 2°C of warming, their potential range could double in area. Pink-footed geese may be among those birds adaptable enough to shift into new areas of suitable climate. In a similar way, other birds may also be able to shift their ranges without detrimental effects, provided they find suitable habitat and the other requirements of their niches.

Dispersal in human-altered landscapes

As bird populations track their niches to keep up with climate change, some may need to disperse considerable distances. This could prove challenging for populations whose future range of suitable climate overlaps little with their present-day range. For birds assessed in *A Climatic Atlas of European Breeding Birds*, for example, this overlap figure averaged 40 per cent. But for 51 of these European-breeding bird species, overlap could be 10 per cent or less, while for a further 27 species there may be no overlap at all.

This overlap question may be critical, since there is no guarantee that all bird populations will be able to disperse fully to track their climate envelopes. Indeed there is great uncertainty about many birds' ability to do so, even though future climate conditions elsewhere may correspond to those of their present-day range. Therefore this zone of overlap between birds' present and future potential range, Huntley and his colleagues theorise, represents the most pessimistic outcome of the range they would occupy under a climate-change scenario. It assumes no dispersal at all. The most optimistic outcome, on the other hand, would be perfect dispersal. This would allow a bird population to fully track climate change, to occupy its entire potential range of suitable climate in future. (Both cases assume birds do not adapt to persist in areas where conditions no longer correspond to their climate envelopes.)

The outcome for most species is likely to lie somewhere between these two extremes. Those likely to tend towards perfect dispersal are apt to be generalists capable of using a wide range of habitats. They are more likely to respond independently of vegetation and other components of their ecosystems. Seasonally migratory birds, as well as dispersive and irruptive species, may also be more likely to expand to new suitable areas in conjunction with the changing climate.

Possible candidates for the 'no dispersal' end of this spectrum are strongly sedentary, resident species. Among birds with specialised habitat or food needs, dispersal would probably be limited by the presence of required trees, food sources or other vital elements of their communities. Yet these elements may shift at a different rate, distance or direction (we will return to this point shortly). Highlighting their sensitivity, one study of birds in France suggests that more highly specialised species are likely to have a negative (spatial) response if their habitat is disturbed or fragmented.[49] However, research on European birds found that while generalist omnivores (along with birds of prey) lagged in their response to range shifts, populations of more specialised birds – insect and seed eaters – were prone to shift the margins of their ranges. One possible explanation is that the latter types of birds are tracking their insect and plant foods, the range margins of which may be more directly influenced by climate-drive shifts.[15] Specialists may rapidly explore appropriate habitats elsewhere if they are adapted to tracking their particular requirements quickly.

The overlap issue also highlights the risk to birds with small ranges as climate envelopes shift. Modelling of European birds suggests that small ranges are less likely to overlap with future potential ranges of suitable climate. Yet it is hard to shed light on this potential threat because it is inherently difficult to model the future ranges of birds with small present-day distributions. This only adds to the uncertainties about the possible effects of climate change on their ranges.

There may be 'climate space', but will it be vacant?

Overlap is not the only factor that could affect birds' ability to disperse and track climate change, as the case of the Spanish imperial eagle, *Aquila adalberti*, suggests. One of the world's rarest eagles, its problems highlight the challenges for birds that survive by virtue of static protected areas. Found on protected 'islands' of forest amid a 'sea' of deforested, farmed and urbanised lands, its small population (253 breeding pairs) makes the Spanish imperial eagle vulnerable to extinction. Its breeding success and distribution pivot on the presence of rabbits, its main prey, but humans also have a powerful influence on the birds. Nesting success drops off when these large eagles are disturbed, and distance from human activity is a significant factor in nest location. Key causes of death are electrocution on powerlines and eating the poisoned baits used to control predators.

With climate change, its entire current habitat – mainly in Spain's forested parks and nature reserves – could have a climate unlike that of today, according to modelling in *A Climatic Atlas of European Breeding Birds*. Its potential future range would generally shift eastwards, to scattered patches across northern Spain, southern France, Italy, the Balkans and southern Russia. Although much greater in total extent than its present-day range, these locations may have insufficient undisturbed and protected land to support the eagle. They are also quite remote from its current range. Conservation efforts fostered the Spanish imperial eagle's impressive recovery from just 30 pairs in the 1960s, but climate change could pose new challenges for those who seek to preserve it.

Today's large human populations have made the world a very different place than during past episodes of rapid climatic change. Bird populations may face not only natural barriers as they disperse to track global warming, but human obstacles as well. On their forced march, they may need to negotiate habitats fragmented by farms, plantations, highways, urban development and coastal fortifications.

In fact, future climate-change scenarios that also account for different scenarios of habitat loss indicate that increased habitat loss leads to higher numbers of bird extinctions from climate change.[6] What is more, the fragmentation problem is likely to be further exacerbated by climate change because ranges, as they shift, are likely to contract and fragment. Taken together, these various synergies between habitat loss and climate change imply that assessments made so far could underestimate the true extent of future range contractions under climate change.

Ecological brick walls

Conservationists are entering a new era of conservation, one in which last-ditch stands to save species where they currently exist may not be enough . . .

Lee Hannah et al., 2005

The case of the Spanish imperial eagle suggests how climate change may force some protected bird species into areas made inhospitable by human activity. Protected areas, the centrepieces of most bird conservation efforts, tend to be established in zones with high numbers of endemic, threatened and rare birds. The combination of range shifts driven by climate change and habitat loss poses a major new conservation challenge. As Lee Hannah of Conservation International and his colleagues put it,

. . . letting natural processes operate unfettered may result in species or whole associations running into the ecological equivalent of a brick wall, as natural processes take the system toward range shifts and re-association, while habitat loss prevents migration or replacement of species.

Establishing static protected areas can be a daunting task. Yet with global warming, conservation promises to become more challenging still, as conservation planners are compelled to account for the changing needs of birds and their communities, across landscapes and into the future (chapter 7).

Comparing the threats: habitat destruction and climate change

Given the conservation challenges likely to be thrown up by the 'deadly anthropogenic cocktail'[50] of habitat loss and climate change, it is helpful to compare these two threats as drivers of range reductions in birds. The point of departure is that today habitat loss is the greatest threat to biodiversity, with roughly 60 per cent of the ecosystems evaluated being used unsustainably or suffering from degradation.

In effort to compare the two threats, Yale University ecologist Walter Jetz and his colleagues took an optimistic climate-change scenario, and combined it with predictions of habitat loss due to human activity. Of 8750 land birds assessed, roughly 400 species could lose more than half their ranges by mid-century, with this figure rising to more than 900 species by the year 2100.[51] But the relative contribution of these two threats would vary with latitude. Climate change would affect birds' ranges most at the high latitudes (above 30° latitude) of Siberia and North America, they argue, due to the relatively greater temperature changes expected in these zones. Range contractions in the tropics and subtropics would be driven to a greater extent by human land conversion than by climate change. And because species diversity is greater in tropical and subtropical zones than at high latitudes, they suggest habitat destruction may be expected to cause greater overall losses of bird species in the near future.

Others believe that climate-change effects in tropical zones will also be profound (chapter 6), and could even exceed habitat destruction in some regions. Studies of climate-change effects on tropical wildlife are relatively few, but as evidence accumulates there is mounting concern that this threat may be underestimated.

Will birds keep up with climate change?

Given that some species may need to disperse considerable distances to track climate change, the rate of warming could be critical to their capacity to cope. Life on Earth has endured periods of very rapid climatic change in the past. In future, the *global* average rate of warming is not expected to be greatly different than during past periods of rapid and abrupt climatic change. Yet in many of the world's *regions*, the velocity of future climate change is likely to be unprecedented in the past million years or more.[52] Moreover, because this warming will be superimposed on a relatively warm period, temperatures may rapidly exceed those of the past million years or more in many regions. This new climate stressor will moreover be imposed on wildlife already affected by habitat loss and other human impacts.

Will birds and other wildlife keep up? Although extinctions did occur, many species were able to track past periods of rapid climatic change. This demonstrates an important built-in capacity of life to adapt. Nonetheless, the actual rates at which animal and plant species can expand their ranges are still poorly known. Some clues may be had by looking back over recent geological history to the rapid climatic changes between glacial and inter-glacial stages of the Quaternary. These are likely to be the most rapid periods of climatic change that many of today's species had to tolerate over their evolutionary history. During these periods, the predominant response of land-based species was range shifts, with the expansion rates for various types of plants estimated at 200 to 2000 metres per year. The role played by adaptation is thought to have been more minor.

The Earth's climate has been unusually stable for the past 11 000 years, providing few precedents from the more recent past for the rapid changes to come. Nonetheless, some species known to be excellent dispersers, like goldenrod, *Soldago* spp., and coyotes, *Canis latrans*, can spread at almost 20 000 metres per year. At the slow end of life, earthworms and forest understorey herbs are thought capable of expanding their ranges at less than 10 metres per year.

Looking to the future, forests are expected to lag well behind climate shifts, making them more sensitive to pests, fires and other disturbance. Desert and grassland ecosystems are thought to be capable of adapting more quickly. Nonetheless, modelling suggests species in deserts, mangrove habitats and flooded grasslands would experience some of the highest velocities of temperature change, necessitating shifts of between 710 and 1260 metres per year to track climate change.[53]

The potential gap between species' rates of dispersal and the velocity of climate change explains why some researchers fear ecosystems could in the future be dominated by weedy, fast-moving species that can invade new landscapes and tolerate a wide range of climates (chapter 7). Overall, global warming is likely to outpace the ability of many species, such as long-lived plants, to keep up. If they are unable to persist in their current range, an inability to migrate will contribute to the global extinction or local extinction of some plant and animal species. Birds dependent on specific types of vegetation may shift only as quickly as the plants they rely on. The UNEP Millennium Ecosystem Assessment found that rates of climate change in excess of 0.2°C per decade would have a 'net harmful impact on ecosystem services worldwide'. In fact, climate change is now faster than 0.2°C per decade, suggesting an accelerated decline in biodiversity soon.[54]

Are birds keeping up now? Research in France provides a clue. Breeding bird communities there apparently shifted northwards by an average 91 kilometres from 1989 to 2006. Yet over this period the northward shift in average temperatures caused by climate warming was a far greater 273 kilometres, suggesting these birds communities lagged behind climate warming by 182 kilometres.[55] Such lags are of concern because, as already discussed, birds unable to either shift their distributions or tolerate new climate conditions may ultimately die out.

Individualistic responses and the threat of reshuffled communities

A forced march, but not in step

In *The Origin of Species*, Charles Darwin hypothesised how species responded to past, dramatic changes in climate, as glaciers advanced and retreated. 'The arctic forms, during their long southern migration and re-migration northwards, will have been exposed to nearly the same climate', he wrote, 'they will have kept in a body together; consequently, their mutual relations will not have been much disturbed . . . '

Darwin was quite wrong. In sharp contrast to his tidy vision of assemblages shifting intact, species actually moved different distances, at different rates and even in different directions during parts of the Quaternary and the last glacial retreat. In future, as climate change drives further range shifts, each species is also expected to respond uniquely. Dispersal rates may vary among species, and among broad taxonomic groups.

How quickly and how far any species shifts could depend on its climate sensitivity, as well as its mobility, life span and reproductive capacity. Constraints on movement, including natural and human-imposed barriers, will also play a role. Yet precisely why some populations disperse in response to regional warming and others do not is still not fully known.

Range shifts could reshuffle communities

These individualistic responses could cause problems under rapid global warming. If species shift at different rates and in different directions, symbioses and other ecological relationships could break down or disappear, and new ones could form in their place. Range shifts driven by climate change could destabilise and reshuffle the ecosystems we know today, as their constituent species dissociate, disassemble and come together in new ways.[56]

These inherent risks of climate-driven range shifts are suggested by modelling for the threatened coastal California gnatcatcher, *Polioptila californica californica*. This thumb-sized, insect-eating warbler is a habitat specialist restricted mainly to semi-arid coastal scrublands in California and Mexico. Critically, modelling that also accounted for predicted ranges of the plants that underpin its niche revealed that the gnatcatcher's potential habitat could be greatly reduced under a warmer climate, compared to scenarios that did not account for this type of biotic factor.[57] It will be crucial to consider how birds with such specialised interactions might be limited by other organisms in their ability to track climate change. Yet in nature cases of tight specialisation tend to be the exception rather than the rule.

Seabird-breeding crashes illustrate the threat of reshuffled ecosystems where climate-sensitive ocean prey shift beyond the foraging range of their land-based colonies (chapter 4). Tundra-breeding shorebirds may also face threats where climate warming brings new competitors for food or for breeding areas, as well as new and more abundant predators, parasites and pathogens. Similarly, birds that extend their ranges may cause problems for other groups of animals. Australia's laughing kookaburra, *Dacelo novaeguineae*, known for its extravagant calls reminiscent of rollicking human laughter, is a large member of the kingfisher group. This species is expanding to higher ground in the Australian Alps, where it preys on alpine skinks, including live-bearing skink species. To promote incubation, pregnant female skinks bask for long periods in the sun where they are vulnerable because they fail to recognise kookaburras as a threat.

Climate change could also spur the expansions of exotic birds and other invasive species already introduced by humans outside their native ranges (chapter 7). Birds from warmer climates, such as Egyptian geese, *Alopochen aegyptiacas*, and rose-ringed parakeets, *Psittacula krameri*, have expanded in Central Europe with the help of warmer winters. The rose-ringed parakeet expansion is viewed with concern because these birds may aggressively compete with native species for nesting cavities and food.

Another concern related to reshuffled ecosystems is the spread of disease-carrying organisms. These organisms are greatly affected by temperature, rainfall and humidity, and many fare better under warmer conditions than do their hosts. Climate change and disease, some fear, will have a profound impact on wildlife, both on land and in the oceans. The spread of diseases such as avian malaria (chapter 6) to high elevation or high latitude areas where birds lack evolutionary experience of these pathogens could pose a particular threat. Diseases can spread rapidly, but birds need time to build up resistance to new pathogens. A shortfall of research on disease in wild birds makes this yet another climate-change threat that is difficult to gauge.

Finally, some fear that reshuffled communities could in turn drive still stronger distribution shifts of their own. The complex and cascading inter-actions likely to be triggered pose a serious challenge to those striving to predict how birds and other wild nature will respond to climate change. Surprises are likely, because the manifold and indirect effects of climate change on food webs may be dramatic and unexpected, and evident only after lags in time. Though hard to predict, understanding the effects of reshuffled communities is important, because they could prompt extinc-tions beyond those suggested by the initial climate-change-driven range shifts (chapter 5).

No-analogue assemblages: 'Here there be Dragons'

In more extreme cases, communities reshuffled by climate change could transform into 'no-analogue' assemblages. This concept is based on the observation that groupings of species today may be very different to those seen during the last glacial retreat when large range shifts occurred. The formation of these past, very different groupings of species and biomes is thought to have been driven by climate conditions unlike those found today, from temperature to patterns of burning or flooding. Palaeoecologists who reconstruct a picture of these past communities, using fossils of animals and plant pollen, call these very disparate groupings no-analogue assemblages.

In future, unabated climate change could also result in no-analogue communities, if ecological communities are 'torn apart' and reconstituted to the extent that they diverge significantly from those we recognise today. Global warming is expected to bring about novel climates – climates that also lack modern analogues. These novel climates will be warmer than today and concentrated at first in the tropics and subtropics, modelling suggests, and in regions with high ecological diversity and complexity.[58] Novel or no-analogue climates increase the odds for novel species interactions, ecological surprises and rising extinction risk, as already described.

What level of future climate change is required to trigger no-analogue groupings, and what threat do they pose to biodiversity? These questions have only begun to be explored, but a study on 60 California bird species provides a hint. By 2070, individualistic responses to future climate change could lead novel groupings of birds to occupy more than half this US state. Although these communities would probably have analogues outside California, their formation could require new approaches to manage these species, creating conservation challenges.[59] Habitat loss, pollution and invasive species could also conspire with climate change to increase the likelihood of no-analogue assemblages, by pushing stressed ecosystems past thresholds and into new states.

Palaeoecologists John Williams and Stephen Jackson compare future novel climates to the world's uncharted geographic regions of centuries past – potentially dangerous territory thought to have prompted European cartographers to write on maps, 'Here there be Dragons'.

Unknowns and challenges

How birds' ranges will respond to climate change is a critical but still largely open question. One significant obstacle is the pressing need for better data on birds' present-day distributions. A dearth of detailed range maps for non-threatened birds, for example, has hampered the IUCN's efforts to gauge how trends for climate-change susceptible birds vary with geography (chapter 7).

In many cases the current mapped ranges of birds overestimate their distributions. This could lead to birds' extinction risk being underestimated. Bird diversity tends to be high in the tropics, yet mapping their actual distributions in these regions can be logistically challenging, and funding is often lacking. In fact, better knowledge on many forest birds' distributions would probably lead to their reclassification as 'threatened' (from 'non-threatened'), because this would ascertain the small size of their ranges. One way to speed up progress on this front would be to draw on the skills of the ever-increasing numbers of competent birdwatchers. Birds' future ranges could be more successfully modelled if data on climate were available on a finer scale, and if it detailed how climate varies with elevation. Another important and continuing challenge will be establishing whether range shifts are a result of climate change or a response to other human influences.

One critical question is whether bird populations will disperse, and disperse quickly enough, to track climate change. When recent range-margin shifts of European and North American birds were studied for patterns related to their ecology and species-specific traits including dispersal, thermal niche and body size, very few consistent clues emerged as to how to accurately forecast the range-margin changes of bird species.[15] Since bird species and other organisms are unlikely to shift together, in lock step, another key concern is the potential ecological fallout of reshuffled communities. Predicting such complex responses to climate change remains highly problematic.

The need to improve estimates of future range shifts is another important challenge. These efforts will benefit from research that considers birds' dependence on plants and the important interactions they have with other species in their ecological communities. Landscapes modified by people will also pose barriers to dispersal. Gauging the obstacles posed by habitat destruction and fragmentation will be inportant in order to estimate whether, and by how much, birds may shift their ranges. Failure to account for these dispersal barriers could lead predictions of range contractions and extinction risk to be underestimated.

Conclusion

Global warming has the potential to transform temperature, moisture and other aspects of climate that define birds' present-day ranges. Many organisms are already responding – another global fingerprint that reveals the importance of climate change as a driver of range shifts in animals and plants today. There is evidence that their ranges are not only shifting in conjunction with warming, but also contracting in some cases. Modelling suggests that in the future substantial shifts are in store, and that cases of shrinking ranges will not be infrequent.

Some bird species may disperse without detrimental effects, given suitable habitat. But where birds' present-day and estimated future ranges overlap little, populations may be at greater risk if they cannot disperse. This lack of overlap could be a particular problem for birds with small or restricted ranges. Birds' ability to shift to new areas of suitable climate could be constrained by both natural and human-imposed barriers.

Temperature increase alone can unleash complex biological effects in ecosystems, but climate change will also alter precipitation patterns, reduce sea-ice extent, and bring more intense extreme events, all of which may be expected to affect bird distributions. As range shifts are set in train, the responses of plants and other key elements of birds' habitats will influence their chances of successful dispersal. The bird communities we know today may become destabilised and reshuffled, and unabated global warming could even bring about no-analogue assemblages.

Conservation efforts today focus on preserving species in static reserves. But as birds track climate change, they could shift out of sanctuaries and into areas where they may face human threats. This prospect explains why habitat destruction, in combination with climate change, constitutes a potent new threat cocktail, and why predicting range shifts is considered a critically important challenge for this century. The risks and uncertainties of a radical departure from present-day climate conditions underscore the importance of constraining greenhouse gas emissions, to keep climate change within 'charted territory'.

Chapter 4

SEABIRDS HERALD OCEAN CHANGES

Vulnerable and responsive marine indicators

El Niño and the equatorial penguin

On the otherworldly, black lava coasts of the Galápagos Islands, the plight of a small penguin illustrates why seabirds' dual existence could be a liability under changing climate conditions. The Galápagos Islands, famed for Darwin's finches and marine iguanas, are perhaps less well known for the most northerly of penguin species. Endemic Galápagos penguins, *Spheniscus mendiculus*, probably descended from Humboldt penguins, *S. humboldti*, that hitched a ride from Chile or Peru on the cold, northward-flowing Humboldt Current to the Galápagos. The only penguin living and breeding on the equator, it also has among the smallest ranges and populations of any penguin species.

These penguins' continued survival also hinges on the vagaries of ocean currents. Great concentrations of fish occur in the Galápagos Archipelago's western portion, where the bottom-flowing Equatorial Under Current (also known as the Cromwell Current) bumps up against the islands. This cold, nutrient-rich upwelling allows tropical and cold-water life to coexist. It also helps explain the penguins' presence on the equator, and why their numbers are concentrated along the western islands where they have ready access to these productive waters.

When University of Washington conservation biologist Dee Boermsa travelled to the Galápagos in 1970 to study these penguins, they were a little-known species. After overcoming the difficulty of actually finding penguins much rarer than anyone realised, she began to observe them breeding. 'Then eventually none of them were breeding,' says Boersma, 'Everybody failed. I realised, "this is really unusual. There's no food." And it turned out to be the 1972 El Niño.'

The El Niño Southern Oscillation (ENSO) is the strongest driver of natural climate variation from one year to another. The Southern Oscillation is a large see-saw of surface air pressure between the eastern and western tropical Pacific. In tandem with reversals in this air pressure come simultaneous ocean warming events. These ENSO effects vary from region to region, but are most pronounced in the tropics, where they are linked to severe and detrimental effects on seabirds. During El Niño events, the best-known ENSO extremes, the eastern and central Pacific warm. La Niñas are the 'cold' extreme of ENSO events and are characterised by colder-than-normal eastern tropical Pacific waters.

El Niño's heavy hand probably shaped the Galápagos penguins' survival strategies over the course of their evolution. These seabirds breed opportunistically to capitalise on variable and unreliable food supplies, and can produce up to three clutches a year. When food is available they quickly gain weight so they can moult all their feathers and prepare to breed if waters stay productive. Foraging near their 'nests' – shady crevices, lava tubes and holes along rocky shores where eggs are laid – adults dive for small schooling fish. Foraging trips last less than a day, and frequent feeding allows chicks to grow rapidly to independence in just two months.

Only the coldest Galápagos waters harbour prey abundant enough to permit the penguins to reproduce. At times the abundance of fish is so great that their bodies blacken the water, inciting incredible feeding frenzies. 'There are concentrations of seabirds diving – pelicans and boobies diving from the top, cormorants coming in from the sides, penguins swimming through, noddy terns on the surface – and tuna or dolphins from underneath,' says Boersma, 'And that can go on for hours and hours.' These events usually occur when waters are cooler, less than 23°C.

Every three to eight years, however, El Niño conditions prevail. The Equatorial Under Current weakens, surface waters grow warmer, nutrient levels drop and fish numbers plummet. Though adapted to cope with El

Niño's fickleness, Galápagos penguins' tolerances have been sorely tested in recent decades. El Niños appear to have become more intense since the 1970s, and evidence suggests they arrive with two to seven times the frequency they did 7000–15 000 years ago.

Under weak El Niños, penguins' reproductive success plummets.[1,2] During one such event (1972–73), Boersma and other observers located 92 penguin nests, but recorded only a single surviving chick. Adult penguins abandon their eggs or young during weak El Niños, to seek food and ensure their own survival. This strategy, whereby adults forgo raising chicks should this threaten their chance to survive, is seen in other seabirds too.

Strong El Niños, on the other hand, can be catastrophic even for adult Galápagos penguins. The last century's most intense El Niños, during 1982–83 and 1997–98, were followed by population crashes of 77 and 65 per cent respectively, with starvation the likely cause of death of both adult and juvenile Galápagos penguins. But starvation of adults has a more critical effect on the penguin's population trends, because adult survival is generally high in seabirds. The population's failure to rebound after strong El Niños can, in turn, be partly explained by the lack of food and poor breeding success during El Niños. Paradoxically, El Niños bring rains that green the Galápagos' normally desert-like land environment, boosting the breeding success of Darwin's finches and other land birds. So whereas land birds breed and thrive during El Niños, seabirds, marine iguanas, sea lions and fur seals have trouble finding food.

Galápagos penguins feed exclusively within a few kilometres of the coast, on dives of 50 metres depth or less. These habits leave them in the lurch when schooling fish shift out of range during El Niño episodes. Disinclined to leave the islands' coastal waters, probably because they would be unlikely to find any small fish, they tend to rely on reef fish foraged within a few hundred metres of the shore. This makes them extremely sensitive to changes in prey availability, and appears to limit their ability to cope with severe El-Niño-triggered food shocks. 'It's like you live in a very remote place in Utah, and you have one convenience store and that's where you get your food,' says Boersma, 'and that convenience store goes out of business.'

What is the outlook for the penguins? Although some climate models predict more frequent and intense El Niño events, other modelling results suggest no changes, leaving the picture unclear. After its precipitous decline since the 1970s, a mere fraction of the Galápagos penguin's former population remains today, estimated at fewer than 2000 birds. If strong El Niños double in frequency, the Galápagos penguin's odds of extinction this century are estimated to exceed 80 per cent, based on an analysis of their population viability.[3] Even if El Niños do not surpass the strength and frequency seen in recent decades, their extinction risk is estimated at 30 per cent. These analyses do not account for other human threats such as fishing, and so may underestimate the risk to these seabirds.

The freedoms and constraints of a dual existence

Many seabirds are under threat, but their dual oceanic/terrestrial lifestyle will create its own special set of challenges under climate change. Although penguins and other seabirds are a diverse bunch, they are all essentially adapted to spending most of their lives in a marine environment. Crested penguins, *Eudyptes*, may grow barnacles on their feet, so long are they away from land.

Each species is rather specialised in its diet, the highly opportunistic and generalist herring gull, *Larus argentatus*, being notable among the exceptions. Using diverse strategies, different seabirds exploit most levels of the marine food web, from pelagic (open ocean) fishes to crustaceans, molluscs and zooplankton, and even the remains of dead animals. Whereas inshore feeders target abundant resources at the ocean surface, pelagic feeders including shearwaters, petrels and albatrosses roam extensively, seeking dispersed prey. Penguins, the most specialised divers and swimmers, are among those adapted to hunt at greater ocean depths.

Seabirds have a long bachelor period, giving them years to explore their environments and learn about prey locations. Seabird colonies, some speculate, may even function as 'information centres' for foraging strategies. Neighbouring colonies may differ in their local foraging culture, even if they experience similar ecological conditions.

When breeding, many seabirds avoid land-based predators by digging burrows or nesting on small, isolated islands or cliff ledges. They typically lay one or two eggs and invest considerable time rearing young. Seabirds are essentially bound to their land-based colonies until their young are fledged and mobile. This makes them reliant on nesting sites within range of high-quality food sources. The great variety of foraging strategies used by different seabirds means the length of this tie to land varies. Whereas foraging Galápagos penguins return daily, king penguins, *Aptenodytes patagonicus*, have been tracked by satellite up to 1800 kilometres away from their chicks, on journeys longer than 50 days (chapter 5).

Regardless, the need to commute between breeding colonies and ocean-based food resources can impose a severe constraint. Magellanic penguins, *Spheniscus magellanicus*, that are able to forage relatively close to their nests – 150 kilometres or less – have greater breeding success than those compelled to swim further afield. In fact, Magellanic penguins commuting further than 350 kilometres have virtually no chance of raising a chick.[4] Critically, these commuting distances can be affected by climate.[5]

Because seabirds are long-lived, adult survival rates undergo relatively little year-to-year change. This tends to promote stable population levels. As a result, their population size is likely to be less bound to fecundity than that of short-lived species. The other side of this coin is seabirds' low reproductive potential: their advanced age of first breeding, low numbers of offspring, and high mortality rates for young birds. These characteristics, combined with the high fidelity many show towards breeding sites, make seabirds more sensitive to climate change than land birds.

Four seabird species are known to have gone extinct over the past five centuries. Today, the world's approximately 700 million individual seabirds (a conservative estimate) face an array of human threats. They die as unintended bycatch in long-line and gill-net fisheries, suffer in oil spills and other marine pollution, are killed by invasive alien species such as cats and rodents, and have their food supplies threatened by overfishing. Combined, these and other human impacts threaten, or nearly threaten, about half of seabirds with extinction, according to the IUCN – twice the proportion for all bird species averaged.[6]

Climate change poses a major new threat. In 2010, a US Department of the Interior status report on birds revealed that *all* 67 oceanic bird species assessed in the USA have medium or high vulnerability to climate change, suggesting this new threat could push more seabirds towards the brink. Efforts to protect seabirds from global warming must also seek to stem overfishing and other human threats, as these could combine with climate change to cause severe negative effects on seabird breeding success and survival.

Messengers from the depths

Some of the same characteristics that make seabirds susceptible to climate change also make them valuable indicators of its effects on oceans.

Their dual existence affords scientists one of the few easy-to-monitor links to the world's oceans. Seabirds are sensitive to fluctuations in their marine food supplies, and relay these changes from lower down the food web. In essence, seabirds are expected to be sensitive to climate change because their marine ecosystems are also sensitive to it. The responses of seabirds, one of the best-known groups of marine life, have been recorded over long periods. In fact, seabirds provide some of the strongest evidence of the negative consequences of climate-change-driven shifts in prey distributions.

Climate change and the world's oceans

Temperature rising in the global heat sink

Before delving into how climate change affects seabirds, it is helpful to understand how it is 'clearly and fully impacting marine ecosystems'.[7] The oceans have enormous thermal mass. By absorbing more than 93 per cent of the heat added to the climate system over the past 50 years, they have restrained global temperature rise. Nevertheless, the oceans are heating up faster than predicted by climate models. Averaged across the globe, sea surface temperatures increased by 0.68°C from 1901–2004.[8,9] Oceans are expected to undergo considerable change over the next half century. Although they have warmed more gradually than most land surfaces, the repercussions for marine life may be greater than for life on land. This is because the distribution and phenology of key components of the marine food web – plankton and especially phytoplankton – are responding even more strongly to warming than land-based life.

Polar oceans demonstrate some of the most striking effects of global climate change. Warming diminishes the sea ice that underpins the ecology of many polar seabirds and other marine animals. This is also significant because sea ice has an important climate-shaping role, insulating the atmosphere from ocean warmth, reflecting sunlight into space and influencing ocean circulation. Arctic Ocean sea ice has rapidly diminished, and sea-ice free Arctic summers will probably come about sometime during this century. In fact, one estimate finds that nearly ice-free Arctic summers could come as early as 2037.[10] Southern polar ocean sea-ice trends have been less clear-cut, but future warming is expected to generally reduce sea-ice extent there as well.

Another carbon dioxide problem: ocean acidification

... lessons from the Earth's past raise concerns that ocean acidification could trigger a sixth mass extinction event, independently of anthropogenic extinctions that are currently taking place.

Secretariat of the Convention on Biological Diversity, 2009

Warming of the atmosphere and oceans is not the only important effect of the burgeoning carbon dioxide emissions from human activity. Each year, the oceans absorb roughly one-third of these emissions. Dissolved in seawater as carbonic acid, this is acidifying the surface waters of the oceans. Today, ocean surface water is still slightly alkaline with a pH averaging about 8.1 (a pH of 7.0 is considered neutral, neither acidic nor alkaline). But the oceans' surface has acidified by 0.1 units over the past 250 years, a 30 per cent increase in acidity. This and associated ocean chemistry changes, it is argued, have already created ocean conditions more extreme than experienced for millions of years. By 2100, pH of the ocean's surface could drop to about 7.8, corresponding to an approximately 150 per cent increase in the concentration of hydrogen ions.[11] Such rates of change would allow life little or no time to adapt.[12]

Critically, the oceans' acidification reduces the ability of calcifying organisms to build shells and other skeletal structures. Plankton (some of which have tiny shells), corals and marine animals ranging from snails to lobsters are among the ecologically important organisms that could be affected. Effects include weakened skeletons for coral reefs and altered composition for reef communities. The other significant threats possible for marine plankton communities around the world are still being investigated. There is serious concern that these and other ocean chemistry changes may affect marine life survival even more profoundly than temperature change.[13]

Ocean variability complicates climate change diagnoses

The effects of global warming on the world's oceans must be viewed within the context of many natural circulation cycles, spanning seasons, years and even decades. In fact, decades of data may be needed to tease apart the effects of natural climate oscillations from those due to the long-term changes related to global warming. How climate change will affect this ocean variability is hard to know. Because ocean warming is likely to profoundly influence the main current systems that distribute heat and moisture around the globe, even small ocean temperature changes could disproportionately affect marine ecosystems.

The El Niño Southern Oscillation, the most famous – or infamous – of these natural cycles has already been touched upon. Should El Niño events become more frequent and intense with climate change (a much debated point), the productivity of eastern Pacific waters would be reduced. The supplies of open-ocean fish available to seabirds would drop, causing the kind of problems already described for Galápagos penguins. But ENSO events also provide an opportunity to study seabirds' response to climate variations, and gauge how they may respond to future global warming (assuming that responses to short-term El-Niño-driven ocean warming reflect how seabirds might respond to longer-term, regional climate change).

Other well-known climate drivers include the North Atlantic Oscillation and the Pacific Decadal Oscillation. Like ENSO, they are associated with dramatic effects on the breeding phenology, reproductive success and abundance of seabirds.

Narrow limits, bottom-up control

Marine invertebrates live within particular bounds of temperature (and chemistry), making climate a fundamental determinant of where plankton, and therefore fish, are found. Fish also have well-defined thermal niches, and changes of less than 0.5°C can radically affect the ability of some to reproduce, grow and survive. Like life on land, marine organisms may adjust if environmental changes are mild. But if their temperature or other thresholds are exceeded, and they cannot acclimatise, marine organisms may sicken, and their populations decline or become locally extinct. In this way, seemingly minor changes can affect when and where seabirds' ocean food supplies are found.

Climate, by influencing ocean circulation and sea-surface temperature, is thought to control ocean food-web productivity from the bottom up, driving the abundance of phytoplankton like free-floating algae. Zooplankton, in turn, graze on phytoplankton and other small organisms, channelling energy and productivity further up the ocean food web, ultimately to seabirds. Climate-driven upwelling of the cold, nutrient-rich water from the ocean depths is a significant driver of this productivity. Upwelling, and limits on it, is thought to affect the food webs and populations of even top predators like Galápagos penguins. Ocean food-web productivity may also be influenced from the top down. Overfishing by humans in the Southern Ocean, for example, appears to have limited the food available to penguins and other marine predators.[14]

Declining productivity and dramatic shifts

Great changes underway in the world's oceans could affect if and where seabirds find prey. Future climate change is expected to bring about large shifts in marine life abundance and distribution. This expectation is reinforced by records of the past: over the last 100 000 years, changes in climate have caused massive sea-level fluctuations of 100 metres or more, and driven big shifts in the abundance and especially the distribution of marine life.

An extensive cluster of climate change effects are expected to stem from increased stratification of the water column due to warming. Ocean water becomes less dense when it becomes warmer or less salty (if diluted by an influx of fresh water from melted ice, for example). This lower-density layer of water is less likely to mix with deeper, upward-moving, nutrient-rich waters. In this way, strengthened stratification prevents nutrients from reaching phytoplankton at the ocean surface, and can lead to declines in phytoplankton productivity. On the other hand, at high latitudes phytoplankton may become more productive as water temperatures warm.

Ocean warming, stratification and acidification have diverse and complex effects on the marine environment. Although it has increased in some areas, in eight out of ten of the world's oceans, phytoplankton productivity has declined over the past century, in step with rising sea-surface temperatures.[15] The extent of nutrient-poor 'ocean deserts' in the Atlantic and Pacific expanded by 15 per cent from 1998 to 2006, as expected under global-warming scenarios. These profound changes strongly suggest a negative effect of global warming on the oceans' overall primary productivity. They affect the food web from the bottom up, from the timing, distribution and abundance of phytoplankton grazers, up to seabirds and other top predators.

Looking specifically at distribution shifts, there is ample evidence that some species of phytoplankton, zooplankton, fish, seabirds and marine mammals are expanding or shifting their ranges polewards. The relatively rapid shifts seen, some argue, better reflect the response of life to climate warming than do the shifts of land-based organisms, which are more likely to lag in their reactions. Powerful records of large shifts come courtesy of a surprisingly simple instrument. The continuous plankton recorder uses silk thread to capture plankton from ocean waters and spool it into a sampling chamber. Towed behind merchant freighters, these recorders sampled a staggering nine million kilometres of the North Atlantic over 70 years. This record reveals that in cool regions, phytoplankton have increased in abundance when waters warmed. Conversely, where warm regions became warmer still, phytoplankton declined in abundance, possibly due to blocked ocean upwelling.[16]

Zooplankton have made the fastest and most extensive recorded shifts of any recorded group on land or sea in response to climate change. North-east Atlantic zooplankton called copepods shifted by more than 1100 kilometres northwards over the past half-century.[17] Some ocean life is mirroring the upslope shifts of mountain species; North Sea demersal fish (those that dwell near seabeds) deepened by approximately 3.6 metres per decade or shifted northwards as winter bottom temperatures increased by 1.6°C, from 1980 to 2004.[18] But it would be a mistake to expect that marine species will always display a straightforward response to ocean warming. Ocean currents and other complex oceanographic and climate factors may also strongly influence their distributions and abundance.

Critically for seabirds, these potentially large shifts may mean food supplies are no longer located where and when predators expect, affecting their foraging success and productivity. Large shifts in sea-surface temperature, for example, regardless of whether they entail warming or cooling, are associated with declines in Arctic and subarctic seabird populations.[19] Some seabirds may adapt by changing their foraging strategies and target prey, or by shifting their distributions. However, the rapid pace of climate change could test the coping capacity of some. Those with little scope to adapt, like endemic Galápagos penguins 'trapped' within their restricted habitat, may face extinction.

In a similar way, reshuffling of ocean food webs could pose a threat to seabirds. This is possible because marine species, like those on land, are expected to respond to climate change individualistically. New ecological relationships or even new ecosystems could form as warming continues. The loss or addition of species has important consequences for marine ecosystems, especially when the species concerned play a critical role in leveraging or controlling the abundance of other life. Even a small temperature change can produce dramatic effects if it acts on these pivotal organisms. Copepods, bewildering in their abundance, are one such example, and dramatic shifts in their seasonal timing and distribution may have already caused radical disruptions in North Sea marine food webs.[20]

Thresholds and regime shifts

Marine food webs are inherently unstable and may sporadically reorganise themselves. When a region undergoes an abrupt and persistent shift at multiple levels of the ocean food web, across a large geographic area, a regime shift is said to occur. Even subtle climate change may trigger regime shifts from one stable state to another.[21] Return to the original state is difficult. Regime shifts, which drive range shifts, do occur naturally but some evidence suggests recent climate change could make them more frequent, and that marine ecosystems are becoming more chaotic overall.[22]

Warming and rising carbon dioxide levels are also moving towards important thresholds[23] that would seriously threaten coral reefs or could make polar ocean waters corrosive to key marine calcifying organisms.[24] The mounting effects of climate change and other impacts of human activity also make domino effects and feedbacks a concern. In the open ocean, for example, ever warmer and more-stratified surface waters are combining with overfishing and increased ultraviolet exposure to change the structure and function of food webs.

Responses of polar and ice-dependent seabirds

Ice-loving phantoms of a warming Arctic

... a bird the color of deep snow, the color of distant icebergs, a bird of shocking white.

Kenn Kaufman, 1997

Turning to seabirds' responses to climate change we begin at the poles, because species most dependent on (or most restricted by) sea ice are likely to be among the early responders to global warming. A seabird epitomising this threat is the 'phantom of the shifting ice', as naturalist Kenn Kaufman described the ivory gull, *Pagophila eburnea*. Though well known to the

Inuit for its habit of following hunters along ice floes and first noted by European whalers more than four centuries ago, the ivory gull remains among the seabirds least known to science. At home in some of the world's most inhospitable and inaccessible regions, its scientific name (*Pagophila* is Greek for 'ice loving') alludes to its year-round preference for a mainly frozen habitat. This extreme polar bird, the sole member of its genus, may even stay in the Arctic over winter, when it seeks habitat 70–90 per cent covered in ice.

Ivory gulls hunt small fish and shrimps near the ocean surface, along the edges of ice floes and *polynyas*, areas of persistent open water surrounded by sea ice. And because the kills of polar bears provide carrion for these opportunistic scavengers, ivory gulls can often be seen hovering around these top Arctic predators. Ivory gulls' breeding colonies are mainly found on sheer cliffs of spectacular *nunataks*, granite peaks or ridges towering 800 metres or more above vast inland arctic glaciers – remote and inaccessible to predators. Their nests of moss, straw and other debris may also be found on bare, gravelly stretches along remote, low islands. This bird's breeding requirements are actually quite restrictive: high Arctic sites, usually less than 100 kilometres from early-season open water, but associated with sea ice, and safe from foxes and other walking or flying predators.

Some Inuit elders of Arctic Canada, though acknowledging ivory gulls were never common, have memories from their youth of gulls making enough din to keep them awake at their spring camps out on the sea ice. This is no longer the case and some Inuit express concern for the decline of a bird they regard with affection for its tame nature. Their observations are backed up by surveys indicating a 50–80 per cent drop in ivory gull numbers since the 1970s in Canada, down to an estimated 652 birds in 2009.[25] Counts are falling elsewhere in the Arctic, and the IUCN estimates their numbers at 15 000 to 25 000 birds globally.

Climate change is considered an important threat to ivory gulls. Concerns about rising sea-surface temperatures and thinner, less-extensive sea ice are reasons cited for this seabirds' endangered listing in Canada. But the difficulty of studying ivory gulls, especially in winter, makes it impossible to rule out a combination of other important threats, from food-web contaminants to mining-industry disturbance.

The Arctic could warm as much as 9°C by 2100, auguring big changes for the ivory gull and other ice-dependent birds. As sea ice contracts polewards, away from restricted numbers of coastal nesting sites, this future, warmer world would provide severely reduced options for breeding habitat. Modelling suggests that even moderate warming could shrink the climate space of its high-Arctic breeding habitat in Europe by 70 per cent by the century's end. An international conservation plan to tackle its decline notwithstanding, climate change is very likely to have serious consequences for the ice-loving ivory gull.

Sea ice, a meltable platform of polar life

The ivory gull's plight hints at the potentially profound implications of loss of the sea ice. Sea ice hosts surprisingly diverse life, including ice algae that underpin up to a quarter of primary production in Arctic waters. Every summer as the ice retreats and releases algae into the water, an explosion of productivity fuels an enormous Arctic food web. Concentrations of algae on extensive sea ice can also foster 'hotspots' of ocean life far below. The tiny marine animals that drift with sea ice and feed on algae (or the organisms that eat them) may include nematode worms, rotifers and crustaceans, as well as young Arctic cod, *Boreogadus saida*, an important prey item for seabirds.

As these icy platforms for food production contract with climate warming, some seabirds are likely to suffer. Brünnich's guillemots breeding at Coats Island, northern Hudson Bay experience the highest July temperatures of any large Canadian colony of these birds. In the past, sea-ice dependent Arctic cod were an important part of their diet. But as sea-ice coverage diminished in the mid-1990s, the diet of nestlings at Coats Island shifted markedly.[26] Arctic cod has been replaced by capelin, *Mallotus villosus*, and sand lance, *Ammodytes* spp. This shift signals the transformation of their food web, from a typically high-Arctic one, to a state more characteristic of the low Arctic where these latter fish predominate.

Brünnich's guillemots typically deliver fish singly to their nestlings. Food delivery has continued, albeit in smaller portions because capelin are roughly a third the weight of the typical Arctic cod caught by the birds. The new diet of smaller fish probably necessitates more frequent feeding trips, one possible reason for slower nestling growth in years when summer ice is at its minimum extent. These slower-growing chicks are considered less likely to survive.

Some climate models predict Hudson Bay sea ice will disappear altogether this century. If warming continues and prey-driven problems with chick rearing intensify, southern Brünnich's guillemot colonies will probably decline. Yet on high Arctic islands, where heavy ice formerly hindered breeding efforts, breeding success may improve. In this way, Brünnich's guillemots demonstrate one of the most important climate change effects on seabirds – food-web disruptions – and suggest how continued warming may cause poleward range shifts of seabird populations.

As the case of the Brünnich's guillemots suggests, where polar sea ice is lost, food webs underpinned by sea-ice algae may be expected to decline or shift. Polar regions host some of the world's largest colonies of seabirds, animals that have evolved to respond to the seasonal ebb and flow of sea ice, especially ice edges. As we shall see, sea ice also provides seabirds (and mammals) with an important platform for hunting, breeding and migration. While some seabirds may benefit, ice-associated species are very vulnerable to reductions in sea ice. An example is Kittlitz's murrelet, *Brachyramphus brevirostris*. This ice-loving bird is disappearing in the Alaskan fjords of Prince William Sound where tidewater glaciers have declined since the late 1980s. Why this species is attracted to fjords with stable or increasing glaciers is still a matter of speculation.

Ice-dependent in Antarctica: Adélie penguins

Against incredible odds this little warm-blooded creature survives only by being supremely adapted, knowing what is important, and doing whatever is needed, always with amazingly defiant energy.

David Ainley, 2002

At the other end of the globe, another ice-dependent seabird is heralding changes in Antarctica's oceans. Along with the emperor penguin, *Aptenodytes forsteri*, (chapter 5) the Adélie penguin, *Pygoscelis adeliae*, is a truly Antarctic seabird, living within or near pack ice throughout the year. Sensitive to the changes in its icy environment, it was dubbed the 'bellwether of climate change' by marine biologist David Ainley.

Helpfully, records for some Adélie colonies extend back 50 years, providing an unusually complete picture of recent responses to climate. Adélies' particular taste in breeding sites has also helped. Around Antarctica, they choose beaches of exposed rock, gently sloping and free of snow and melt-water, to build nests of small pebbles in the austral spring. Also important is ready access to open water and sufficient prey. Such sites are relatively scarce on an Antarctic coastline largely bound by sheer ice and rock cliffs, towering over ocean locked in continuous sheets of sea ice for much of the year. Adélie penguins' preserved remains littering these sites on cold, dry Antarctic shores show how their populations ebbed and flowed over 45 000 years of environmental change.

Where the Southern Ocean is now devoid of their prey fish (for a variety of reasons including overfishing), Adélies prey on Antarctic krill, *Euphausia superba*, during summer. The reproductivity and survival of Antarctic penguins like Adélies are expected to relay information about predators of krill, a keystone Antarctic species. Krill can lay as many as 10 000 eggs at once, and up to 3000 larval and juvenile Antarctic krill may take refuge in fissures and crevices of just one square metre of sea ice. In summer, krill amass where phytoplankton bloom and can form dense swarms stretching kilometres in every direction, attracting seabirds and marine mammals in spectacular feeding frenzies.

Ice is important not just for krill. Pack ice is ideal Adélie habitat in every season. This zone of ice floes, packed together by wind or separated by stretches of open ocean water called leads, is actually one of Earth's largest habitats. Yet there can be too much ice, even for Adélies. Their legs are only a few centimetres long, and lengthy treks across very dense pack ice or fast ice (ice that has frozen along coasts) consume energy that could otherwise be passed onto chicks. If parents cannot commute effectively between nests and feeding areas, hungry mates may desert nests, leaving the chicks to starve. Furthermore, Adélies can forage only so far beneath the ice surface without returning to ice-free areas to come up and breathe, so ocean totally covered in ice is less useful feeding habitat. New ice, though thin, is thick enough to support the penguins' weight. But leopard seals, *Hydrurga leptonyx* – the largest of all seals – can spot them through this glassy surface and smash through to capture them. Taken together, these challenges explain why Adélie penguin colonies are found close to *polynyas* and absent where November fast ice extends more than 10 kilometres from shore.

An ecosystem on fire

The Adélies' dependency on ice is illustrated by events on the western portion of the Antarctic Peninsula, the long curving arm that reaches towards the tip of South America. This region is undergoing the most rapid warming of any marine area of the globe. Although warming has been rather uneven across Antarctica, average winter temperatures on this peninsula have leaped 6°C since 1950, and the ocean has warmed by nearly 0.7°C. Massive peninsular ice shelves[27] have disintegrated for the first time in recorded history including, famously, the rapid collapse of a huge portion of Larsen B in 2002. These changes prompted biological oceanographer Hugh Ducklow to declare in the journal *Science*, 'This ecosystem is on fire.'

In the western Antarctic Peninsula, Adélies are near the warmest extreme of their distribution. Here their populations fare best under heavier-than-normal winter sea-ice conditions. But sea-ice coverage in waters west of the peninsula declined a dramatic 40 per cent over the past quarter century. Adélies without ice are like ducks out of water, and their colonies along the mid to northern Antarctic Peninsula have generally declined, more steeply after 1990.[28] On Anvers Island, a couple of hundred kilometres south of the Antarctic Peninsula's tip, scientists at Palmer Station watched Adélie numbers plummet over 1975–2003 to less than half their former level.[29]

On the western Antarctic Peninsula, clues about the mechanisms behind Adélie population declines suggest climate change will act via complex effects. The cold, dry, continental Antarctic conditions under which Adélies evolved have given way to a warm, moist, maritime climate, owing to a shift in the track of the polar jet stream. Adélie penguins need snow-free areas to build their nests, yet snowfall has increased over the past century on the Antarctic Peninsula. One hypothesis is that if snow forces Adélies to delay nesting, their chicks' feeding demands may no longer coincide with periods of high krill abundance; this could result in slower-growing chicks less likely to survive. When snow from more frequent and severe spring blizzards melts, Adélie nests may flood – fatal for eggs and chicks.[30] Tellingly perhaps, at colonies where snowfall tends to be scoured away by wind, Adélie numbers appear to be declining less steeply.

A shorter sea-ice season may also hamper Adélies' winter hunts, as they seek out isolated hotspots of krill (and fish) amongst the sea ice. Because they do not hunt at night, short winter days restrict the time and distance they can travel and feed. To stay close to krill hotspots, they walk across the sea ice and use it as a hunting platform. However, off the western Antarctic Peninsula, the annual duration of ice cover is 80 days shorter than a quarter of a century ago. Continued loss of sea ice over the long term will make it increasingly difficult for Adélies to access krill hotspots.

Sea ice declines may also be affecting numbers of Antarctic krill, this penguin's main food in the western Antarctic Peninsula region. Krill abundance declined by as much as 80 per cent from 1976 to 2003 along the northern half of the western Antarctic Peninsula and throughout much of the Southern Ocean's South West Atlantic sector, a trend linked to winter sea ice.[31] Winter sea ice is thought to provide a vital nursery for larval krill, which graze on algae in the safety of ice crevices. When sea-ice extent is lowest, krill abundance is also lowest and breeding Adélies must forage longer.[32] This could negatively affect their growth and reproductive chances.

A southward shift in diatoms, the preferred food of krill, could also be affecting their numbers. Where glaciers have melted and seawater has become less saline, diatoms – phytoplankton that live on sea-ice margins – have been replaced by cryptophytes. These are microscopic algae too small for krill to graze efficiently. Food-web shifts like these would be expected to exacerbate the problem of reduced krill numbers for Adélies in the waters along the northern portion of the western Antarctic Peninsula.[33]

Nonetheless, pinning down the precise causes of change in Southern Ocean food webs is a very complex exercise. Climate change effects must be teased from the long history of human impacts from sealing, whaling and fishing. The expansion of the fishery for krill, which is used as an aquaculture feedstock, has triggered concern since krill may also increasingly affected by climate change.

Food-web dynamics aside, modelling suggests that, with 2°C of warming[34] over the period 2025–2052, Adélie colonies would experience the negative effects of declining sea ice; those north of 70°S would decrease or disappear, affecting 70 per cent of their total breeding population.[35] Further towards the pole, south of 73°S, limited growth might be expected. Adélies may be helped at their more polar colonies where concentrated sea ice diverges or where coastlines are exposed as ice shelves are lost, opening up more locations where they can establish colonies. Yet during winter, one constraint could be diminished pack ice north of the Antarctic Circle (66.5°S), where light still reaches during the darkest Antarctic winter days. Adélies need at least few hours of light and twilight each day to forage, and a lack of winter pack ice in waters below this latitude and further north would limit their ability to migrate and survive through winter.

Responses of temperate seabirds

Climate trouble in a Pacific seabird paradise

Far from Antarctica, events off Canada's southwest coast illustrate how climate change could disrupt the food webs that sustain seabirds in temperate waters. Remote Triangle Island, off the northwest tip of Vancouver Island, rises from rocky, wave-pounded shores to a high, slab-like plateau naked of trees. It is so rugged and remote that attempts to staff a lighthouse there were abandoned after just 10 years. Life lines strung between the lighthouse keepers' buildings helped keep people on terra firma during hurricane-force winds, but were of no assistance to one lighthouse keeper's dog dispatched by a gale. Fog so frequently obscured the lighthouse beacon that sailors close enough to spot its beam in bad weather were said to be already doomed.

Though perilous to sailors and purgatory to lighthouse keepers, Triangle Island is a paradise for seabirds, and one of the North Pacific's most significant colonies. Its low-lying vegetation flourishes in the moist climate and the surrounding waters abound with life, from fish to seals and orcas, underpinned by pulses of plankton abundance. Each spring, Triangle Island explodes into life, veiled by clouds of breeding auklets. Twelve seabird species nest there, including Canada's largest colony of tufted puffins, *Fratercula cirrhata*, its second-largest colony of rhinoceros auklets, *Cerorhinca monocerata*, and the world's largest colony of Cassin's auklets, *Ptychoramphus aleuticus*.

Protected as an ecological reserve (strictly off limits to those without permits), Triangle Island is also the site of Canada's most intensive seabird monitoring program. Its valuable insights have demonstrated that there is trouble in seabird paradise. Sea-surface temperatures in this region generally increased since the 1970s, peaking in the late 1990s at some of the century's highest recorded levels, before dropping off again after a regime shift took hold in late 1998.

Rhinoceros auklets return without full bills

Warming oceans are a concern for the rhinoceros auklet, named for its horn-like beak extension. This seabird forages for fish up to 60 kilometres away from its colony, to depths of 60 metres, and returns under the cover of darkness, possibly to avoid thieving gulls or preying raptors. At Triangle Island, its catch is typically a bill load of up to eight small fish. Key among them is Pacific sand lance, *Ammodytes hexapterus*, which provides a lipid-rich food that helps nestlings grow rapidly and fledge successfully.

In warmer springs with higher-than-usual ocean surface temperatures, the amount of sand lance in the chicks' diet drops off, as do chicks' growth rates.[36] Why is not fully understood, but a likely mechanism is the type of bottom-up effects on the ocean food web already discussed, driven by warming. When ocean temperatures soared during the 1990s, nutrient levels at the water's surface plummeted. Zooplankton abundance is thought to be lower in such years, as is the recruitment of sand lance that feed on zooplankton.

Curly prey problem for tufted puffins

Warming may be affecting not just the abundance of sand lance around Triangle Island, but also where and when they are found. In other regions, warmer waters have been shown to cause sand lance species to shift their distributions, vertically or horizontally. At Triangle Island this may already be causing problems for tufted puffins, one of the most beautiful auks. Their Latin name means 'curly headed little brother', a reference to the long, curled yellow tufts behind each eye, and the bold white face masks and glossy black body plumage evocative of hooded friars. Complemented by bright orange legs and bills, these puffins are dressed to impress during the breeding season. After mating, a single egg is laid in a burrow.

An Triange Island, breeding is most successful when sea-surface temperatures range from 8.9 to 9.9°C, and drops off outside this range. This decline is especially precipitous when the upper boundary is breached. Fledgling success of almost zero beyond 9.9°C implies that these seabirds, or more likely their prey, are sensitive to higher sea-surface temperatures.[37] Tufted puffins' extreme response may be explained by their habit of foraging relatively close to their colony. This strategy might make them more vulnerable than other auks if their prey shifts in abundance or distribution, as they may be less able to find alternatives nearby. Yet these relationships, along with tufted puffins' population biology, remain poorly understood.

This abrupt cut-off for breeding success emphasises how even a slight change in climate may trigger a severe and disproportionate response in this ecosystem. Near-complete reproductive failures were frequent for Triangle Island's tufted puffins during the 1990s, and during 2003 and 2007. Though tufted puffins are long-lived birds, burrows counts at study sites on Triangle Island suggest a decline of 1.7 per cent per year between 1984 and 2004. If ocean warming continues, Triangle Island's tufted puffin numbers may be severely reduced within a few decades, and the site could eventually become unsuitable for breeding. North of its Canadian Triangle Island stronghold, suitable predator-free breeding islands for tufted puffins are scarce.

Colder is also better for Cassin's auklets

The case of a third Triangle Island auk shows how shifts in the timing of food species can be highly detrimental to seabirds. The gregarious Cassin's auklet is a dark-feathered seabird that mainly eats krill-like zooplankton. This plankton preference means its fate is more directly tied to ocean productivity than that of tufted puffins and rhinoceros auklets (larger birds that concentrate on fish during the breeding season). Among their zooplankton prey are copepods species that peak briefly in abundance during spring and early summer in the upper 100 metres of the ocean. They include the large-bodied *Neocalanus cristatus*, an especially important item in the Cassin's auklet's diet.

During early and warm springs,[38] zooplankton biomass peaks early and ends early in the waters around Triangle Island.[39] This allows for less overlap between earlier, narrower *Neocalanus* abundance peaks and chicks' demands. The proportion of copepods in the nestlings' diets decreases, and nestlings grow more slowly than during years with cold ocean temperatures or late springs. Lighter chicks, in turn, are generally less likely to survive their first year at sea.

In temperate oceans especially, plankton food webs are characterised by highly synchronous pulses of abundance, each level being vital to transfer production efficiently from the lower to higher trophic levels. However, different trophic levels of this food web respond to warming differently.

In the North Sea, for example, dinoflagellates are peaking 23 days earlier, diatoms 22 days and copepods 10 days earlier.[40] Mismatch and uncoupling of phenology at different levels of the plankton food web could have ripple effects that alter the dynamics of entire food webs.

If Cassin's auklets fail to adapt to shifts in plankton pulses, their long-term survival could be jeopardised. Climate-driven changes in zooplankton availability are already thought to be a factor in the decline of the numbers of Cassin's auklets breeding at Triangle Island. Future ocean warming, and possibly more frequent ENSO events, are expected to increase this mismatch, and further reduce their ability to produce nestlings.

Shockwaves in the California Current

Triangle Island lies at the northern end of the California Current, an ocean current system with a broad and generally southward-meandering surface flow, finishing at Mexico's Baja Peninsula. The current makes this domain's southerly waters relatively cool for their latitude. However, since the 1950s, zooplankton biomass in the California Current declined markedly, by 80 per cent. The birds that characterise this system have undergone an essential long-term shift, from communities typical of highly productive waters to those more characteristic of the low-productivity waters found in subtropical regions. Cassin's auklet, rhinoceros auklet and other populations of cold-water seabirds have declined.

At the Gulf of the Farallones, located in the Pacific Ocean west of San Francisco, Cassin's auklet populations have dropped 75 per cent in the past three decades.[41] In 2005 these seabirds abandoned their colony at Southeast Farallon Island en masse, and for the first time in 35 years of study researchers witnessed their complete failure to breed. The same year and far to the north, scientists visiting Triangle Island, accustomed to being greeted by the din of the Cassin's auklets, were instead met with eerie silence. Most seabirds abandoned their burrows just days after their chicks hatched, and breeding success was close to zero. These widespread failures show why these seabirds are considered susceptible to climate change across the entire California Current system.

The extreme 2005 events are blamed on unfavourable winds that apparently delayed coastal spring upwelling of nutrient-rich ocean waters.[42] This delay is thought to have radically reduced plankton availability in the unusually warm surface waters, with repercussions up the food web to fish and seabirds. The root causes of this 2005 weather anomaly are unknown, but its powerful effect emphasises the critical consequences of changes to ocean currents and upwelling for seabirds and other marine life.

Black-legged indicators of the sea

Far from the California Current, the breeding problems of temperate seabirds in the United Kingdom are also being blamed, in part, on warming seas. Prospects for these seabirds were cause for optimism during the 1960s to 1990s, as their ranks grew from around 4.5 to seven million birds. However, since 2000 total numbers have fallen by about 600 000 birds. Fewer adults are surviving, and numbers of new recruits are too low to compensate, according to the Joint Nature Conservation Committee, the UK government's wildlife adviser. The situation was especially dire in 2004, the worst seabird breeding season on record.

The immediate culprit has been a lack of food, but ultimately climate change, and warmer winters in particular, could be a one of the key factors in decreasing seabird numbers. Declines are pronounced among seabirds dependent on small fish, like lesser sandeels, *Ammodytes marinus*, an abundant, lipid-rich fish closely related to the sand lance so crucial to some Pacific auklets' breeding efforts.

Sea temperatures in the east Atlantic and around the UK coast have risen by approximately 0.2–0.9°C per decade since the 1980s, most rapidly in the southern North Sea and English Channel. Huge shifts in the location of North Sea plankton communities, already described, have dramatically affected the food web and greatly reduced the abundance of zooplankton upon which sandeels prey.

Because their breeding efforts in the North Sea hinge on sandeels, black-legged kittiwakes, *Rissa tridactyla*, are highly sensitive to changes in the abundance of these fish, one reason they are carefully observed by the UK Seabird Monitoring Programme. By 2008, UK black-legged kittiwake numbers had dropped to about half their 1986 levels. Whereas a pair of black-legged kittiwakes in eastern Britain could be expected to successfully fledge one chick in 1986, by 2008 only about one in every three pairs could be expected to produce a chick, on average. In breeding seasons following warm winters, their reproductive success is poorer, and so is adult survival; in these poor years they catch fewer and smaller sandeels.

But exactly why are sandeels declining? Though these fish are difficult to study, growing evidence links lower sandeel recruitment to warmer sea-surface temperatures, an effect that has been especially noticeable in the south-west North Sea, where these fish are near the southern limit of their distribution.[43] Specifically, there appears to be a shift in the plankton communities they rely upon for food, from cold-water to warm-water or sub-tropical species. Human fishing may also reduce sandeel numbers enough to affect the seabirds, although an east coast UK ban on fishing sandeels close to seabird colonies failed to stem the seabirds' decline (despite some initial improvement). Unless sea-surface temperatures begin to drop instead of rise, the decline of black-legged kittiwakes and other seabirds dependent on sandeels is expected to continue.[44]

Tropical seabirds, El Niño and climate change

Across the world and far to the south, birds of blue reef waters are helping to clarify the threat of ocean warming, showing that Galápagos penguins are not the only tropical seabirds affected by the El Niño Southern Oscillation. In fact, ENSO operates with a heavy hand in tropical systems, where it drives the greatest ocean temperature fluctuations and has powerful effects. Among tropical seabirds mainly negative responses have been observed so far. In addition to ENSO, decade-long and even century-long climate cycles drive tropical ocean-surface temperatures.

Australia's tropical seabirds powerfully demonstrate the effects of changing climate conditions. Lying off the continent's northeast coast, the Great Barrier Reef hosts a quarter of Australia's tropical breeding seabird population. Terns, noddies, shearwaters, boobies and tropicbirds are among the 22 species found at colonies on the region's granite islands and coral cays.

Peak seabird breeding events create spectacles. 'Michaelmas Cay is only two hectares, but during peak breeding it's completely covered in seabirds,' says James Cook University biologist Carol Devney, 'Some are on the ground, some are up in the air, and as you approach it's just a swirling mass of life.' During an El Niño event, a very different picture presents itself. 'You get an empty, quiet breeding colony,' says Devney, 'Usually the birds just don't bother, or they might attempt but the chicks die.'

Tropical waters tend to be nutrient-poor, so seabirds may need to seek prey in small, shifting patches where food webs are relatively more productive. Where fish are found, however, may be changing due to warmer sea temperatures linked to climate change. The marked prey declines that accompany intense El Niño events suggest how breeding seabirds like wedge-tailed shearwaters, *Puffinus pacificus*, could be affected if sea-surface temperatures warm further. Wedge-tailed shearwaters are monogamous and tend to return to their natal colonies on coral cays and other islands, where they nest in burrows. They forage for fish and squid by day, returning at night to feed their chicks.

During 2002, an El Niño event brought abnormally high sea-surface temperatures to a wedge-tailed shearwater colony at Heron Island in the southern part of the Great Barrier Reef. As the birds' food supplies dropped to one-third normal levels, parents foraged up to four times as long to capture the same quantity of food. Yet they were unable to compensate, and the colony suffered an almost total breeding failure.[45] Moreover, at least 2000 adults died,[46] cause for concern since these shearwaters are typically long-lived.

In fact, throughout the Great Barrier Reef, all the big rookeries of tropical breeding seabirds have probably suffered significantly from El Niño-driven ocean warming; future climate change is expected to magnify these effects.[47] Serious population declines at its four most important colonies led the Great Barrier Reef Marine Park Authority in 2009 to grade the outlook of its seabirds as 'poor'.

Here again, the well-known link between El Niño and seabird breeding failures is probably governed by the mechanisms described earlier: unfavourable temperatures block nutrient-rich upwelling, disrupting phytoplankton abundance and distribution (see figure 2). This impairs productivity for months or more, ultimately affecting the recruitment of seabirds' prey.

Dinner delivered from the thermocline

It is also thought that seabirds' prey may shift, horizontally or vertically, out of their foraging range during ENSO events. This could affect the fish-eating birds that congregate where prey is found in thermoclines. Thin but distinct layers, thermoclines essentially form a boundary between relatively warm and cold water masses (such as the boundary between two different ocean currents). Within a thermocline, which is a semi-permanent feature in tropical ocean waters, the temperature gradient with depth tends to be relatively steep, compared to layers above and below.

Importantly for seabirds, prey fish may concentrate at thermoclines, and different seabirds are known to hunt prey at specific thermocline depths. Yet climate can affect thermocline depth or stratification and when it does, the abundance, distribution and availability of seabirds' prey may be affected, too. Remarkably, by responding to thermocline changes, some seabirds can signal a coming El Niño event up to one year before it arrives. At Michaelmas Cay in the northern Great Barrier Reef, the number of breeding sooty terns, *Sterna fuscata*, and common noddies, *Anous stolidus*, declined as the 20°C thermocline deepened in this vicinity, well in advance of an ensuing El Niño.[48] Seabirds in temperate south-west Pacific waters and on southern African coasts display similar responses.

Precisely how changes to thermoclines affect seabirds' access to prey is unknown, but tuna and dolphins may be implicated. Off the Great Barrier Reef, most tropical pelagic seabirds do not actually dive down to the thermocline to reach their prey. In this zone the thermocline is quite deep, 200 metres or more below the surface. Instead seabirds rely greatly on sub-sea predators to drive prey to the ocean surface, where they can glean fish while flying. In the tropical Pacific, tuna are the most important such sub sea predators.

In El Niño's early stages, changes in the thermocline cause productive foraging waters to shift from the western tropical Pacific to the central Pacific.[48] Tuna can disperse to track these food-rich zones, but breeding seabirds must remain near their colonies, presumably with less access to prey. How future changes in ocean temperature will affect these important relationships between seabirds and sub-sea predators is little known.

Getting to know the devil through the details

... it is likely that relatively small increases in average sea surface temperature or in the number and duration of large hot water incursions into the GBR will cause repeated and catastrophic reproductive failure of many seabird species.

Bradley Congdon et al., 2007

Relatively small and fleeting warming events can shed light on how more sweeping climate change could operate in future. At Heron Island, seabirds' efforts to breed were affected as prey availability fluctuated in concert with short-term changes in sea-surface temperature. When the sea surface warmed by 1°C, wedge-tailed shearwaters fed their chicks only once every five nights, instead of every two nights, and the amount of weight gained by growing chicks fell by six to seven per cent (of their body weight) per day.[49] 'There is an immediate response by the seabirds,' says Devney, 'When sea surface temperatures go up, the amount of food chicks are getting goes down; it's a direct relationship.' These effects, also shown in other species, appeared regardless of whether of El Niño or other ocean anomalies were present.[50]

These fine-scale changes may also shed light on the kinds of temperature thresholds already noted earlier for the tufted puffins of Triangle Island. Tropical wedge-tailed shearwaters, sooty terns and black noddies, *Anous minutus*, all have a temperature threshold for feeding, below which their chicks' growth simply stops and weight loss begins. This zero-growth window appears to occur within a 2–4°C increase in background sea-surface temperature. The duration of warm periods also counts. Chicks of many species of open-ocean wanderers like albatrosses, shearwater and petrels (procellariiform seabirds) can physiologically cope for days without food. Yet even wedge-tailed shearwater chicks, though particularly well-adapted to deprivation, are likely to perish after eight to 10 days with no provisioning. Sea-surface temperature increases of 4°C or more, for two weeks or longer, are therefore expected to wreak repeated catastrophic breeding failures.

Some of the mechanisms already described are also speculated to operate at these fine scales. If prey prefer specific temperatures, they may shift out of seabirds' ranges as waters warm or cool on a daily or weekly basis. It is also possible that day-to-day temperature changes influence the numbers of sub-sea predators that seabirds greatly rely on. These fine-scale events show how daily changes, summed over a period of time, affect seabirds even in a 'good' breeding season. During El Niño events, however, these impacts may compound themselves over weeks of sustained temperature increase. Evidence that major breeding failures are possible even for wedge-tailed shearwaters is sobering, because these ocean-going foragers are considered resilient to short-term prey changes.

Dual foraging strategies

To overcome poor local food resources in waters near their colonies, some procellariiform seabirds use a remarkable dual feeding strategy. At Heron Island, breeding wedge-tailed shearwaters make a number of short, one- to four-day foraging trips, then a single long-distance foraging trip of eight to ten days. After short trips to resource-poor waters near their colony, they are likely to pass most food onto chicks, since adults are known to lose body fat and muscle in the process. On long trips they visit zones of consistent high productivity, such as seamounts or oceanographic fronts, to feast on abundant food and shore up their body reserves. Shearwaters breeding on Heron Island, for example, use a small number of sites up to 1000 kilometres away near Coral Sea seamounts.

Wedge-tailed shearwaters' use of this dual feeding strategy at tropical Heron Island colonies is actually a local adaptation. (Birds at Lord Howe Island, a more southerly colony in temperate waters, forage locally.) It suggests intensive local foraging cannot compensate for poor local prey resources at Heron Island. Instead, these birds rely on two separate and independent food sources to breed successfully.[47]

These flexible strategies will probably be stretched further with climate warming. 'As temperatures go up, adults are either going to lose more body condition, or they're going to have to spend more time away from the chick,' says Devney, 'It's unlikely to bode well for either adult survival or reproduction.' How future climate change will affect the ocean conditions around their at-distance sites is unknown, but their critical role in seabird breeding highlights the importance of their conservation. Yet over the past decade, increasing ENSO and sea-surface temperature variations appear to have affected at least one of these small but very rich at-distance food areas in the Coral Sea.

Open-ocean foragers not primed for change

Open-ocean foragers breeding in the Great Barrier Reef and Western Australia are thought to be especially susceptible to changing ocean conditions. These vulnerable pelagic feeders, which include tern and shearwater species, tend to form large breeding populations and breed synchronously. They also tend to breed at their natal colonies, and other suitable locations are few and far between. This means that when conditions are not right at a given colony, a large number of birds are apt not to breed. And since they generally have single-egg clutches, conditions in a given season determine whether they will produce either one chick or none.

Some of these open-ocean feeders also have a limited capacity to increase foraging. Their chicks may endure relatively long intervals between feedings, grow more slowly and take longer to fledge, traits that make them vulnerable to El Niño. Research on black noddies, for example, suggests they have limited plasticity in terms of adult provisioning behaviour and the development of chicks, constraints that could limit their ability to respond rapidly to future ocean warming.[51]

Taken together, these factors explain why pelagic terns and shearwaters tend to fare worse than inshore foraging terns when ocean conditions have changed. They also imply that small food supply changes can greatly influence pelagic seabirds' ability to produce chicks, prompting concern that future climate change could bring about catastrophic failures at their breeding colonies.[47]

Chipping away at the Great Barrier Reef

Coral reefs are the world's most diverse marine ecosystems, harbouring a third of known marine species. Yet most reefs worldwide are predicted to decline even at current atmospheric greenhouse gas levels, due to mass bleaching during warming episodes, along with other impacts. Further acidification of the oceans is expected to weaken coral skeletons and alter the composition of reef communities. By 2099, 70 per cent of the world's known cold-water corals – important feeding grounds and refuges for fish – could experience seawater that is corrosive.[12]

The Great Barrier Reef's current status as one of the world's healthiest reef systems will not shield it from climate change. In 2009, global warming was named its greatest long-term threat by the Great Barrier Reef Marine Park Authority. The combined threats of coral bleaching, ocean acidification and sea-level rise led the Authority to conclude that, 'the overall outlook for the Great Barrier Reef is poor and catastrophic damage to the ecosystem may not be averted'.

It could also be speculated that their deterioration could affect prey species reliant on coral reefs, with possible adverse effects up and down seabirds' food webs. Yet this question remains largely unexplored. How seabirds respond at any one coral reef will probably depend on their feeding strategies. Whereas inshore foragers such as crested terns feed on coral-reef fish, for example, pelagic foraging sooty terns may travel 250 kilometres or further to feed offshore.

On coral cays, nests face stormy future

Storms and tropical cyclones can damage seabird nesting sites by bringing wind, waves and currents that inundate and erode coral cays, for example. Storms can also be an important source of direct stress and mortality to seabirds. If they cannot fight powerful winds to return to breeding colonies, their young may starve or die of exposure during tropical cyclones. During storms, seabirds may also have trouble finding prey on the rough sea surface. Tropical cyclones can have catastrophic effects on seabird colonies, and many climate models project that the most intense events will become more frequent under climate change, even as the overall frequency of cyclones may decrease (chapter 5).

Sea-level rise, especially in combination with tropical cyclones and other storms, could also cause problems for seabirds. Their low-lying habitat on islands and coastal areas could be vulnerable as vast areas, including the mudflats of estuaries, are inundated. Especially vulnerable are tropical seabirds nesting on coral cays, low islands formed from deposits of broken coral and the remains of other ocean life. At Australia's Great Barrier Reef, seabird abundance goes hand in hand with the abundance of coral cays. Expected sea-level rise of 0.8 metres by 2100 threatens colonies because most cays lie less than three metres above the high water mark.[52] Seabirds prefer to breed on low-lying coral cays, but in future these could be flooded even at high tide. Seabird nests at the interior of coral cays could be at risk when sea-level rise combines with storm surges. During 2009, for example, Cyclone Hamish caused a four-metre high tide and storm surge on parts of Heron Island.

Pioneers and poleward shifts

As tropical waters warm, will seabirds shift polewards? In contrast to the picture of decline at many of Australia's northern tropical seabird colonies, some populations in the south-west are expanding. Marine life on the mid to southern part of the continent's west coast is far more tropical than its southerly latitude would suggest, thanks to the warm, southward-flowing Leeuwin Current. Nonetheless, tropical seabirds including common noddies and red-tailed tropicbirds, *Phaeton rubricauda*, are now recorded further south than a century ago.

The new southerly colonies show how little-studied aspects of seabird behaviour, such as dispersal and selection of breeding habitat, play a role in their ability to adapt to a more unpredictable world. When now-frequent El Niños cause food failures in their established breeding areas, seabirds are thought to disperse further south, attracted to islands where they find prey.

Among species that are very faithful to their current breeding areas, new colonies are likely to be pioneered by pre-breeding individuals. In species with low site fidelity, the pioneers may be adults. At Lancelin Island, for example, just off Australia's south-west coast, five pairs of common noddies pioneered a colony in 1991. Numbers built in a period of rapid colonisation, after which immigration slowed, while at the same time new noddies were reared on the island. By 2008, numbers stabilised at around 1200 pairs, sustained by new recruits from within the colony.[53]

Along with El Niños, rising ocean temperatures (a relatively high 1°C sea temperature increase off mid-western Australia) may be driving this demographic shift. During El Niño years, these new colonies tend to perform better than long-established ones. However, the ability of seabird colonies to expand southwards in future may run up against limits on available habitat and prey.

Unknowns and challenges

'Penguins are like icebergs,' nature writer Diane Ackerman has quipped, 'a scintillating mystery, most of which is hidden from view.' Seabirds may be easy to observe on land, but their ocean feeding grounds are Earth's most complex and difficult-to-study biomes. How climate change will affect ocean ecosystems is still poorly understood. Information is especially sparse for tropical oceans, even though they make up half the planet's open water.

Crucial questions, such as how intense and how frequent El Niño events will be under climate change, remain unanswered. Precisely why El Niño is so detrimental to many temperate and tropical seabirds is still under study. Teasing apart the effects of natural ocean climate cycles from those of global warming is another great challenge, with the impacts of human overfishing adding further layers of complexity. The scarcity of long-term biological records on seabirds' responses also hinders efforts to understand how they might cope with climate change. Moreover, the biology and ecology of many seabirds are still poorly known. This includes their feeding behaviour, since it is inherently difficult to untangle marine food webs. However, a recent boom in tracking seabirds, aided by new technology, is helping to fill the main knowledge gaps.

Seabirds species are expected to respond to climate change individualistically. Even different populations of a single species may respond uniquely where their foraging ecology is attuned to local ocean conditions. Yet this inherent capacity to modify their behaviours and adapt makes it more difficult to predict how they might shift their distributions in response to global warming.

Conclusion

From the poles to the tropics, some seabirds are proving highly sensitive indicators of climate change. They are vulnerable to its effects not only on land, but also in their marine environments, where life responds strongly to temperature and chemical changes. Ice-dependent seabirds are likely to be early responders to climate change, because ice is highly sensitive to warming. Even in Antarctica, long viewed as a huge planetary heat sink, 'the Adélie penguin is showing us that no habitat on Earth will escape'.[28]

Regarding seabirds' ocean food webs, global warming is associated with the declining primary productivity of most world oceans since 1999. Warming-driven reductions in the upwelling of cold, nutrient-rich waters is thought to be a common mechanism behind some changes in productivity. Plankton are vital for funnelling energy and productivity up the marine food web to seabirds, but some of these organisms have undergone the most rapid and extreme distributions shifts observed in the living world. Climate-driven shifts in the timing and abundance of prey species are critical for seabirds.

When breeding, seabirds are bound to their land-based colonies, and constrained in their ability to track prey should changing ocean climate conditions drive prey to shift in space, time or abundance. The breeding success of tufted puffins drops off precipitously when sea-surface temperatures rise above a critical threshold. For tropical seabirds at the Great Barrier Reef, a 2–4°C increase in background sea-surface temperature impairs parents' ability to forage to the extent that chicks stop growing. Sea-surface temperature increases of 4°C or more for two weeks or longer are expected to wreak repeated catastrophic breeding failures on these tropical seabirds. Understanding the causes of disastrous seabird breeding crashes will help scientists better attribute and predict climate-change effects.

Many seabirds can adapt their foraging behaviour and diets to cope with changes to their preferred prey, but there are limits beyond which their ability to reproduce and even survive is threatened. Some are relatively more vulnerable, like tropical seabirds that feed in the open ocean and cannot increase their foraging rates.

Some seabirds appear to be undergoing distribution shifts of their own, or at least abundance shifts headed in that direction. Yet their capacity to track climate change will depend on their ability to find suitable, predator-free habitat. Some ice-dependent seabirds are expected to face range contractions under climate change, and restricted range species like the endemic Galápagos penguin may face extinction.

Chapter 5

CLIMATE CHANGE, ABUNDANCE AND EXTINCTION

Human fingerprints on Earth's coldest crèche

Take it all in all, I do not believe anybody on Earth has a worse time than an Emperor Penguin.

Apsley Cherry-Garrard, 1922

The ice-dependent emperor penguin is an Antarctic icon that has come to symbolise the threat of a warming world. Yet on the first winter visit to any emperor colony, a too-warm Antarctica is a scenario English explorer Apsley Cherry-Garrard probably never considered. A frail man with terrible eyesight, 24-year-old Cherry-Garrard was an unlikely choice for Robert Scott's 1910 Terra Nova Expedition to Antarctica. As Cherry-Garrard himself acknowledged, 'doctors had nearly refused to let me go because I could only see the people across the road as vague blobs walking.' Yet chosen he was, and in the months before Scott's fateful trek to the South Pole, Cherry-Garrard was given the task with retrieving eggs from a colony of incubating emperor penguins, *Aptenodytes forsteri*, in the coldest breeding environment of any bird. The young Oxford graduate described the mid-winter trip in his book, *The Worst Journey in the World*.

The trek from the Cape Evans expedition base camp on Ross Island to the emperor colony was only about 108 kilometres, but it took Cherry-Garrard and his two companions almost three weeks to reach it, manhauling two sleds laden with almost 345 kilograms of supplies in temperatures down to about minus 60°C. When the weather rendered his spectacles useless, Cherry-Garrard was compelled to travel half-blind, causing him to stumble and fall. Arriving near the emperor colony at Cape Crozier, Cherry-Garrard found an alien world, 'a breeding-place of wind and drift and darkness. God! What a place!' The men finally laid eyes on the birds after a dangerous climb across ice ridges and crevasses. As they disturbed the milling penguins, the birds lost purchase of their eggs and called out, 'trumpeting with their curious metallic voices'.

Although Cherry-Garrard's poor vision caused him to fall about and crush two emperor eggs stowed in his mittens, the men still managed to return with three eggs – but at great personal cost. Blizzards of 'indescribable fury and roar' blew away their tent (later retrieved) and shredded the canvas roof of their stone 'igloo'. Horrifically exposed, they huddled in sleeping bags, singing hymns above the storm's blast to sustain their spirits. The return journey was also wretchedly slow, and Cherry-Garrard shattered his teeth, so hard did they chatter. Their five-week ordeal ended when they stumbled back into their Cape Evans base as the expeditionary force was getting ready for bed. In a fog of exhaustion Cherry-Garrard watched pyjama-clad men cut away his ice-stiffened clothing, weighted down by kilos of frozen moisture. 'We slept ten thousand years . . . '

The Winter Journey, as it became known, confirmed that emperor penguins choose the coldest, darkest winter months to breed. But the hard-won eggs failed to provide the hoped-for evolutionary insights. Emperors turned out not to be the world's most primitive birds, nor could they reveal a missing link between birds and reptiles to allow scientists to elaborate on the now-defunct theory that ontogeny recapitulates phylogeny (the embryo, as it grows, passes through each adult stage of its evolutionary history, or phylogeny). Ironically, the remains of an adult emperor (they had burned its blubber for warmth) left by the trio at their stone igloo proved an unexpected boon to 1960s environmental science. The blubber from this bird that died decades before DDT was ever used provided an uncontaminated sample to compare with that of more modern birds, revealing that this persistent organic pollutant had subsequently infiltrated even Antarctica's food chain.

Polar exploration, Cherry-Garrard declared, was 'at once the cleanest and most isolated way of having a bad time which has been devised'. Ironically, the frozen wastes that left him cold may prove to be one of the emperors' final sanctuaries, as the most polar of colonies in a warming world. Climate change has penetrated even parts of Antarctica, planet Earth's 'refrigerator', and over the next century could threaten many emperor penguin colonies.

This chapter explores global warming as a driver of changes to bird abundance and community composition, and as an extinction threat. Natural climate variations are already known to bring about massive fluxes in plant germination, rodent outbreaks and predator responses in some parts of the world. So there is good reason to expect that climate change will also drive significant population changes.

Like shifts in phenology and distribution (chapters 1 and 3), changes in bird abundance and community composition are important fingerprints of climate change, although they can be more challenging to monitor and detect against the backdrop of other human threats. Crucial questions – which species may thrive and which may decline to extinction in the face of climate change – have only begun to be addressed. Nonetheless, a picture is fast-emerging of the novel risks to many among the world's almost 10 000 bird species. These climate-change risks are being superimposed on the other human impacts that already threaten roughly one in eight bird species with global extinction. Climate change, warns Mike Rands of BirdLife International, may prove the most serious long-term stress of all. One assessment revealed that climate change and associated severe weather already threaten at least 24 critically endangered bird species, a figure expected to rise rapidly in future.

Fewer surfers of an endless summer

As is true for so many examples of population declines linked to climate warming, the case of sooty shearwaters, *Puffinus griseus*, raises as many questions as it answers. Some sooty shearwater populations traverse the entire Pacific in spectacular figure-of-eight annual journeys of about 64 000 kilometres. These medium-sized, long-lived seabirds pursue an endless summer, flying from breeding grounds located mainly in New Zealand to the North Pacific where they feed on fish, squid and krill. Thanks to miniature geo-locating tags (chapter 2) that record light levels, pressure and temperature, the shearwaters' extraordinary pan-Pacific journeys have been confirmed, and their vertical movements as they forage ocean depths revealed.[1] The vast majority of foraging dives (95 per cent) are in the food-rich waters of both hemispheres, with far fewer taking place in the warm tropical Pacific where productivity is low. Their wide-ranging lifestyles may be a strategy evolved to buffer against year-to-year disruptions of their food supplies, like those driven by ENSO events.

Despite this buffering strategy and its status as one of the world's most abundant birds (20 million adults), the sooty shearwater was listed as 'near threatened' by the IUCN in 2004. A population that spends North American summers in the California Current declined by about 90 per cent from 1987 to 1994 as sea surface temperatures rose.[2] This decline may have levelled off in recent years (it is possible the birds shifted their distribution as well as declined). Trends at a range of New Zealand breeding colonies also indicate a falling population, pointing to a rapid decline in both hemispheres.

Long-line fishing and direct harvesting of young birds take a toll on sooty shearwaters, but ocean warming is suspected of reducing their marine food supplies. Yet precisely how food supply or other possible climate effects might translate into population declines is uncertain. Are more adult birds dying, or are fewer chicks and juveniles being recruited? Do adults simply abstain from breeding? Unanswered but increasingly pressing questions like these are all too common when the effects of climate change on population are raised.

Today evidence for global warming as an important driver of abundance changes is mounting. In Europe, this was gauged by combining climate-envelope modelling with observed population trends for common and widespread European birds. This revealed a strong link between expected range changes associated with climate change and observed population changes of individual bird species. The results indicate a detectable influence of climate change on bird populations after the mid-1980s, during a period of rapid warming.[3] Birds predicted to fare well under climate change increased in number after the mid-1980s, while those expected to do badly declined. Worryingly, however, the declining group encompassed 75 per cent of the 122 species assessed.

Climate change and adult survival

Survival: direct climate-change effects

Population levels are a function of birth and death rates. Therefore climate-change effects on birds' overall abundance will aggregate on their breeding periods, which determine productivity, and non-breeding periods, when adult survival is critical. Climate and weather strongly influence both these stages in myriad direct and indirect ways. Each bird's response will reflect its unique ecology, habitat and life history. In migratory birds especially, dependence on multiple habitats means global warming is likely to affect their populations via diverse mechanisms (chapter 2).

We begin by asking, 'How will climate change affect birds' survival outside the breeding period?' Where cold winters grow less severe, survival may improve. A bird's inability to meet the energy demands of staying warm can have fatal consequences, and snow, frost or ice cover can also restrict foraging and threaten its survival. Grey herons, *Ardea cinerea*, for example, cannot hunt when ice covers wetlands. This may explain why milder European winters have coincided with the higher survival rate of some European birds. These beneficial warming effects may melt away where winter precipitation increases. Among Eurasian treecreepers, *Certhia familiaris*, mortality rates rise with increasing winter rainfall, possibly due to hypothermia as a result of their breast feathers becoming wet from brushing against tree trunks, as these birds scale trees from top to bottom in their quest for insects and spiders.

In hot climates or during warm seasons, more extremely hot days and more heat waves could harm birds' survival chances. In hot deserts, heat waves can dramatically affect survival (and reproduction), because even a small rise in temperature can greatly increase the amount of water lost from birds' bodies through evaporation. Small desert birds, modelling suggests, will need 150–200 per cent more water during the day's hottest period to survive the predicted increases in maximum daily temperature. Hotter weather due to climate change is expected to make it harder for birds to sustain their water balance, and will lead to more frequent cases of catastrophic mortality by the 2080s.[4]

In Europe, some birds less tolerant of heat may already be showing detrimental effects. Among 110 common species with the lowest thermal maxima (those typically experiencing the lowest mean spring and summer temperature at the hottest part of their breeding ranges) showed the sharpest population declines during 1980–2005.[5] Conservation authorities have already deemed extreme temperatures and droughts to be a climate-change threat to some critically endangered birds.

Survival: indirect climate-change effects

Climate change can also affect birds' survival indirectly, mainly via its effects on their food supplies. Such indirect effects may be even more pervasive and powerful than direct ones. In northernmost Alaska warming may be the factor that initially allowed black guillemots, *Cepphus grylle*, to breed in the Point Barrow area sometime during the 1960s. Yet between 1989 and 1997, numbers at one colony monitored in this area halved. These seabirds hunt arctic cod along the pack-ice edge, but sea ice has been decreasing throughout the Arctic. Other prey in ice-free waters near shore is lacking. Immigration to one colony has decreased and fewer adults are surviving. Boding ill for this population's future, anticipated warming could cause pack ice to retreat more than 100 kilometres from mainland Alaska in this region, well beyond the typical 15 kilometres foraging range of black guillemots at their colonies.

Climate change could also affect birds' survival by influencing predators (chapter 2), competitors, pests and disease-carrying organisms. Climate may affect where pathogens are found, and when and how quickly they reproduce (chapters 3 and 6). Birds need time to build up resistance to new pathogens and, until they do, their survival could be jeopardised. Birds' behaviour may also play a role; if flocks increasingly concentrate at limited water and food sources during droughts, disease could spread more easily. Climate change, by bringing more frequent summer heatwaves, will probably lead to more harmful cyanobacteria blooms in freshwater lakes. These are implicated in the mass kills of birds and fish.

Productivity: climate-change effects during breeding

Ready or run down? Climate and the pre-breeding period

Global warming may act broadly across all phases of the breeding cycle, from pre-breeding effects on adult body condition through to the survival of young.

The timing of birds' arrival on the breeding grounds, and the condition they arrive in, are two factors that can greatly influence their reproductive success and population dynamics. Climate-change impacts on birds' pre-breeding migrations are expected to have a greater effect on their population size than on post-breeding migrations, since pre-breeding migration fatal-ities directly reduce the number of potential breeders. Generally speaking, many of the effects that influence adult survival described above may also detract from their breeding efforts if they draw down birds' body reserves. Seabirds dramatically illustrate the importance of body reserves when they strategically defer or abandon breeding efforts if environmental conditions weigh against their survival.

Climate-change effects may also improve birds' body condition in some cases. Where milder winters reduce energy demands, birds may be able to invest more energy in breeding. The body condition of eiders breeding in southwest Finland, for example, is better after warmer winters. However, warming that is uneven across regions or seasons may cause problems for other waterfowl. Asymmetric climate change could lead some Arctic-breeding geese to arrive at breeding grounds to find spring less advanced than conditions along their flyways might indicate (chapter 2). High-Arctic breeders might also face a problem with increased precipitation linked to climate warming. If breeding waders arrive to find extended spring snow cover, they may perish, or delay laying eggs in an environment where the chances for breeding success has abrupt cut-offs.

Climate effects at the nest: brood number, clutch size and eggs

Thermoregulation and egg production are both activities that exact a consid-erable toll on birds' energy reserves. The need to balance these two demands explains why, under colder conditions, birds tend to produce smaller eggs. In Finnish Lapland, for example, warmer springs have apparently allowed female pied flycatchers to produce larger eggs. Bigger eggs are more likely to hatch and produce chicks with better survival prospects.

Some birds, so-called 'facultative multi-brooders', produce more than one clutch per breeding season if conditions are right. And in Europe, multiple brooders are advancing their spring migrations more strongly. In Poland, marsh-breeding reed warblers, *Acrocephalus scirpaceus*, start their first clutches two weeks earlier than they did in 1970. And whereas at most 15 per cent of warbler pairs produced a second clutch during the 1970s and 1980s, up to 35 per cent were doing so during 1994–2006. Their lengthened breeding season, along with beneficial habitat changes during warmer years (like earlier growth of marsh reeds that conceal nests), could allow these warblers to produce more nestlings.[6]

Highlighting the complex responses birds are likely to show to climate change, an opposite outcome is seen in a facultative multi-brooder in the Netherlands. The proportion of great tits producing second broods declined strongly over the past three decades in four study populations around this country. Where second clutches were laid, numbers of young recruited also decreased during 1973–2004. At the Hoge Veluwe, their egg laying has failed to track earlier food supplies (chapter 1). In these great tits, the chances of producing second clutches were lower when this mismatch (between food demand and food supply) for first clutches was greater.[7] These results suggest that climate change will lead to a drop in the number of double broods for some birds.

When climate change bites at Achilles's heel

How might climate change affect very young birds? Seen as the 'Achilles heel' of population stability, this vulnerable stage is well illustrated even among the most aggressive of birds, like great skuas, *Catharacta skua*, dusky-coloured seabirds with curved beak tips. They breed at high latitudes in the Northern Hemisphere and can have trouble dissipating heat in warm weather. Adults bathe in fresh water near their nesting areas, apparently to cool down, but this absents them from their nests. When air temperatures surpass 14°C and food supplies are low, parents are particularly likely to be absent. This leaves unprotected chicks vulnerable to fatal attacks from neighbouring great skuas. Fewer chicks have survived in such years.[8]

Adult common guillemots, *Uria aalge*, normally never leave their chicks unattended. Yet in 2007, declines in food availability are thought to have compelled many adult pairs to forage simultaneously from their North Sea colonies. With half of the nests left unattended, unprecedented numbers of chicks were killed by neighbouring common guillemots.[9] Although colonial breeding is normally considered advantageous for seabirds, these examples suggest how climate change could create environmental conditions that lead costs to outweigh benefits.

As for temperature effects on young birds, climate warming could improve their survival in some cases. In the Arctic, cold weather saps the energy of shorebird chicks, at the expense of their tissue formation. To stay warm, they spend more time being brooded by parents, leaving them with less time to forage for insects. This explains why Arctic shorebirds' repro-ductive success improves in warmer springs with earlier snow melt. Warmer

(**Top**) Prime breeding habitat … ivory gulls mainly breed in colonies found on *nunataks*, granite cliffs towering above inland glaciers. Canada's ivory gull population has plummeted 50–80 per cent since the 1970s, and climate change is one of several important threats.
Image: Mark Mallory, Canadian Wildlife Service

(**Above**) Some ivory gulls also nest on gravelly stretches of remote, low islands, as seen here at Canada's Seymour island colony. Image: Mark Mallory, Canadian Wildlife Service

(Main picture) Tufted puffins and a single horned puffin (far left) at Buldir Island, Alaska. At Triangle Island, burrow-nesting tufted puffins suffered a number of total or near total reproductive failures in recent decades. Some fear ocean warming could make Canada's largest tufted puffin breeding colony unsuitable for these seabirds. Image: Ray Buchheit/USFWS

(**Inset top**) A tufted puffin at Buldir Island, Alaska. At Canada's Triangle Island, tufted puffins' chances of raising fledglings drop to virtually zero when ocean surface waters are warmer than 9.9°C. Image: Ray Buchheit/USFWS

(**Inset above**) Endemic Galápagos penguins can suffer breeding failures and even adult mortality when El Niño disrupts the cold, nutrient-rich upwelling that underpins their ocean food web at the Galápagos Islands. Image: Çağan Şekercioğlu

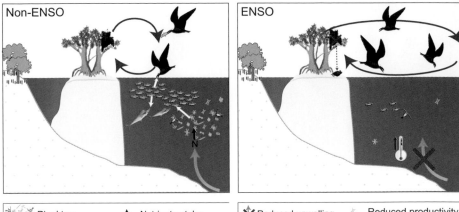

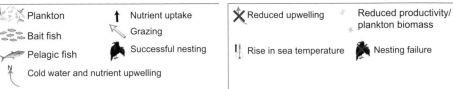

Figure 2 In the tropical waters of the Great Barrier Reef, El Niño Southern Oscillation (ENSO) events affect seabirds' ability to breed. The warm ocean conditions that accompany El Niños probably block nutrient-rich upwelling, reducing the productivity of the phytoplankton that underpins the seabirds' marine food web. © GBRMPA: Reproduced with the permission of the Great Barrier Reef Marine Park Authority.

(**Below**) UK-breeding whitethroat numbers crashed by about 70 per cent after a serious 1968 drought in the western Sahel, where this warbler winters. Image: Çağan Şekercioğlu

(Below) Australia's critically endangered mallee emu-wrens persist in small, fragmented pockets of habitat, from which they rarely disperse more than five kilometres. Even small bushfires pose a risk if they wipe out habitat patches that effectively host separate populations. Image: ©Tony Crittenden, TCPhotos.net

(Bottom) The red-capped manakin, *Pipra mentalis*, and orange-collared manakin, *Manacus aurantiacus* (overleaf), are among the roughly 45 manakin species found in American tropical forests. Many of these species could face local extinctions if they are unable to disperse to track climate change. Image: Çağan Şekercioğlu

(**Above**) The orange-collared manakin, *Manacus aurantiacus*. Image: Çağan Şekercioğlu

(**Top right**) King penguins at Possession Island, Crozet Archipelago. With their low reproductive rate and long generation time, some long-lived birds like king penguins are expected to be limited in their ability to evolve in response to climate change over the long term. Image: ©Yves Handrich – CNRS/DEPE.

(**Right**) True Antarctic penguins, emperor penguins rely on sea ice to forage, moult, and carry out their winter breeding strategy. Image: © Samuel Blanc: www.sblanc.com.

(**Above**) With 2°C of warming, colonies harbouring 40 per cent of emperor penguins could decline or disappear. Image: © Samuel Blanc: www.sblanc.com.

weather also boosts the activity of arthropod prey, and therefore the amount of food chicks can collect.

Conversely, excessive heat may be hard on the cold-adapted chicks of greater snow geese, *Chen caerulescens atlantica*, one of North America's most northerly breeding geese. Sunny, windless weather later in summer is thought to stress the goslings as they walk about foraging for long periods, and breeding success is lower under these conditions. Chicks in warmer climates, such as the Mediterranean, may also be vulnerable to heat stress. Where warming is not consistent across seasons, this too may create problems. Due to asymmetric climate change, the vulnerable phase of earlier-hatching black grouse chicks in Finland now often coincides with adverse and cold conditions (chapter 1).

Not just high heat but other extremes, including strong winds or heavy rain, can also stress or kill young birds, and have a disproportionate and negative effect throughout the birds' first year. In winter wrens, *Troglodytes troglodytes*, adverse weather reduces first-year survival rates by a quarter. Extreme weather is a topic we shall return to shortly.

Teasing apart mismatch mechanisms

Mismatch is believed to be another consequence of climate change that can affect birds' ability to successfully raise chicks. In the Netherlands, lighter chicks less likely to fledge are one apparent consequence of mismatch among great tits (chapter 1). Mismatch has also been linked to population declines of up to 90 per cent in some long-distance migratory pied flycatchers, also in the Netherlands. Here we attempt to unpack some of the mechanisms behind these mismatch effects.

Pied flycatchers in Central Spain provide a glimpse of these mechanisms. These birds have not bred earlier despite experiencing warming spring temperatures, and it is possible they are mismatched with earlier-emerging caterpillar prey. Even though birds provisioned their young at a higher rate, nestling survival decreased by 15 per cent from 1982 to 2001. This may be because available prey, like beetles and grasshoppers, had less nutritional value. Despite higher provisioning rates for the overall study period, on warmer days the parent birds seemed to expend less effort. Overall this population, at the southern extreme of pied flycatchers' geographical range, seems unable to cope with the energy demands of feeding young in a warmer climate with poorer quality food.[10]

Mismatch may exact a high energetic toll on parents, as shown by blue tits, *Parus caeruleus*, in France. A Corsican blue tit population, synchronised with its caterpillar food supply, was compared to a mismatched population from continental France (climate change did not cause the mismatch in this instance). The mismatched blue tits work as much as twice as hard to feed their young, running at five to seven times their basal metabolic rate – compared with about 3.5 times for synchronised blue tits. The mismatched parents in fact operated at among the highest metabolic levels recorded in breeding birds. The demands of chick rearing apparently pushed mismatched adults beyond their sustainable limits; they were less likely to return to breed the following year, possibly because the extra effort burned up their fat reserves and made them more vulnerable to winter starvation.[11]

In the common cuckoo, *Cuculus canorus*, climate-change-induced mismatch is foiling a time-tested strategy of trickery. Evocative of early summer in Europe, the morning song of the common cuckoo is fading. A 59 per cent decline since the 1960s in the UK (along with an apparent global decline) led the Royal Society for the Protection of Birds to red list[12] this cuckoo in 2009. As brood parasites, common cuckoos famously pawn off the task of raising young to other birds. They lay eggs only in the nests of other species, a strategy that permits a single female common cuckoo to visit up to 50 nests in a breeding season.

Though the common cuckoo is a long-distance migrant to Europe, it counts both short- and long-distance migrants among its hosts. Long-distance migrant host species have not advanced their arrival in Europe more than this cuckoo, but some resident and short-distance migrant hosts have. Mismatch is possible if host parents nearly finish incubating their own eggs before the cuckoo arrives, leaving it insufficient time to get away with its trick. This may explain why, after 1990, common cuckoos across 23 countries in Europe counted relatively fewer resident and short-distance migrants amongst their hosts, especially where spring temperatures showed greater increases.[13] Different 'host races' or 'gentes' of common cuckoo depend on different species of host, and even breed at different times. Among common cuckoos, changes in abundance of gentes reflected a trend towards more frequent use of long-distance migratory birds as their hosts. Increasing mismatch with their hosts due to climate change may cause some gentes of common cuckoo to decline, perhaps even to extinction. This cuckoo's current decline may also reflect the declining fortunes of its host species and adverse conditions in its African wintering grounds.

Population dynamics: tubs, taps and density dependence

Will climate change empty tubs or turn off taps?

Breeding Eurasian golden plovers, *Pluvialis apricaria*, provide an intriguing test case for the question, 'will climate change more strongly influence breeding success or adult survival?' When these plovers dart forwards to seize prey, more often than not their invertebrate victims are craneflies, of the family Tipulidae, also known as daddy-long-legs. In spring, huge pulses of craneflies and other invertebrates are critical to the breeding success of golden plovers and other upland, subarctic and Arctic birds. In the UK, the plovers' first clutches hatch when adult craneflies emerge, both these events being strongly related to temperature.

Craneflies are cold-adapted insects, and hot, dry spells can kill their larvae and eggs. When August temperatures are high, the numbers of adult craneflies emerging the next spring can plummet as much as 95 per cent. Many chicks starve or die without this vital food, explaining why these climate conditions are associated with a lower golden plover population two years later. Unabated warming at Snake Summit in the UK's South Pennines, modelling suggests, could reduce prey abundance enough to cause a local golden plover population to become extinct by 2100.[14]

Formerly, severe winter weather was the dominant constraint on this golden plover population. But as winters warmed and plovers' overwinter survival improved, the negative effects of hotter summers became the more significant population driver. This population now appears limited more by weather effects on its breeding success than its winter survival.

As to whether climate-change effects on breeding success or adult survival will generally prevail, we turn to the 'tub' and 'tap' hypotheses for illumination. According to the tub hypothesis (originating from the 1954 writings of evolutionary biologist David Lack), population changes would be bound to weather effects on birds' survival during their non-breeding period. Individuals may face adverse weather, as well as density-dependent factors (we will come to these shortly) such as food shortages during this phase. In Britain, for example, changes in resident farmland bird populations correlate well with winter weather. By contrast, the 'tap' hypothesis emphasises the inflow of new individuals into a population. Climate variation, it predicts, will have its greatest effect on populations during the breeding season, by affecting numbers of new recruits.

Bernt-Erik Sæther of the Norwegian University of Science and Technology and his colleagues examined both possibilities.[15] Of course, each bird species' ecology and life history will determine which effect reigns. However, climate effects on the breeding season (the tap hypothesis) may prevail for birds (especially passerines) breeding in arid environments where limits on food and other resources are severe. Tap effects may also be dominant for temperate birds with precocious young (so-called nidifugous species). Among northern temperate birds with highly dependent offspring (so-called altricial species), on the other hand, climate is likely to have a strong effect in the non-breeding season (tub), when density-dependent losses will be most important.[15]

Density thickens the plot

Population responses to climate change may not be straightforward or intuitive, especially when effects of population density come into play. The density of bird populations may be limited by food supplies, predation, disease and space, because the environment does not have an endless capacity to support an ever-increasing abundance of life. The influence of climate change on a population may therefore hinge on its density, as climate variables interact with these limiting factors. When a population is at relatively low density, for example, it may decline very little if reduced rainfall restricts food abundance, since individuals may still find sufficient food. On the other hand, for a population close to the limits of its environment's carrying capacity for food, the same rainfall change might undermine the efforts of many individuals to survive or reproduce. Density dependence will complicate efforts to understand how climate change affects birds' abundance.

Extreme weather and bird populations

The disproportionate toll of extremes

Severe weather events that exceed birds' tolerances, on the other hand, are classic examples of density-independent factors. Extreme events like severe storms, cold snaps and droughts powerfully influence local population dynamics, and may affect adult survival and productivity regardless of how dense or sparse their populations may be, as the fortunes of California arid-land birds show to devastating effect. The Coastal Sage and Chaparral ecoregion is a landscape of terraces and foothills hosting a diverse but rare scrub community. It has a Mediterranean climate of winter rain and summer drought, and in normal years breeding is possible for the great majority of birds, including wrentits, *Chamaea fasciata*, spotted towhees, *Pipilo maculatus*, California towhees, *P. crissalis*, and rufous-crowned sparrows, *Aimophila ruficeps*. One such year was 2001, when almost nine of every 10 breeding pairs among these species nested and successfully raised at least two fledglings per pair, on average.

During the next year, 2002, productivity withered under the driest year in the area's 150-year climate record. Only one in 15 (6.7 per cent) pairs among these four species attempted to breed.[16] Near-total reproductive failure ensued, with severe food supply reductions the likely cause. Craneflies, an important early-season food, were almost completely absent, and the grasshoppers and caterpillars needed to feed chicks also declined dramatically. The drought's negative effects on plant productivity probably caused these insect shortages. The decision by most pairs of birds not to breed could reflect a strategy to optimise adult survival in bad years, and focus reproductive efforts instead on wetter years.

Extreme events like droughts already have an extensive effect on local bird population dynamics. Yet with climate change these events will become still more extreme, more frequent, or both. In 2008, BirdLife International found extreme events to be the top climate-change threat to critically endangered birds. Some extremes have probably already increased with climate change, including the risk of heatwaves and drought. Events like these, some argue, may explain the unexpectedly swift response of ecosystems worldwide to climate change so far. In future, even if climate change is moderate, extreme events can be expected to have devastating effects on ecosystems and species.[17]

Exacerbated drought could play a critical role in arid and semi-arid ecosystems. With their low and unpredictable rainfall, these ecosystems have inherently variable climates. The above California arid-land birds' decision to breed or not hinges on rainfall changes that are actually quite minor. Even a modest increase in the frequency of arid conditions, such as a string of dry years, would make their populations vulnerable to dying out.[16]

Droughts' effects can be enduring, as the fate of a common and widespread warbler called the whitethroat, *Sylvia communis*, suggests. A drought in its overwintering areas in the western Sahel is thought to be behind a 70 per cent crash in the numbers of whitethroat returning to breed in the UK between 1968 and 1969. Numbers have since fluctuated at this new lower level, with only slight recovery since the mid-1980s. With these effects in mind, one must view with concern the IPCC's finding that areas affected by drought globally are expected to increase under climate change, including at mid-latitudes. This increase is expected to affect birds' survival, driving large shifts in their abundance and the make-up of their communities.[18]

Tropical cyclones are another class of extreme event with powerful effects on birds. Future changes in the frequency of tropical cyclones under climate change remain a topic of considerable debate. Yet while some models indicate that the global average frequency of tropical cyclones will decrease, global warming is likely to cause their intensity to increase, bringing about a shift towards stronger events; the most intense cyclones, many models suggest, would become more frequent.[19] The projected changes vary considerably from one ocean basin to the next.

If severe cyclones do become more frequent, this could increase the vulnerability of some migrating birds. Among Nearctic–Neotropical songbirds migrating over water through the hurricane belt, 25 species declined over the period from 1966 to 1996. Breeding populations of red-breasted grosbeaks, *Pheucticus ludovicianus*, and mourning warblers, *Oporornis philadelphia*, for example, were lowest when previous autumns were stormiest.[20] These birds migrate across open water in the Gulf of Mexico or West Atlantic, where hurricanes have become more intense. Yet among those songbirds that breed in western North America and migrate southwards only over land, only three species declined over this period. These birds can rest on land when the weather turns stormy.

Where extreme events occur with greater frequency or intensity, extinction risk is likely to increase. Yet gauging this risk is very difficult because extreme events are rarely accounted for in climate projections, due to the difficulty of estimating their frequency. This implies that current estimates may understate the climate-change threat to biodiversity.[17]

Not trivial: extremes hurt avian risk takers

The population dynamics of European shags, *Phalacrocorax aristotelis*, emphasise the importance of considering extreme events as drivers of bird abundance. Seabirds are typically very conservative and 'prudent' breeders, making European shags and other cormorants with 'risky' lifestyles somewhat unusual. As deep divers, these shags prefer to hunt in clear waters and have adaptations thought to aid their sub-sea pursuit of fish, including very low body-fat stores and partially wettable plumage. This probably reduces their buoyancy and increases underwater efficiency, but also means they habitually roost on rocky shores to dry out after foraging.

Yet these same adaptations and habits make European shags vulnerable to winter gales, and they endure large swings in adult survival. When conditions turn cold and windy, their plumage remains drenched from waves and spray. Chances to forage and shore up their energy reserves deteriorate in turbid water and strong onshore winds. In the North Sea, this vulnerability to gales plays out in winter 'wrecks', mass mortality events that become apparent to people when dead seabirds wash up on beaches, peaking in late winter for shags.

Cormorant populations are apparently able to compensate for such mortality events by producing up to four chicks per brood, and occasionally two broods in a single breeding season. Their populations can grow rapidly, by up to 20 per cent in a good year. This has permitted European shags to ride out past variability in survival in areas of abundant food. In the UK, however, numbers of breeding European shag populations have declined by a third since the late 1960s.

Research on an Isle of May population of European shags casts doubt on their capacity to ride out more extreme weather in the future. In 1994, this population off Scotland's east coast suffered a bout of severe weather and mortalities spiked. Modelling suggests that one more winter with survival as low as that during 1994, per 40-year period (corresponding to a 50 per cent increase in survival variability), would probably cause this population to go extinct.[21] However, uncertainty about the future frequency of North Sea winter gales precludes making a precise estimate of the Isle of May birds' extinction risk.

Storms, along with heatwaves and droughts, can cause changes in numbers of births and deaths to fluctuate across an entire population at once. This so-called environmental stochasticity can affect the growth rate and extinction risk of populations large and small. Importantly, as the case of the European shag suggests, the greater environmental variations and extremes expected with climate change are likely to increase these fluctuations in adult survival and productivity. Critically, greater variability in death rates, even if their average rates do not change, can still reduce population growth rates. One poor year for adult survival followed by one good year is in effect worse than two medium years – even if the mean is the same. For bird species with highly variable survival rates, the impact is far from trivial.[22] This greater variability is another way climate change could reduce population viability and bird abundance, posing an extensive conservation challenge.

Nature, she does jump

There was a natural history belief held from Aristotle's time, and summed up by the 17th century German thinker Gottfried Leibniz as *Natura non facit saltum*, that 'nature makes no leap'. But it is now amply clear that nature, and notably climate, does indeed take leaps. Earth's climate has changed abruptly in the past, and in the future climate change may also drive sudden and radical shifts. Global warming may bring about both large and abrupt changes in climate, and lead to radical changes in ecosystems and other non-climate systems.

Hurricanes, floods, droughts, wildfires and other large-scale extreme events can trigger rapid and fundamental changes in the way entire ecosystems function, and alter the numbers and types of species within them. Ocean regime shifts are marked by radical changes in the abundance or productivity of important marine species (chapter 4). Even small or gradual changes, once thresholds are crossed, can unleash abrupt and drastic responses in the climate or ecosystems (chapter 7). The possible rapid, non-linear responses of the climate system are often referred to as 'surprises' in the scientific literature because their occurrence, size and timing are difficult to predict.

Community effects: complexity, cycles and competition

Within ecosystems, the diverse responses of plants and animals to climate change may result in complex and even unexpected effects on bird abundance. From the rugged escarpments that crease the Mogollon Rim of Central Arizona come rare insights into the cascading effects climate change can trigger in ecological communities. More than 20 years of careful observation in this high-altitude riparian habitat allowed Thomas Martin of the United States Geological Survey to link decreasing snow levels to some local bird declines.

Winters with low snow levels have become increasingly frequent in this region, permitting elk and deer to remain at higher elevations, where they continually browse plants. Over time, they greatly reduced a once-thick understorey of deciduous woody vegetation. The birds dependent on this habitat also declined. Predators consumed the eggs and young in nests more frequently as the vegetation in this habitat declined, and this was the greatest cause of the birds' reproductive failure.

MacGillivray's warbler, *Oporornis tolmiei*, for example, depends on canyon maple for nesting. It declined in tight synchrony with this plant, becoming locally extinct.[23] These yellow and olive-coloured birds still pass through the study area, but no longer settle to breed. Three other bird species also declined, two of them severely, while two others showed no clear change, and one species became more abundant. These community shifts shows how climate change may trigger a cascade of changes that alter the structure of ecosystems and how they function.

Population cycle meltdown

... when the Bible was translated into Norwegian, mention of plagues of locusts was replaced with plagues of lemmings.

Tim Coulson and Aurelio Malo, 2008

Declining snowy owls, *Bubo scandiaca*, are prominent actors in a wider ecological story of collapsing population cycles. With large, yellow eyes, thick, white plumage and feathery, sharply taloned feet, this distinctive owl is a predator fine-tuned for life in the Arctic. Snowy owls specialise in preying on lemmings, hamster-like rodents whose numbers once regularly peaked with such teeming abundance that, in Norway, snowploughs were used to clear their squashed bodies from roads. Boom–bust population cycles like those of lemmings have provided valuable insights into how populations are regulated and how different levels of the food web interact. Though a textbook example, the lemming boom–bust cycle may soon be relegated to history in some regions. At northern latitudes, these cycles are ultimately related to climate, and climate warming is implicated in the flattening or collapse of some.[24]

Long, cold winters are critical to lemming population cycles. These rodents can live under the snow pack because ground warmth melts a narrow layer of light and fluffy snow. This creates space for them to move about under the snow, feeding on ground vegetation, insulated from cold and concealed from predators. In Norway, however, a changing climate is creating the wrong sort of snow conditions for lemmings. A shorter snow period now limits how much time lemmings spend in sub-snow labyrinths. Warmer temperatures also promote alternating freeze–melt cycles, creating an icy ground layer that impedes lemmings' access to moss. Less insulated from cold, less able to access food and more vulnerable to predators, lemmings no longer occur in large-scale population peaks in some areas.[25] Their collapse also affects populations of predators adapted to capitalising on years of peak lemming abundance.

In Greenland, modelling suggests climate change could flatten lemming cycles enough to reduce the breeding success of lemming predators, and lead to the local extinction of some. The collapse of lemming population cycles in eastern Greenland suggests these events may already be in train.[26] In Fennocscandia, their collapse has already been accompanied by the decline of some specialist lemming predators, such as snowy owls and Arctic foxes, *Alopex lagopus*.[27]

The fortunes of geese, waders, grouse and ptarmigan are indirectly bound to lemmings. Generalist lemming predators, including skuas and Arctic foxes, are thought to turn their attention to the nests of breeding birds in years after lemmings peak, thereby reducing the breeding success of these birds and driving their demographic cycles as well. Especially vulnerable are ground-nesting shorebirds and geese. Intriguingly, snowy owls may further reinforce this cycle. They do not hunt near their nests but fiercely defend these breeding territories against Arctic foxes. This makes snowy owl territories safer places for nearby geese, sandpipers and other ground-breeders whose nests are indirectly defended by the owls. Yet when lemmings are scarce, snowy owls tend to be absent from the tundra.

These various trends mean that climate change, by influencing lemming abundance and owls' presence or absence, is likely to severely change Arctic wader populations. This illustrates how changes in birds' abundance and diversity have important consequences of their own, since birds can influence ecosystems in important ways, from both the top down and the bottom up.[28,29]

Climate tips the balance of bird wars

Yet another way climate change may drive abundance changes is by tipping the balance of competition between bird species. In the warm lowland areas of central and eastern Europe, collared flycatchers, *Ficedula albicollis*, dominate pied flycatchers in competition for nest sites, evicting them from their territories. This delays or altogether prevents pied flycatchers from breeding, or relegates them to marginal habitat. The density of collared flycatcher populations, on the other hand, appears to be limited by relatively colder climate conditions, like those of alpine areas. These same cool conditions do not constrain pied flycatchers to the same extent, and in this way permit more balanced competition between the two species, allowing them to coexist. Temperatures in the Czech Republic, however, are warming and this may explain the rising density of collared flycatchers during the 1985–97 period. This trend may signal 'a march towards competitive exclusion of pied flycatchers during warm periods'.[30]

Competition between pied flycatchers and another foe, great tits, can turn deadly. These two species compete for tree holes and nest boxes, and rely on the same food sources. Because they are resident birds in many parts of Europe, great tits can breed earlier and occupy available nest holes before pied flycatchers, long-distance migrants, can interfere. Yet the physically weaker pied flycatchers may attempt nest-holes takeovers. Although they cannot dominate through force, they may interrupt their foes or quickly build their own nests atop great tit nests when they are absent. But this risky strategy may see pied flycatchers killed by great tits.

In Finland, the closer these two species breed in time, the more frequent these deadly interactions become. A shorter lag time means fewer great tits reach the incubation phase of breeding, a stage when their nests are continuously occupied and harder to usurp, before the arrival of pied flycatchers in their territories. Higher population densities of the birds also increase the likelihood of fatal takeover attempts. Since climate change can affect both the timing of breeding and population density of birds, it could tip the balance of competition between such species.[31]

The climate-change extinction threat

By the end of the century, climate change and its impacts may be the dominant direct driver of biodiversity loss and changes in ecosystem services globally.

Millennium Ecosystem Assessment, 2005

A fast-ice survival strategy wears thin

Turning to the question of the extinction risk posed by global warming, we return to the ice-dependent emperor penguin, a seabird whose relatively well-studied population dynamics can provide better insights than most. Today's scientists, unlike those of Cherry-Garrard's day, can keep tabs on emperor penguin breeding colonies without making gruelling mid-winter treks. An important breakthrough was possible because sea ice, where nearly all emperor colonies are found, is free from impurities that discolour ice on land. British Antarctic Survey scientists are exploiting this fact to use satellite images to spot colonies from space. Individual black and white penguins are almost impossible to discern on low resolution satellite images, but their accumulated droppings at colonies leave tell-tale brown stains in their otherwise pristine white world.

A tally of 38 such stains around most of the Antarctic coast provided both good news and bad.[32] Ten previously undiscovered colonies were revealed, and six known colonies were shown to have relocated. On the bad side, six previously known colonies seem to have disappeared (although colonies of fewer than 500 penguin pairs were not detectable in these satellite images). Now that most larger colony sites are known, high-resolution satellite images and other techniques can be used to get an accurate count of individual penguins, improving on rough estimates by other methods that put total emperor numbers at 270 000 to 350 000 mature birds.

Monitoring this least-common of Antarctic penguins is important, because climate change could put ice-dependent emperors on a march towards extinction. Warming events diminish the sea ice crucial to emperors' ability to forage, moult and carry out their winter breeding strategy. So critical is their requirement for fast ice – stable, landfast sea ice, locked in place by grounded icebergs, islands or capes – that breeding birds endure treks of up to 150 kilometres across ice to reach it. In a ritual now familiar to many, the female lays her single egg at these colonies by early June, and transfers it carefully to the male before returning to *polynyas* to feed. Huddling together to conserve energy in temperatures as low as minus 50°C and winds of 200 kilometres per hour, incubating males may have fasted for 115 days before females return with a regurgitated meal for newly hatched chicks. The emaciated males, which may have lost almost half their body weight, then take their turn to feed on krill, fish and squid, but only after walking and 'tobogganing' over extensive winter sea ice. Parents alternate feeding duty through winter and spring. In December or early January, with the arrival of the austral summer, melting sea ice opens up water close to the colony and chicks fledge, embarking on independence when food is most plentiful.

This breeding strategy of epic endurance may also make emperors highly susceptible to climate change. At Terre Adélie, an exceptionally long record of local emperors' response to changing climate conditions gathered by researchers at the French Antarctic base of Dumont d'Urville has yielded important insights. Between 1972 and 1981, emperor numbers at this colony halved in association with abnormally warm winter temperatures and reduced sea-ice extent.[33] Reduced sea-ice extent, in turn, has been linked to lower numbers of krill, a key species for the entire Antarctic food web (chapter 4). This could explain why higher sea surface temperatures and these particular sea-ice conditions in the colony's foraging area coincided with increased mortality of adult emperors. On the other hand, during years of extensive sea ice, emperors hatch fewer chicks, possibly because this lengthens treks between hunting grounds and emperor crèches.[34] If females take too long to return, starving males may abandon their eggs to save themselves.

Although reduced sea ice has both advantages and disadvantages in terms of emperor population growth, its negative influence on adult survival trumped its effect on fecundity. As with other long-lived birds, the growth rates of emperors are very sensitive to changes in adult survival.

After 1981, sea-ice extent and temperatures returned to former levels, but for some reason the emperor numbers did not. Although adult survival rates recovered to levels seen before the abrupt environmental change, breeding success became more variable and dropped to a point that makes population recovery unlikely.[35] Possible causes include severe blizzards or early blow-outs of sea ice, of the kind described by Dee Boersma at Terre Adélie in 2006:

> In September, when the chicks were a little more than half grown, the adults started marching with their chicks across the ice. After several days, the colony had moved more than 5 km from where the eggs had hatched. . . . In late September, a large storm hit, and the strong winds and waves broke up and blew out the remaining sea ice and the penguins. . . . Chicks in late September are downy, not waterproof, and are unable to survive in the sea for any period of time. The storm most likely caused the reproductive failure of the entire colony.

Over this century, increasingly frequent warming events are expected to give this Terre Adélie emperor colony a 36 per cent chance of collapsing to a level unlikely to ensure its persistence – a potential decline from 6000 breeding pairs today to a mere 400 pairs by 2100.[36]

The Terre Adélie colony is not the only 'northerly' emperor population with problems. On the Antarctic Peninsula, where this continent's warming is most pronounced, a colony declined from 150 breeding pairs in 1950 to just a few pairs at present. Moreover, all six of the former colonies that could not be found in satellite images are lower-latitude ones, lying north of 70° South. The pattern of decline hints at an inevitable contraction of suitable climate conditions towards the South Pole, and climate modelling suggests this will continue in future. With 2°C of warming above pre-industrial levels (reached sometime between 2025 and 2052) colonies north of 70°S could decline or disappear, yet these colonies currently harbour 40 per cent of the emperor penguin breeding population.[37]

The need for fast ice, adjacent to land, constrains emperors' long-term capacity to track climate change. These particular requirements mean the continent could act as the ultimate barrier to their poleward dispersal. The most polar and stable emperor populations are found where the Ross Sea cuts deep into the heart of Antarctica. This region now harbours about a quarter of all breeding emperors, and may prove their final sanctuary. Ultimately, however, even Ross Sea ice is expected to diminish as greenhouse gas emissions rise.[35]

To avoid the threat of extinction, ice-dependent emperors would need to somehow adapt by changing their breeding timing or by evolving. Yet unlike some other Antarctic birds at Terre Adélie, emperors have not shifted their timing of arrival or egg laying at their colonies. And with their long generation times, these penguins are considered unlikely to adapt to a rapidly changing climate via microevolution.

Extinctions, but where? Novel and disappearing climates

The well-studied emperor penguin belies the nascent state of efforts to quantify the climate-change extinction threat to life on Earth. Climatic changes have extinguished species across time, and no less can be expected with the rapid climate change now underway. Not all bird species will be losers with global warming, but significant numbers of extinctions are possible. This threat will apply to species now considered safe, in areas far from direct human influence.

Global warming is not uniform across the planet, and its threat to birds will depend on how, and by how much, important aspects of their climate changes. If global warming tracks at the upper end of the IPCC's 2007 scenarios, the current climates of up to almost half (10–48 per cent) of Earth's land surfaces could disappear by the end of the century. Furthermore, up to more than a third (12–39 per cent) of land surfaces could experience new, no-analogue climates under the same scenarios (chapter 3).

Where existing climates disappear, extinctions are possible, especially for species with narrow climatic or geographic distributions. Roughly corresponding to biodiversity hotspots, disappearing climates are concentrated in tropical mountain regions (chapter 6), but also at poleward continental boundaries. New climates are expected to be concentrated in the tropics and subtropics, and in regions with high ecological diversity and complexity. Yet how species will adapt to new, no-analogue climates is uncertain and difficult to predict.

...and how many?

The ecological details may be sublime, and the models of them worry-ingly simplistic, but the overarching conclusion is chilling. Large numbers of species, thus-far largely unaffected by human actions, are in danger of extinction from climate change.

Stuart L. Pimm, 2008

The threat of climate-change-driven extinctions is not just a future possibility – it is a present danger. Global warming has already been implicated in animal extinctions, including those of the golden toad, *Bufo periglenes*, in Costa Rica's Monteverde cloud forests,[38] and of dozens of species of harlequin frogs, *Atelopus* spp., endemic to the American tropics.[39] Although outbreaks of chytrid fungus, *Batrachochytrium dendrobatidis*, infection were the immediate cause of their extinction, large-scale climate warming is thought to have fostered favourable conditions for this fungus in the frogs' highland ranges.

As to future extinctions, one of the first efforts to tackle this question produced an answer surprising to many. University of York biologist Chris Thomas and his colleagues estimated that 15–37 per cent of plants and animals would be committed to extinction under moderate climate warming (1.8–2.0°C by 2050).[40] Based on data from a fifth of the Earth's land surface, their analysis assumes extinction would follow if a species were to lose its suitable climate space; they also consider the possibility that species might be unable to track suitable climate conditions across habitat altered by humans. Climate change, they conclude, 'is likely to be the greatest threat in many if not most regions'. These findings were widely covered by the world's media and their approach, though criticised for its methods and assumptions, advanced this field because it showed that the question of extinction due to climate change could, in fact, be tackled.

Another intensive effort sought to gauge the effect of climate change on 25 global biodiversity hotspots. British environmental scientist Norman Myers characterises hotspots as zones where 'exceptional concentrations of endemic species are undergoing exceptional loss of habitat'. Twenty-five such hotspots harbour about 44 per cent of the world's vascular plants and 35 per cent of its mammals, birds, reptiles and amphibians, in just 1.4 per cent of the planet's land area.[41] Moreover, these hotspots have already lost

70 per cent or more of their natural vegetation. Yet if carbon dioxide levels double, climate change would cause extinctions ranging from 1 to 43 per cent (11.6 per cent on average) of endemic hotspot plants and vertebrate species over this century.[42] At the high end, this could mean the loss of some 56 000 endemic plants and 3700 endemic vertebrates. Extinction rates in tropical hotspots would in some cases exceed those due to deforestation, again implicating global warming as one of the gravest threats to biodiversity.

In 2007, the IPCC also weighed in on the extinction question. It found that, possibly within this century, '20–30 per cent of species assessed are likely to be at increasingly high risk of extinction' if global average temperatures increase by 2–3°C.[43]

The extinction threat to birds

Though great unknowns remain, some important inroads have been made on gauging the climate-change extinction risk to the world's bird fauna. By 2009, climate change was already a firmly established threat to birds, according to the first systematic assessment by the International Union for the Conservation of Nature. Among the 9856 living bird species assessed, the IUCN deemed 35 per cent (3438 species) to be susceptible to climate change.[44] Highlighting the hazard to birds now suffering from a range of other human impacts, four out of every five bird species already listed as threatened were also deemed to be vulnerable to climate change. Ominously, however, the IUCN also found nearly 30 per cent of non-threatened species to be susceptible to global warming.

The IUCN also sought to identify the most vulnerable families of birds. Their results underscored the climate-change threat to seabirds (chapter 4); all species of the Spheniscidae (penguins), Diomedeidae (albatrosses), Procellariidae (petrels and shearwaters), Pelecanoididae (diving petrels) and Hydrobatidae (storm petrels) families were deemed susceptible. Apart from seabirds, high proportions of species in the Scolopacidae (sandpipers and allies), Thamnophilidae (antbirds), Formicariidae (antthrushes and antpittas), and Turdidae (thrushes) families were also found to be at risk.

Looking to the future, Şekercioğlu and colleagues found that with 2.8°C of surface warming, 400 to 550 of the world's 8459 land-bird species could be committed to extinction by 2100 (see figure 3).[45] By combining a worst-case surface warming estimate of 6.4°C with a worst-case habitat loss scenario, they estimate that nearly 2500 land birds could become extinct by 2100.

Depending on the amount of habitat loss, each degree of surface warming is expected to lead to an additional 100 to 500 bird extinctions. Yet only 21 per cent of these birds are currently on the IUCN Red List, again showing how climate change can be a risk to large numbers of species now considered 'safe'. This drives home the urgency of large cuts in greenhouse gas emissions to avert bird extinctions.

Profiling the climate-change-susceptible bird

What specific characteristics might make any bird species more vulnerable to extinction from climate change? Some of the criteria used to assess their susceptibility to other human threats could also address this question. But these criteria will need to be refined to accurately evaluate this newer threat of climate change. They will also need be augmented by new climate-change criteria, such as narrow elevational range.[45] Here we explore some of the characteristics likely to increase birds' susceptibility to climate change.

Small is risky: population and range size

The best indicator of a population's extinction risk is its size, although its population trend is also important. Small populations also face greater risks if they have low genetic variation. This can lead to inbreeding, reducing birds' fitness and rendering them less able to respond to selection pressures in their environments. Another set of risks arises because births and deaths of individuals are random events, in that different individuals produce varying numbers of young and may die at different ages. Small populations are vulnerable when chance events that affect the numbers of young born or adults expired influence their growth rate. Demographic stochasticity, as these chance fluctuations are termed, may be easily withstood by large populations, but can trigger extinctions in small populations.

Because small populations often have small ranges, local catastrophes can wipe out a large proportion of individuals and lead to extinctions. In the mountain forests of Puerto Rico, the critically endangered endemic Puerto Rican parrot, *Amazona vittata*, had a brush with oblivion in 1989, when Hurricane Hugo reduced its single wild population of about 45 birds to 25 stragglers. A succession of severe hurricanes could easily drive it to extinction. Smaller, isolated, and less genetically diverse populations are also less likely to recolonise zones damaged by extreme events. Taken together, it is unsurprising that these consequences of small and declining populations are also expected to increase birds' vulnerability to climate change.

As to risks associated with small range size, where birds' ranges contract with climate change, their populations will probably decline, too. In this way, range contractions could elevate birds' extinction risk, especially those with smaller distributions. *A Climatic Atlas for European Breeding Birds* found 10 out of 40 endemic or near-endemic[46] European bird species to be at particularly high risk, if unable to disperse or adapt. The birds' already-small ranges could shrink to a tenth of their present size by 2100. True endemics in this group include the citril finch, *Serinus citrinella*, the azure-winged magpie, *Cyanopica cyanus*, and the Spanish imperial eagle (chapter 3).

Bird species with small ranges tend to occur in rare climates that are cooler, drier and higher (or lower) than their surrounds. These species may be cold-adapted relicts of the last glacial period, persisting in today's warmer world thanks to cool refugia on mountain tops or in canyons (chapter 6). Climate models suggest these centres of rarity will shrink markedly and disproportionately with climate change, leaving the populations they harbour highly vulnerable.[47]

Exactly how climate-change-driven range contractions will translate into declining bird numbers is a largely unanswered question, despite it being a pivotal one for biodiversity conservation. A bird's abundance is unlikely to be uniform throughout its range. In the Wet Tropics of Queensland, accounting for birds' uneven abundance across different elevations of mountain habitat revealed extra cause for concern. For nine of 12 endemic species, total population size could drop faster than range contractions driven by warming.[48] The grey-headed robin, *Heteromyias albispecularis*, would not only lose habitat, but it would also undergo a population reduction in its remaining range. This is possible because the climate types supporting dense numbers of this bird are expected to shrink as they shift towards mountain tops.[49] Insights like these suggest bird populations may become extinct well before their habitat disappears. They also suggest that estimates based solely on loss of distributions could be overly conservative.

Range shifts may also trigger flow-on and feedback effects as communities are reshuffled, changes that could drive further range shifts of their own. The difficulty of predicting such complex effects makes it extremely challenging to estimate their contribution to birds' extinction.

Specialists, generally speaking, face greater peril

Specialised needs may also increase the climate-change threat to some birds, like the globally threatened spoon-billed sandpiper, *Eurynorhynchus pygmeus*. Its breeding range is restricted to a north-east Russian coastal strip, where it nests only on lagoon spits covered with crowberry-lichen, dwarf birch and willow sedge. This bird is virtually never seen more than five kilometres from the seashore. Yet warming of just 1.7°C by 2070 could reduce this habitat by more than half.[50] (Other short-term human threats are likely to be more pressing, however, given this enigmatic sandpiper's dramatic population decline to just 120–200 breeding pairs in 2009.) The IUCN identified specialised habitat or microhabitat needs as a vulnerability in almost half (46 per cent) of climate-change-susceptible birds. Even if birds can disperse to new areas of suitable climate, those that require particular habitat types may not find what they need.

Highly specialised and evolutionarily unique birds are generally more likely to go extinct. Where the relatively new threat of climate change transforms their habitats and disrupts their interactions with symbionts, hosts, prey and competitors, their extinction risk will only increase. Take Cape sugarbirds, *Promerops cafer*, endemic South African birds that face range contraction with climate change. When breeding, they are highly reliant for food on the nectar of the Proteaceae, a family of slow-growing plants. Yet climate change is expected to cause range contractions and even extinctions of some Proteaceae species that Cape sugarbirds depend on. In this way climate change could accelerate the extinction of the food-specialised Cape sugarbirds beyond what is expected from their climate-driven range contractions alone.[51]

At particular risk are birds so highly specialised that they may be unable to switch to alternatives to meet their survival needs. Their extinction could be followed by that of plants dependent on them for pollination or seed dispersal.[52] If sugarbirds decline or disperse away in response to climate change, this could lead to reduced seed set among rare or specialised Proteaceae species, causing these plant populations to decline as well. Even less specialised birds, such as the southern cassowary, *Casuarius casuarius*, may have unique and irreplaceable roles in their ecosystems. This very large flightless bird is a long-distance disperser of fruits with large seeds in Australian tropical rainforests (chapter 6).

In contrast to specialists, climate change is expected to favour mobile, widespread generalists.[44] Birds able to use a wide range of habitats are considered most likely to disperse to suitable new areas (chapter 3). Those that tolerate a wider range of climate conditions may breed successfully even when subjected to heatwaves or other extremes. Generalists may also switch to alternative prey if their reproductive timing falls out of synchrony with one food species. Factors like these may explain why, in North America, warming so far appears to have favoured opportunistic birds that are likely to be better dispersers, in this case widespread species that tend to be large-bodied. Such species have become more common from 1975 to 2001.[53]

Deadly together: habitat fragmentation and climate change

The plight of southern Australia's endangered mallee emu-wren, *Stipiturus mallee*, illustrates why climate change and habitat destruction are seen as a particularly dangerous combination. This diminutive bird, numbering at most 2800 adults, can be seen darting quickly about in patches of mallee eucalypt scrub and spinifex grass. Crop and livestock farming have drastically reduced its distribution, and fire is a devastating and growing threat in its remaining fractured and fragmented habitat islands.

Though periodic fire is essential to maintain the mallee emu-wren's habitat, larger and more frequent wildfires are expected under global warming. Big fires eliminate birds from large areas, isolating them in small, scattered habitat patches where they are vulnerable to subsequent fires. Mallee emu-wrens' virtual disappearance from the isolated Billiatt Conservation Park was blamed on a large 1988 fire. This pattern of loss has been repeated in other habitat patches, including those in conservation areas. Mallee emu-wrens rarely disperse more than five kilometres, so a habitat patch may for all intents be an isolated subpopulation. Even single fires can therefore prove catastrophic.

In fact, some of the most severe repercussions of climate change may occur as it combines with the well-established threats biologist Jared Diamond terms the 'evil quartet': habitat destruction, introduced species, over-exploitation and chains of extinctions.[54,55] Another important realm of interaction includes the direct effects of rising carbon dioxide levels, in particular altered plant growth and ocean acidification (chapters 3 and 4). Although such effects could conspire to trigger destructive synergies, current estimates of extinctions generally fail to account for them.[56]

Poor dispersers may lag dangerously

The greatest global warming threat, the IUCN finds, is an inability to disperse to suitable habitat, a potential hazard for about two-thirds (69 per cent) of climate-change susceptible birds. Constraints to poleward or upslope dispersal may come in the form of oceans, rivers or mountain ranges and mountain tops – not to mention ever-expanding human barriers.

A key consideration here is the degree of overlap between the present and future ranges of suitable climate. If overlap is small or non-existent, this could constrain birds' ability to disperse and track climate change (chapter 3). In this regard, birds with small ranges face a particular challenge because their chances for overlap may be reduced, thereby increasing their odds for dispersal failure. This is yet another reason why birds with small ranges could face elevated risk from climate change.

A small population, because it inherently limits the pool of potential colonists, could also make dispersal more difficult. One could also speculate that sedentary and territorial birds may be more vulnerable to dispersal failure than migratory and nomadic species pre-adapted to moving frequently to find productive patches of habitat. Even some migratory birds may be poor candidates for dispersal if they display the sort of inflexible migratory behaviour seen in many wader species.

On the risks of being migratory

Climate change could significantly affect the abundance of migratory birds. Yet whether 'migratoriness' is a characteristic that increases birds' susceptibility to climate change is still a matter of debate. Currently, sedentary species are 2.6 times more threatened or near threatened with extinction than migratory species,[57] and sedentary birds are five times more likely to go extinct than are long-distance migrants from a combination of climate change and habitat loss by the year 2100.[45]

Nonetheless, migratoriness could constrain some birds' phenological response to rapid changes in climate.[58] Among 100 European-breeding migratory birds, earlier spring migration timing was associated with stable or increasing bird populations over the 1990–2000 period. Yet among species that did not change their spring migration timing, or even delayed it, populations declined. This suggests that 'ongoing climatic changes will increasingly threaten vulnerable migratory bird species, augmenting their extinction risk'.[59]

Factors besides climate change, such as habitat loss, also influence the decline of migratory birds. And whereas most bird species in the well-studied regions of North America and Europe are migratory, in the less-studied tropics where most species are found the majority of birds are sedentary. It seems possible that we are underestimating the climate-change threat to most tropical, sedentary bird species (chapter 6).

Other behavioural and life-history traits

A wide range of other behavioural traits may influence birds' susceptibility to climate change. One possible example is the use of exposed nest sites that might increase vulnerability to heat stress. And the open-cup nests of small passerines could be a liability where storms and floods increase. Birds reliant on specific environmental cues to time their breeding and migration may also be susceptible if these triggers no longer accurately predict food resources or other ecological processes. Changes in phenology due to climate change could threaten birds when this desynchronises migration, uncouples mutualisms and predator–prey relationships, and brings about interactions with new pathogens (chapters 1 and 2). Species that use different cues at different life-history stages may be particularly susceptible, as might those whose males and females relying on different cues. Birds highly faithful to their breeding sites, like some seabirds, could be vulnerable where climate change causes food resources to shift out of a colony's foraging range.

Life-history characteristics may also affect birds' susceptibility to climate change, as the case of king penguins, *Aptenodytes patagonicus*, suggests. These long lived, slow-reproducing birds are not currently listed as a threatened species, and their population of roughly two million adult birds even appears to be increasing for the time being. Yet their responses to warming at the Crozet Archipelago (lying in the southern Indian Ocean between Africa and Antarctica) hint at trouble to come. There, where two-thirds of the world's king penguins breed, even small environmental changes during sensitive phases of their life cycle could seriously affect adult survival and breeding performance.

Like the emperor penguin, the only other living member of its genus, the king penguin is a large bird with an exceptional breeding strategy. Most king penguins do not breed until about five years of age. And because they require more than a year – 14 to 16 months – to complete their reproductive cycle, they generally breed successfully only twice in three years. Females lay a single egg some time between November and early March, and hatchlings are initially fed every 3–14 days on lanternfish, myctophyds, caught within 300 to 600 kilometres of the penguins' colonies. Yet as winter gets underway, prey move to deeper waters and food may become very scarce and its occurrence unpredictable nearby. At this stage, adult king penguins depart on extended foraging trips to seek alternative prey, and have been tracked by satellite to a distance of 1800 kilometres south of their colony in Crozet. The adults ensure their winter survival by foraging at the marginal ice zone, the transition area between open ocean and solid sea ice.

Remarkably, king penguin chicks, left in crèches over winter, often go unfed for three months and commonly lose half their body weight. They endure these cold-weather fasts by decreasing energy expenditure, gathering together into crèches to conserve body warmth and relying on stores of body fat. With the arrival of spring, parents return and feed chicks frequently until they fledge.

Despite such remarkable adaptations, the responses of king penguins at the archipelago's Possession Island reveal that warm events can have complex but detrimental effects on their breeding success and adult survival. These warm events affect food supplies at both the seabirds' distant winter foraging sites and around the Crozet Archipelago. The warmer the surface waters, the fewer the fish near Crozet. When parents need to forage further afield, this reduces chick survival, or interferes with the adults' ability to restore their fuel reserves after incubation fasts. Adults may either abandon breeding attempts or choose to sustain their young and thereby reduce their own survival chances.[60]

Nine years of observations at Possession Islands showed that, with 0.26°C of sea surface warming, adult survival declined by about nine per cent. In a long-lived species such as the king penguin, this level of decline in adult survival cannot be sustained. Current global warming predictions, it is argued, imply that king penguin populations are under heavy extinction risk.

Generally speaking, the low reproductive rate and relatively long generation time common to long-lived birds like emperor and king penguins may indicate a limited ability to adapt to long-term climate change. These life histories are characterised by advanced age at first breeding, small (often single-egg) clutches produced yearly or less frequently, and an extended period of parental care. In contrast, birds with shorter generation times (typically smaller-bodied species) have the potential to evolve more rapidly and may better adapt to climate change over the long term.

Unknowns and challenges

Climate change is expected to affect birds' abundance and ramp up the extinction threat to many species, but elucidating this risk remains a huge challenge. Insights are hampered by many of the knowledge gaps covered in previous chapters, including a dearth of long-term data sets that show how birds' productivity and survival rates vary with climate – the kind of records that would help predict their future responses to global warming.

If birds' distributions were better known, range contractions due to climate change could be estimated with more accuracy, along with the implied population consequences. This question is especially critical for birds with small and declining ranges. Understanding how birds' abundance varies across their distributions is also needed to better gauge the population impacts of range shifts (chapter 6). The ripple effects likely to follow on from reshuffled ecological communities is another wide knowledge gap; complete understanding of these complex effects on bird populations may not be unattainable.

Shifts in phenology are increasingly well studied but, despite being recognised as a climate-change threat, their implications for bird abundance are still poorly understood. Another crucial question is how productivity and survival rates will be affected by an increasingly variable environment, characterised by more extreme weather. Knowledge on how climate change will interact with other extinction drivers will also be critical, especially since the final path to extinction is often driven by synergies that may not have prompted a species' initial decline.

To better estimate possible extinctions from climate change, population models that account for this threat need to improve. More accurate estimates of extinction will also hinge on efforts to better understand the characteristics that increase birds' susceptibility to climate change.

Conclusion

Growing evidence suggests that climate change is already among the most important drivers of changes in bird abundance, and its influence can only be expected to increase as warming gathers momentum. Climate change is expected to affect birds' survival directly via changes in temperature, precipitation and extreme weather, and in numerous indirect ways, including effects on prey, pests and disease. It is also expected to affect birds' productivity, from their ability to reach pre-breeding condition and make timely migrations, to the number of clutches laid, and indeed whether some choose to breed at all. If it results in a mismatch between reproductive demands and food supplies, climate change could reduce the fitness and number of young, and possibly draw down parents' energy stores.

Large seabird population declines have been linked to ocean-warming events, but unambiguously establishing climate change as their cause is difficult. Density-dependent factors may mask, filter or delay climate-change effects on populations, complicating efforts to understand its contribution. Species-specific responses will probably determine whether climate change exerts a greater influence on population levels via effects on adult survival (tub effects) or via the numbers of new recruits (tap effects).

Some extreme weather events are already on the rise, and are considered today's top climate-change threat to critically endangered birds. Extreme events, or even gradual changes in climate, can cause climate regimes and ecosystems to shift to new, possibly unwanted states. These shifts may bring about surprises and new threats to bird populations. If they cause adult survival to fluctuate more widely, extreme events and more variable climate conditions could lead some populations to decline to extinction. Despite their disproportionate effect on populations, extreme weather events are not accounted for in most climate-change predictions. This implies that future impact levels are likely to exceed current estimates.

Climate change may also trigger changes that cascade through birds' ecosystems. By causing lemming populations cycles to flatten (as may already be the case in some regions), global warming could lead to population declines of predators like snowy owls, and more indirectly to increased predation of ground-nesting tundra-breeding birds. Climate change could also influence the dynamics between different bird species as they compete for limited resources.

Some bird species are likely to profit from climate change, but widespread extinctions are more likely. Estimates based on modelling of future range contractions suggest a significant share of plant and animal species could become extinct by mid-century. In some regions climate change could exceed the threat posed by habitat loss, today's greatest biodiversity threat. Already considered a firmly established threat to birds, climate change and associated severe weather now threaten 24 critically endangered species. A preliminary assessment suggests that more than a third of all known bird species are susceptible to climate change, many of them not formerly considered threatened; seabirds emerge as a particularly vulnerable group. Modelling on land birds indicates that 2500 species may go extinct by 2100, if the worst projections of climate change and habitat loss are realised.

Chapter 6

TROPICAL WARMING AND HABITAT ISLANDS

Habitat islands in a warming world

Bird architects of dinosaur forests

... the playing passages of bower-birds are tastefully ornamented with gaily-coloured objects; and this shews [sic] that they must receive some kind of pleasure from the sight of such things.

Charles Darwin, 1871

Golden bowerbirds, *Prionodura newtoniana*, of the Wet Tropics of Queensland embody the uniqueness of tropical mountain wildlife, and its vulnerability in a warming world. An undulating landscape of warm lowlands and cool highlands in north-east Australia, this bioregion abounds with rainforest life found nowhere else on Earth. As its climate changed over millions of years, forested upland islands of coolness were isolated from one another by warmer lowland barriers, accelerating the rise of new species. Home to some of the world's oldest continually surviving tropical rainforest, it also harbours descendents of archaic Gondwanan forms of life. Today, at least 700 vascular plants are endemic, found only in the Wet Tropics.

The golden bowerbird is one of 13 endemic birds. It courts and breeds in patchy tracts of cooler, upland and highland rainforest between altitudes of 700 and 1500 metres, sharing an unusual mating strategy with other bowerbirds, medium-sized passerines of Australia, New Guinea and their adjacent islands. To attract mates, bowerbird males build displays, or bowers. Charles Darwin concurred with English ornithologist and artist John Gould that these 'must be regarded as the most wonderful instances of bird-architecture yet discovered'. Papuan men are said to admire bowerbirds for their adeptness in acquiring what they see as the avian equivalent of a 'bride price', the wealth accumulated to pay for a wife.[1]

Though golden bowerbirds are the smallest of Australia's bowerbirds, they build the largest displays. The yellow and brown males invest immense energy to construct two towers up to three metres high, structured around vertical sapling trunks, connected by a display perch and decorated with flowers, fruits, moss and lichens. Here they await the attention of discriminating females; only males with the most impressive bowers actually mate and father young. Bowers can also be battlegrounds where males ransack and pilfer rivals' work, leaving the victims to spend time rebuilding instead of courting.

Golden bowerbirds' contests of construction, pilfering and song may have an uncertain future. Though much of it is protected as a World Heritage Area, the Wet Tropics bioregion is considered one of Australia's most vulnerable to climate change. With future warming, the area with climate conditions characteristing the cool mountain refugia that have fostered diversity across millions of years will contract markedly. Modelling suggests that 2°C of warming would cause the area with the golden bowerbirds' current climate to shrink by almost 90 per cent, to just 163 km^2, assuming a 10 per cent decrease in rainfall. With future warming beyond 3°C, this area of suitable climate would completely disappear.[2]

Consider the tropics

... it is time to question the conventional wisdom that tropical climates are biologically benign by taking a closer look at the challenges that climate change poses for tropical species.

Robert Colwell et al., 2008

Tropical ecosystems are cradles of biodiversity. They harbour the highest concentrations of species, and abound with centres of endemism and restricted-range species. Avian diversity also reflects this pattern, and most (77 per cent) endemic bird areas are found in the tropics and subtropics.[3,4] Yet the highest rates of forest clearance are in the tropics; if current trends continue, most remaining tropical forests will be destroyed, fragmented or otherwise degraded within this century. It is therefore unsurprising that extinction rates are highest in the tropics, and many more tropical species are also threatened with extinction.

An optimistic view of the tropics as having a benign and unchanging climate has persisted since 1878, when Alfred Russel Wallace wrote in *Tropical Nature* that, '[i]n the equable equatorial zone there is no such struggle against climate. Every form of vegetation has become alike adapted to its genial heat and ample moisture, which has probably changed little even throughout geological periods'. Similarly, climate change has been viewed as mainly a threat to life at higher latitudes, where the rate of warming is generally more rapid. This notion is being quickly dispelled.

In fact, 'the tropics have been engulfed in continual climate change throughout the past 2 million years'.[5] And although evidence suggests most life in the tropics was resilient to past episodes of climatic change, future scenarios are likely to differ. During the past two million years, most tropical species experienced climate conditions that were mainly cooler than today's. Some species may already be approaching the upper limits of their tolerance for heat. Furthermore, tropical palaeoecology suggests that warming will far surpass the bounds experienced in the past 100 000 years.[5] In the future, novel climates are expected to concentrate in tropical and subtropical regions, creating conditions unlike those experienced anywhere today (chapter 3).

Some tropical species may actually be more sensitive to future warming and temperature extremes than those at higher latitudes. Most species in the moist tropics are thought to have narrowly restricted niches; that is, they range across narrow elevational zones and have more specific requirements for moisture, and for food or hosts.[5] Furthermore, the relative constancy of tropical temperatures across seasons is thought to favour reproductive strategies of smaller clutches, lower productivity and longer life spans. These birds with 'slower' lives may be less able to evolve in response to climate change.[4]

When tropical populations' adaptation to low year-to-year temperature variability is considered, modelling suggests that tropical regions are likely to be affected by climate change just as much as temperate regions, and perhaps even more so in some cases.[6] In fact, some fear climate-change will pose an even greater threat to tropical species than habitat destruction in some regions. Although awareness of this threat has grown in recent years, in the tropics where the need for understanding is greatest, climate-change effects on wildlife are less well studied.

Islands, peaks and patches

The analogy between tropical mountains and islands has pertinence on multiple levels. Both mountain regions and islands tend to host relatively high numbers of endemic species (including those with restricted ranges[7]). But mountains are also effectively 'habitat islands'. In place of the saltwater barriers that isolate islands, arid lowlands may isolate separate mountain habitat islands. The island analogy also extends to remnant patches of natural forest and other unaltered habitat that form 'pockets within a sea of altered habitat', as Robert Whittaker and his colleagues observe in *Island Biogeography*. Forest fragments and the species they harbour may function as habitat islands isolated by inhospitable agricultural land.

Insights like these have led scientists to use the theory of island biogeography to better understand the effects of habitat fragmentation and extinction. The same features that promote endemism and evolution of new species on islands (isolation and, in some cases, long-term stability of their environments) also make their wildlife extremely vulnerable to sudden environmental change. These insights into habitat fragmentation, insularisation and extinction may also help illuminate the conservation threat climate change poses to the birds of mountains, islands and forest fragments.

Tropical mountains and islands: vulnerable foundries of diversity

Tropical mountains store and generate diversity

Key characteristics of mountains make them important for bird diversity, yet vulnerable to climate change. Covering almost a quarter of the planet's land surface, mountains are among the world's most species-rich zones. From bases to peaks, they feature a wide range of warm-to-cool climatic gradients that permit diverse, stacked ecological communities, concentrating diversity into a relatively limited geographic area. In the tropics, mountain peaks and high tablelands provide crucial refuge for heat-intolerant species, creating archipelagos of coolness in seas of warmer lowlands. On top of these climatic gradients, the complex topography and ground cover of mountains superimpose another layer of habitat diversity. Overall, these features afford a buffer against climatic change that may promote the persistence of lineages over time.

Mountains also tend to be relatively rich in endemic species. Forty-two per cent of continental endemic species are found in mountains, while another 24 per cent are found in areas that at least partly include mountains.[3] Yet endemic-rich tropical mountains are more than mere storehouses of biodiversity. Their isolation, along with the long-term climate stability engendered by their topography, actually promotes the evolution of new species.

The staggering diversity of the Albertine Rift Mountains is a case in point. From lowland tropical forests to bamboo stands, montane forests, moorlands and up to the highest, the 5000-metre ice-capped Rwenzori peaks, their slopes host Africa's greatest concentration of vertebrate species. This includes 1061 bird species, among them 36 range-restricted endemics like the regal sunbird, *Nectarinia regia*, whose riotously colourful males sport green heads, blue collars, yellow sides and orange breasts.

Increasingly, mountains are also refuges for endemic species threatened by a broad range of human influences. Yet even as habitat destruction progresses ratchet-like up mountain flanks, high elevational habitats will be increasingly under threat because mountain regions are expected to be among the world's most vulnerable to climate change.

Mountain zones have already warmed more than the global average, a trend likely to continue. Species-rich tropical mountains could be among those regions suffering the majority of extinctions if cooler, upland habitat is greatly reduced in extent due to climate change. Disappearing climates (chapter 5) are expected to concentrate in tropical mountain regions, in areas that closely correspond to critical biodiversity hotspots, including the Andes, Mesoamerica, the Himalayas, the Philippines, southern and eastern Africa and Wallacea.[8,9]

On a more optimistic note, mountains may provide a spatial buffer against future climate change, just as they have done in the past. Mountains, with their steep climate gradients and complex topography, may permit species to disperse overland at speeds which fall within historic rates (chapter 7).

Islands: extinction history and future vulnerability

A gun is here almost superfluous; for with the muzzle I pushed a hawk off the branch of a tree.

Charles Darwin, 1839

Madagascar's flora and fauna epitomise the uniqueness engendered by 60 to 80 million of years of isolation – and the vulnerability of island wildlife to new threats like climate change. Of the more than 300 birds on Madagascar and its neighbouring islands, almost 60 per cent are endemic to this remnant of the ancient Gondwanan supercontinent. Madagascar still yields new surprises and surrenders ancient curiosities. In 1992, the cryptic warbler, *Cryptosylvicola randrianasoloi*, a species unique enough to be placed within its own new genus, was discovered. It was found in eastern Madagascar's subhumid forests, habitat islands in a now-denuded landscape that once hosted a remarkable array of endemics. Among them was the elephant bird, *Aepyornis maximus*, an avian colossus possibly weighing up to 450 kilograms. It succumbed to the island's human occupation centuries ago, but fragments of its eggs are still found in southern Madagascar.

Though islands tend to host fewer species than similar-sized continental lands, they are generally eight and nine times as rich in endemic vertebrate animals and plants, respectively, as mainlands.[10] This explains why about half the world's endemic bird areas are located on islands. Their isolation limits the exchange of species with mainlands and promotes the evolution of new island lineages. Whereas new, volcanic islands like Hawaii tend to be textbook examples of how adaptive radiation generates new species, the ancient continental fragments of Madagascar and New Zealand host descendants of ancient lineages now extinct elsewhere. Isolated from ever-evolving mainland competition, predation and disease, lineages on islands may persist long after their mainland counterparts are extinguished.

Yet some of the same features that make islands foundries for evolution also leave their endemic species vulnerable to human influences. Although most (more than 80 per cent) of bird species are found on continents, the majority (88 per cent) of the 153 bird extinctions[11] since 1500 have taken place on islands. Most island birds evolved without the pressure of animal predators or competitors. More 'ecologically naive', they tend to be captured easily and to succumb to human-assisted invasions of disease, alien predators (like snakes, cats and rats) or grazing animals that degrade their habitats. (Recent efforts to control invasive alien species may now be helping to slow island bird extinctions.) Along with small range size, another island trait associated with extinction risk, these vulnerabilities explain why a high percentage of birds on oceanic islands are threatened.

With their species-rich but threatened ecosystems, almost all tropical islands are found in a biodiversity hotspot. Madagascar, together with Mauritius and its associated islands, is classed as one of the world's three 'hottest' hotspots. Humans have destroyed about 80 per cent of this hotspot's original vegetation, and 32 of its bird species have gone extinct. They include the dodo, *Raphus cucullatus*, of Mauritius, an icon of extinction that had followed in the elephant bird's footsteps by end of the 17th century.

Climate change brings new threats to birds on islands, especially small islands. On Madagascar, the warming trend is at least as great as the global average.[12] This island also has highly fragmented habitats and some areas of dense human populations. These threats are expected to compound the dangers of future warming for this hotspot's more than 55 threatened endemic birds. Birds now confined to habitat fragments may be forced southwards by warming, into lands already transformed into veritable deserts by unsustainable agricultural practises. Wildlife attempting to shift upslope to higher elevations may be prevented from doing so by habitat fragmentation.[12] Despite these pressing concerns for the birds of Madagascar and many other tropical islands, the threat of climate change has only begun to be explored.

Elevational range shifts and extinction

Tropical, protected, but very climate-sensitive

In tropical zones, birds may face particular limits on their capacity to cope with climate change, and these constraints could ramp up their extinction rates, even in areas like the Wet Tropics of Queensland. A world apart from the Madagascar's rapidly fragmenting and vanishing forests, 90 per cent of this bioregion's remaining forests are protected as a World Heritage Area, with 29 per cent of this area explicitly managed for conservation. Yet climate change could prove a potent spoiler of these efforts to safeguard unique wildlife.

With 1°C of average warming, the endemic golden bowerbird, mountain thornbill, *Acanthiza katherina*, and Atherton scrubwren, *Sericornis keri*, would lose more than half of the area of suitable climate that now underpins their core environments, climate envelope modelling suggests. When both expected range shifts and birds' abundance are accounted for, models suggest that, under mid-range (1.4–3.6°C) regional warming, up to 41 species (74 per cent) of Wet Tropics' rainforest birds could be threatened.[13] If average warming reaches high levels (5.8°C) this century, all 55 of the rainforest birds studied would be threatened, and seven species could become extinct.

Taking into account aspects of ecology, as well as abundance and climate reveals a more complex picture for Wet Tropics birds. In upland areas above 500 metres, bird numbers may be limited by the net primary productive of their forests. This productivity is, in turn, limited by lower temperatures and, at the highest elevations, by excess precipitation. The threatening scenario described above could be less severe if warming temperatures increase the productivity of upland forests. In this way, the highly diverse bird fauna now found at 600–800 metres might be accommodated at higher elevations, even if temperatures warm by several degrees.[14]

This suggests how temperature and precipitation effects on net primary productivity, and thereby on the energy sources available to birds, could be important to understanding how they track their niches under climate change. These additional possible determinants of ranges need to be considered alongside birds' physiological tolerances to climate extremes,[15] and could help explain why not all species might move poleward or upward in elevation in response to climate change.

Less latitude for shifts in the tropics

In the tropics, the ability of wildlife to track climate change may face a special constraint. The extent of climatic cooling, as one progresses away from the equator and towards the poles, is relatively limited in the tropics. This shallow temperature gradient could present a great obstacle to the poleward dispersal of populations under climate warming, especially among species with restricted ranges and a limited capacity to make rapid shifts. In fact, some consider successful poleward range shifts to be unlikely in the tropics.[16]

However, for every 1000 metres climbed in elevation, air temperatures typically drop by 5–5.5°C in the tropics (and by somewhat more, about 6.5°C, in temperate and boreal zones). This lapse rate allows for a vastly greater rate of temperature decrease, for a given dispersal distance, than is achievable via poleward shifts.[17] It explains why some believe tropical species are more likely to disperse along elevational than latitudinal gradients in response to warming.[16] Indeed distribution shifts documented so far in the tropics mostly entail upslope shifts, although the small number of studies involved requires cautious interpretation.

The climate escalator to extinction

... extinctions will increase in an accelerating fashion, not linearly, and will be especially severe for tropical mountain species, most of which are endemic and have small ranges.

Şekercioğlu et al. 2008

The view from mountain summits, however, betrays the abrupt limits to upslope range shifts. Climate warming will effectively place some mountain bird species on an 'escalator to extinction'.[18] The distances required to reach cooler zones upslope may be relatively small, but mountaintops, plateaus and ridges impose absolute limits on upward dispersal. Moreover, an inescapable fact of mountain geometry is that peaks are smaller than bases. Potential habitat, therefore, decreases in extent with elevation. As zones of suitable climate rise, contract and then possibly disappear off mountaintops, some birds may be able to disperse to other, higher peaks with suitable conditions. But for others, these areas may simply be too distant to colonise.

When Şekercioğlu and his colleagues factored elevational limits into estimates of range shifts, projections of bird extinctions under climate change were greatly increased (see figure 3).[19] The endemic black and gold cotinga, *Tijuca atra*, of south-east Brazilian cloud forests illustrates why. It is found in an Atlantic Forest biodiversity hotspot, an area of scintillating bird diversity, including 144 endemics, that has already lost 92 per cent of its original forest cover. The black and gold cotinga occurs between 1200 and 2050 metres above sea level. These elevational limits to its range were used to determine the actual area this bird might occupy, which turns out to be a mere fraction of its broader 'field book guide' geographical range. (Because the broader estimate does not account for elevation, it includes lowland areas this bird would not actually populate.) With 2.8°C of warming, the black and gold cotinga's range would shift upslope by 560 metres, contracting markedly and fragmenting into discontinuous patches.[20] Elevational effects like these help explain why expected habitat loss, combined with moderate warming of 2.8°C, could lead to 400–550 land-bird extinctions by 2100.

A study of the upslope dispersal potential for 1009 mountain bird species emphasises its importance under climate change. If they are not constrained at all in their ability to shift, the extinction risk of these birds is strongly affected by the location and structure of their mountain environment. Their ability to disperse upslope emerges as a key factor; generally speaking, if a species's vertical range extent is doubled, its projected average range loss would be reduced by 23 per cent. If mountain birds cannot disperse upslope at all (admittedly an unlikely scenario in many cases) very high range contractions are possible, especially among species with narrow elevational ranges. A total of 327 mountain bird species (versus 184 for the above-mentioned unconstrained dispersal case) would lose 50 per cent or more of their range, with the greatest proportions of such species being in the Afrotropics and the Nearctic, and the highest numbers in the Neotropics.[21]

On narrowness, and lapse rate revisited

... Mother Nature is unkind. Small-ranged species are typically both locally rare and have narrow elevational limits.

Stuart L. Pimm, 2008

Some key characteristics of tropical birds' ranges could heighten their vulnerability to climate change. Range size generally tends to be smaller towards the equator (Rapoport's rule), and birds with small ranges are more susceptible to threats. Endemic tropical species' ranges tend to be narrow in both the geographic and the climatic senses. Elevational ranges are narrower in the tropics than in the temperate regions. These narrow ranges reduce the likelihood, under global warming, that a population's current distribution will overlap with its range of suitable climate in the future. This could constrain a population's ability to disperse, and elevate its extinction risk (chapter 5).

The escalator effect described above poses a particularly high risk to birds of endemic-rich tropical mountains. The threats to the upland birds of the Wet Tropics of Queensland are predicted, in part, because the distribution of its wildlife is defined largely by elevation, and because temperature increases will be most noticeable across these gradients of altitude. If climate change causes the ranges of these birds to contract, the genetic diversity of their populations will probably diminish, and the chance of extinction due to other sources of stress would probably increase. Events like these have occurred in past eras of climatic change.

Moreover, compared to other zones, the potential for upslope range shifts in the tropics may be somewhat constrained due to lower regional lapse rates compared to other mountain zones (5–5.5°C versus 6.5°C for temperate and boreal mountain zones). This means that, for the same level of temperature increase, tropical birds would need to shift further upslope to track the suitable climate conditions. This could increase their extinction risk where higher elevation habitat is unavailable.[19]

Warming in the lost world

There falleth over it a mighty river which toucheth no part of the side of the mountaine, but rusheth over the top of it, and falleth to the ground with a terrible noise and clamour, as if 1,000 great belles were knocked one against another: I think there is not in the world so strange an overfall, nor so wonderful to behold.

Sir Walter Raleigh, 1596

The unusual topography of the spectacular Pantepui region makes its bio-diversity particularly vulnerable to the escalator effect, and highlights the climate threat to 'sky islands'. This inaccessible and almost pristine area of the Neotropics straddles the borders of Guyana, Venezuela and Brazil, and inspired Arthur Conan Doyle's book, *The Lost World*. Conan Doyle's land of pterodactyls and dinosaurs is a romp through scientific fantasy, but shares with the real-life biogeographical province of Pantepui a dramatic and ancient landscape of table mountains, populated with rare and diverse life – including carnivorous plants.

These table mountains, known as *tepui*, are remnants of ancient sand-stone plateaus that were eroded away by rivers. The highest *tepui* tower to elevations of 3000 metres, some banded by precipitous pink or red cliffs and graced by stunning waterfalls, including the world's highest, Angel Falls at Auyantepui. Encompassing roughly 50 *tepuis*, this archipelago in the air includes the 2810-metre high Mount Roraima, likely to have inspired the above rapt description in Sir Walter Raleigh's account, *The Discovery of Guiana* after this English explorer's 1595 visit to the region. The climate of relatively flat *tepui* tops, which may tower up to 2400 metres above the tropical lowlands at their bases, tends to be colder and significantly wetter. Some *tepui* summits are also topographically isolated by sheer bands of cliffs.

Pantepui is among the more ancient of the world's roughly 20 sky island complexes. Sky islands are analogous to oceanic islands in that lowlands, like oceans, may hinder or prevent the dispersal of species among them. Isolated from one another by savannah or forest plains, some *tepui* may host concentrations of endemic species so high that their proportions approach that of oceanic islands. So far 2500 Pantepui plants are known, about 770 of them endemic; a quarter of *tepui* plants may be unique to a single mountain,[22] and many are thought to have evolved on site among the *tepui*.

Also like oceanic islands, sky islands have long fascinated biologists because they are natural evolutionary laboratories with quantifiable, discrete and repeated habitats that help distil the natural world's complexity. In the 'Galápagos of the mainland' that is Pantepui, birds and plants have permitted important tests of influential theories on tropical biodiversity evolution. Again like oceanic islands, Pantepui generates diversity. This Neotropical biodiversity reservoir is an important speciation centre for the Guayana and Amazon regions, and could generate more biodiversity in the future.

Among the 100 or so Pantepui bird species described so far, 10–20 per cent are endemic to the highlands.[22] The eastern part of the Pantepui, where plateaus tend to be higher and closer together and bird diversity is greater, hosts species endemic to only this area. They include the fancifully named ruddy tody-flycatcher, *Todirostrum russatum*, rufous-breasted sabrewing, *Campylopterus hyperythrus*, and greater flower-piercer, *Diglossa major*, all found above 1200 metres in elevation. Many have small ranges, but the saffron-breasted redstart, *Myioborus cardonai*, takes this to the extreme. This bird is found on just a single *tepui* further to the west in Venezuela, in cloud forest between 1200 and 1600 metres.[3]

Future climate warming is expected to threaten Pantepui biodiversity. The flat summits of *tepui* impose a finite and abrupt limit to upslope dispersal. With 2°C of warming, the overall area of climate now typically found at 1500 metres on Pantepui would migrate upwards by 330 metres, fragmenting and shrinking by more than 68 per cent over this century. With 4°C of warming, this climate would persist in only 10 per cent of its former land area.[23]

So far, modelling has been carried out only for Pantepui's vascular plants, for which very high losses are considered possible. Around 80 per cent of plants (roughly 1700 species) could become locally extinct by 2100 under the 2–4°C of warming predicted for the Amazonia region. This extinction figure includes 200–400 Pantepui endemics.[23] Loss of keystone species, invasion by lowland species and dispersal problems could exacerbate this climate threat.

Information on the elevational ranges of Pantepui birds is available for only a few species, and studies on their responses to warming are lacking. Yet their high levels of endemism and limited ranges imply a threat as suitable climate conditions shift upslope. Field observations by palaeoecologist Valentí Rull, of the Botanical Institute of Barcelona, suggest that Pantepui birds' fortunes are tightly bound to the local plant communities that provide their food and physically structure their niches. With warming, he believes, birds face not only loss of suitable climate space, but also a secondary threat posed by the fragmentation, critical reduction or even disappearance of their ecological communities.

Although Pantepui features prominently in historical studies of South American birds, its future is uncertain, and some fear its unique biodiversity will vanish into thin air even before it is fully understood.

Precipitation and vulnerability to fire

In the tropics, rain drives seasonal change

In addition to warming, changes to precipitation, moisture and fire regimes will also be critical in the tropics. Although tropical birds' life cycles have been thought of as aseasonal, it is increasingly evident that birds and other wildlife respond to the wet–dry seasons typical of many tropical regions. In fact, plants and animals in humid tropical mountain zones are sensitive to water stress. Rainfall can be a critical constraint in the tropics, because dry seasons create bottlenecks of important bird food supplies including nectar, fruit and insects. In the Wet Tropics of Queensland, dry-season length and intensity are suspected to strongly influence birds' food supplies and so their abundance. In the lowlands of this region, it is hypothesised that the more seasonal the rainfall pattern, the less dense the populations of Wet Tropics birds – especially insect-eating birds.[14,24]

With climate change, rainfall is expected to become more intense in the tropics, but the periods between rainfall events are expected to lengthen. Should this pattern hold true for the Wet Tropics of Queensland, dry spells and dry-season severity would increase, even as intense flooding rains become more frequent. These changes may be expected to cause the bird population densities of the Wet Tropics to decline in the lowlands. And this would exacerbate expected population declines due to possible warming-driven range contraction and fragmentation. Changes to precipitation patterns could also lead to mismatches between food supplies and reproductive timing among tropical birds that breed seasonally.[4]

Lifting the veil from cloud forests

Changes afoot in the cloud forests of Monteverde, Costa Rica highlight how altered levels of moisture and precipitation can subtly and indirectly affect tropical birds. Here, rich biodiversity is sustained not only by wet-season rains, but also by a life-giving shroud of cloud and mist. Moisture-laden air from the Caribbean trade winds travels up the continental divide, rising and condensing into a large cloud deck that feeds mountain forest moisture, even during the dry season.

This extra moisture is a defining – and limiting – characteristic of the many tropical mountain cloud forests around the world, including those in Madagascar, Sri Lanka, the Philippines, New Guinea and the Hawaiian Islands. Tropical mountain cloud forests on islands, though relatively small in size, are reservoirs for island endemics and comprise important sources of fresh water.

Though their impressive diversity defies strict definition, tropical mountain cloud forests are rare habitats spanning a narrow band of altitude, typically featuring lush and abundant vegetation blanketed by constant, frequent or seasonal clouds. A multitude of ferns, mosses and orchids find purchase on every available surface. Like giant sponges, these forests strip water from cool, moisture-laden air and slowly release it, boosting overall precipitation levels significantly beyond what rainfall alone provides. This extra moisture affects nearly every aspect of forest ecology.

Though constituting a tiny 2.5 per cent of tropical forests, these mist-shrouded ecosystems feature explosive speciation and disproportionately high and concentrated biodiversity. Isolated and unique, tropical mountain cloud forests are exceptionally rich in endemic and specialised species with very specific requirements. These forests are already some of the world's most threatened ecosystems, and their endemics are among the mountain species at disproportionately high extinction risk from global warming. Even relatively small changes in climate can prompt extensive changes in local cloud cover, humidity and precipitation, affecting forest life.[25] Epiphytes, for example, occupy fine-grained niches on the trunks, crooks and branches of trees. These plants provide birds with food and nesting materials, and help regulate their microclimates. But epiphytes may decline or die when climate conditions change slightly, sending cascading effects through cloud forest communities.[26]

At Monteverde, these highly climate-sensitive forests provide rare insight into the effect of global warming on tropical mountain birds. Cloud height depends on humidity, which in turn depends on temperature. Warming, particularly since the mid-1970s, is suspected to have increased the altitude at which clouds form. Where the cloud base shifts away upslope, forests no longer receive as much ecosystem-defining moisture. During the 1970s at Monteverde, Pacific slopes at elevations of 1540 metres rarely went more than two days without mist. By 2005, mist-free periods persisted as long as three weeks. Superimposed on this general drying, El Niño events brought extreme dry episodes in 1983, 1987, 1994 and 1998. Another possible contributor to these drying trends may be lowland deforestation in the vicinity of Monteverde.

From 1982 to 1999, changes to the lower montane cloud forest community fluctuated in virtual lockstep with climate change.[27] Lizard populations retreated upslope in concert with this drying trend, and many frog and toad species disappeared, including the now-extinct endemic golden toad (chapter 5). Breeding birds also shifted their distributions and abundance. The total number of dry days during the previous year's dry season turned out to be the best predictor of upslope shifts.

In 1979, when biologist J. Alan Pounds first began to document Monteverde birds, species intolerant of cloud forests including keel-billed toucans, *Ramphastos sulfuratus*, nested below 1470 metres. Yet over time, and especially in the late 1980s, some of these birds had extended their ranges upslope. By 1998, 15 species of cloud-forest-intolerant birds had established breeding populations upslope in the territory of lower-montane cloud forest birds.[28]

As for typical cloud forest species, population trends varied over this period. Some of the original breeding birds of the lower mountain cloud forest, including resplendent quetzals, *Pharomachrus mocinno*, simply declined. Several of those best characterised as mountaintop species, like hairy woodpeckers, *Picoides villosus*, vanished from the lower montane cloud forest study site and receded upslope.[27]

Pounds suspects many mechanisms, from food availability to competition, are working to cause these upslope shifts. In fact, biotic interactions like these are thought to be important determinants and reinforcers of range boundaries in tropical mountains. Evidence suggests that competition between birds, such as aggressive interactions, can lead one species to replace another along elevational gradients. This has important implications under climate change. One hypothesis is that climate warming could allow a more aggressive lowland species to expand, causing higher-elevation, subordinate species to retreat into progressively smaller mountain top zones.[29] A possible reason for the local decline of cavity-nesting resplendent quetzals in Monteverde, for example, may be increased competition and predation due to the presence of keel-billed toucans (these toucans are both cavity nesters and nest predators).

Alternatively, if a higher-elevation bird is dominant, it could hypothetically prevent the subordinate species' upslope dispersal. In this way, middle-elevation birds could be held in check at their upper boundary, but squeezed by their upslope-contracting lower boundary if the climate conditions they require deteriorate. If dominant, high-elevation species are able to fend off the upslope movement of competitors, they may remain as 'kings of the hill' much longer than climate models alone suggest, according to Jill Jankowski and her colleagues at University of Florida. Should interactions like these prove important under climate change, many species could be affected. When threatened birds alone are considered, an estimated nine per cent of these are tropical mountain species with elevational ranges that border alongside those of widespread, lower-elevation species from the same genus.[29]

Returning to the climate threat for Monteverde's cloud forest, its future looks less misty still under the warmer, drier scenarios predicted by climate models for the region. Other tropical mountain cloud forests are expected to share Monteverde's problems of reduced cloud cover, less water capture and drier ecosystems. In the Wet Tropics of Queensland, for example, each degree Celsius of warming is predicted to be accompanied by a 100-metre upslope shift in the cloud base. By mid-century, should the climate warm by the expected 1.0–3.0°C, the mountain area in this bioregion receiving critical moisture from clouds could contract by up to 40 per cent.[30]

As this pattern is repeated around the world, bands of cloud forests would be replaced by habitats now found at lower altitudes. Those now on mountaintops would simply disappear. Ultimately, many cloud forests now cloaking mountain peaks may be consigned to extinction, with major implications for their diverse wildlife.[31]

Harried by fire on New Guinea

Hotter, drier conditions could also cause problems in New Guinea. This large and remarkably biodiverse tropical island harbours 708 species of birds, 47 per cent of them endemic. The implications of climate change for its rich birdlife are little understood, but recent observations of the Papuan harrier, *Circus spilothorax*, suggest fire is a growing threat.

Prior to 2007, only one Papuan harrier nest had ever been documented, and even the evolving classification of this bird epitomises a lack of knowledge surrounding species-rich tropical zones like New Guinea. The Papuan harrier has been treated as a subspecies of eastern marsh harrier, *Circus spilonotus*, a bird that almost never visits New Guinea. In 2007, University of Cape Town conservation biologist Rob Simmons led a research expedition to the island to learn more about threats to the Papuan harrier, and resolve its status as a separate and endemic species.

New Guinea's estimated 3600 Papuan harriers are thought to prefer grasslands and swamps, habitat found on just seven per cent of the island. During the dry season they breed in damp grassland and floodplains. In Papua New Guinea's swampy lowlands, Simmons and his colleagues recorded some of the first harrier ground nests, eggs, downy white chicks and likely food sources, and observed adults sky dancing – aerial courtship displays featuring acrobatic diving and spiralling.

Yet they also observed wildfires, up to 38 in one month, consume all the available grassland in their study area. The harriers, it turns out, are even attracted to fires to hunt fleeing prey. Within five weeks of discovering two Papuan harrier nests, the researchers found both destroyed by fires.[32] If all these raptors breed at the start of the dry season, as is believed, their nests will be vulnerable to grass fires. This is likely to be the greatest threat to their breeding success now and in the future. Thus fire is a double-edged sword, creating grassland habitat as it pushes back the tropical forest, yet consuming harrier nests as it goes. Because climate change could increase grassland fire frequency in a hotter, drier Papua New Guinea, accelerating its habitat loss, researchers suggest the Papuan harrier should now be listed as 'vulnerable'.[33] Sea-level rise, which could inundate low-lying grasslands and freshwater swamps, poses an additional potential threat.

Forest fires are extreme events that can dramatically reduce the density and productivity of tropical bird populations, and raze plants they rely on for food. Fires powerfully reshape birds' communities, and can trigger sudden collapses or shifts in ecosystems – one of many possible ecological surprises (chapter 5). Blazes also fuel climate change by releasing the vast quantities of carbon dioxide stored in forests. The fire-prone nature of tropical and subtropical vegetation is further exacerbated as humans fragment forests. On many islands, for example, forests have been converted into more flammable shrublands and grasslands.

Tropical forest fires are becoming larger, increasingly severe and more frequent even in forests where they were previously rare.[34,35] Tropical blazes are more severe during El Niño events, like the devastating 1997–98 South-East Asian wildfires that also swept through part of New Guinea. The hotter, drier conditions expected with climate change would increase forest fires dramatically this century, even with global warming of less than 2°C.

Splendid, but dangerous, isolation

Far from New Guinea, fire and drought are also affecting some forested oases of coolness in south-western USA and northern Mexico. The Madrean sky islands tower serenely above what is now lowland desert or prairie, but prior to 10 000 years ago was mostly woodland. As the climate warmed, lowlands were transformed into the grasslands and desert ecosystems found today, and pine-oak forests and cool-adapted species contracted upslope to cool refugia. As they did so, their subpopulations of plants and animals became increasingly fragmented and isolated.

Though geologically much younger than the timeless sky islands of Pantepui, these Madrean summits still have impressive stores of biodiversity. As stepping stones between the Sierra Madre massifs and the Rocky Mountains, the 35 Madrean sky island mountain ranges are at the nexus of temperate, tropical and subtropical climates. Their diversity reflects this collision of zones. Climbing one of these peaks, which may tower almost 2000 metres above valley floors, one might travel from the radiant heat of cactus-scattered, subtropical desert, through to arid oak woodlands, pine-oak forests and, in the loftiest, summits of cool, seasonally snowy, boreal conifer forest. On the way one can see both Neotropical and Nearctic birds.

Among them is the Mexican jay, *Aphelocoma ultramarina*, a blue–grey bird with pale breast and underparts. These jays are at the 'stay-at-home' extreme of North American birds in terms of dispersal capability. They rarely leave their natal flocks, and the exchange of individuals between different sky islands is thought to be infrequent or non-existent. Whereas the *arizonae* subspecies populates sky island archipelagos in south-eastern Arizona and northern Sonara, *couchii* birds are found in south-western Texas and northern Coahuila. Evidence suggests their populations diverged genetically 2.5 million years ago, and the different sky islands' archipelagos have played an important role in maintaining their distinction.[36]

Climate change could pose a unique and insurmountable threat to these sky islands, with devastating consequences for their present biodiversity, and for their potential to generate diversity in future. Changes including droughts, fire and invasive insect outbreaks are already radically altering the Madrean sky islands.[37] Their compressed diversity is sensitive to fire and drought; in the western USA the wildfire season has lengthened by 78 days in response to spring–summer warming of 0.87°C, and large fires are burning longer. In 2003, a month-long blaze consumed 343 square kilometres on Mount Lemmon, a sky island in the southern Arizona desert; another fire followed the next year.

Although Mexican jays are also found outside the Madrean sky islands (mainly in pine-oak woodlands of Mexico's highlands), their disappearance from isolated sky island populations would mean the loss of genetically distinct populations, reducing the species' overall diversity. A similar situation might exist for some birds of the Wet Tropics of Queensland. Among golden bowerbirds, songs of males from the same population are similar, and provoke aggressive displays in competitors. Yet songs of males from separate upland rainforest blocks are sufficiently different that birds fail to recognise these foreign dialects.[38] This implies an extent of isolation between these populations – although whether it also reflects their genetic isolation remains to be seen. Examples like these suggest how loss of isolated mountain populations could lead to reduced genetic diversity under climate change.

The climate threat to birds of islands

Under the volcano, the disease line creeps higher

On the Hawaiian Islands, the threat of an introduced disease suggests the complex ways global warming may affect island biodiversity. Like some other islands with large volcanoes, they feature mountains with climates ranging from almost tropical to alpine, helping explain why the Hawaiian Islands host 150 distinct ecosystems, rich in endemic species. Over time, a spectacular burst of adaptive radiation saw a single ancestral Hawaiian finch species evolve into more than 50 honeycreeper species (including those known only from fossils) filling virtually every possible songbird niche on the islands. The story of Hawaii's endemic honeycreepers has been called an evolutionary triumph – and an ecological tragedy.[39] At least 11 species have become extinct since their discovery by Europeans, and most of the 21 remaining honeycreeper species (tallies of extant species vary because some honeycreepers have not been seen sighted for a decade or more and may already be extinct) are threatened by habitat destruction, invasions of exotic species and a range of other human threats.

One pernicious honeycreeper threat is avian malaria. Caused by the parasitic protozoan, *Plasmodium relictum*, it is spread from bird to bird by the southern house mosquito, *Culex quinquefasciatus*, introduced to the formerly mosquito-free Hawaiian Islands in the early 1800s. This disease is thought to be responsible for native Hawaiian forest birds' relegation to higher elevations, where they find cool refuge from the disease. Mean summer temperatures lower than 17°C slow the parasite's development, making only seasonal transmission of avian malaria likely; at 13°C or lower, the parasite's development is inhibited and disease transmission stops. This may explain why native Hawaiian bird populations are densest at elevations of 1800 metres, corresponding to the 13°C isotherm.[40,41]

Warming, however, would cause the disease line to rise over the next century. Importantly, this would reduce optimal native bird habitat (the area above the 13°C isotherm). In this way, regional warming of 2°C, a level in keeping with climate-change predictions, could cause a 57 per cent reduction in bird habitat in the Hanawi Forest on the island of Maui, and a massive 96 per cent reduction in the Hakalau National Wildlife Refuge on Hawaii.[41] These reserves have some of the Hawaiian islands' largest remaining tracts of protected forest.

At a third important forest refuge, the Alakai Swamp region on Kauai, there is currently no area free of malaria. Protected lands top out at 1600 metres in a broad plateau where disease transmission should now be limited (corresponding to the 13–17°C isotherm). Expected warming would reduce this current habitat by 85 per cent. As temperatures rise, Kauai's endemic honeycreepers will have no higher ground to move to. Their populations are expected to decline or become extinct within this century, unless steps are taken to manage the disease.

Returning to Hakalau Wildlife Refuge, climate change may combine with human land use to create another challenge for this sanctuary on Hawaii. The area above the refuge has been used as cattle pasture, and almost no native forest remains. Unless the forest is restored, upslope dispersal may be impossible for honeycreepers there. Affected birds include an endemic to this single island, the rare and declining akiapolaau, *Hemignathus munroi*. With its curious mismatched bill, this honeycreeper exploits the island's woodpecker niche to prey on insects, but also feeds on nectar and sap.

Taken together, these challenges illustrate how several of the remaining honeycreepers could become extinct under this climate scenario. In fact, avian malaria prevalence may have already doubled during the 1990s to 5.4 per cent in a sample of forest birds at 1900 metres in the Hakalau reserve, in association with the presence of breeding mosquitoes and warmer summer temperatures.[42]

Avian malaria is also found in other world regions, and if warming permits it to move into new areas, it could threaten birds that lack evolutionary experience with the disease. Yet there are few long-term studies to help gauge this threat. Nonetheless, the case of Hawaiian honeycreepers emphasises how, quite apart from direct climate-change effects, birds of cool mountain refuges may ride an escalator to extinction on the back of complex interactions with pests and disease.

Why stay-at-home islanders may be at sea

Birds offer us one of the best means of determining the law of distribution; for though at first sight it would appear that the watery boundaries which keep out land quadrupeds could be easily passed over by birds, yet practically it is not so ... [they] are often as strictly limited by straits and arms of the sea as are quadrupeds themselves.

Alfred Russel Wallace, 1869

The Berthelot's pipit, *Anthus berthelotii*, suggests how dispersal challenges could be important climate-change threats to island wildlife. Though it is a small, plain-looking, grey–white bird, the Berthelot's pipit has the distinction of being one of the few island endemics with some sort of climate-change prognosis. Named after Sabin Berthelot, a 19th-century French naturalist and ethnologist who studied the Canary Islands' natural history, this small songbird is restricted to the North Atlantic's Madeira, Canary and Selvagens islands, lying off the coast of north-west Africa.

This pipit has persisted on the islands since it colonised them 2.5 million years ago, marking its separation from its closest relative, the tawny pipit, *Anthus campestris*. However, climate models suggest the future climate of its current range will be unlike that experienced at any time in its evolutionary history, according to *A Climatic Atlas of European Breeding Birds*. Moreover no habitat of a similar climate will exist anywhere in Europe.

Even if habitat of suitable climate did exist on continental Africa or Europe, this very sedentary bird's isolation could pose a severe extinction risk under climate change. Despite the presence of similar habitat on the African coast 160 kilometres distant, nary a Berthelot's pipit has been recorded there. This raises wider questions about the climate-change threat to range-restricted island endemic birds. Island species' legacy of isolation may leave them poorly equipped to track climate change.[43] Even if they can disperse to appropriate habitat on neighbouring mainlands, suitable niches may already be occupied by sister species.

Wildlife on islands, and especially small islands, faces a range of global warming threats. Island-breeding seabirds are vulnerable to reproductive crashes linked to ocean warming events (chapter 4). Sea-level rise, coupled with more extreme weather events, is expected to cause coastal flooding and reduce the extent of coastal wetlands on small islands. Increases in extreme weather, including possibly higher numbers of the most intense tropical cyclones (chapter 5), could destroy tropical island forests. These forests may be small in extent, slow to regenerate and already degraded by a range of human influences.

The IPCC is 'virtually certain' that warming will step up invasions of islands by exotic species at mid and high latitudes where colder conditions formerly discouraged them. This already appears to be happening on islands. Native island species may be particularly vulnerable because their isolation has provided them with little evolutionary experience of new predators or competitors. Their tendency to have lower genetic diversity could also make them vulnerable to changes in their ecosystems. Some argue that this legacy of isolation will make island species, and especially those of oceanic islands, acutely vulnerable to the brunt of climate change.[43]

The climate threat to birds of forest fragments

Flightless and fruitless after the storm

Moving from oceanic islands to forest fragments, the case of the southern cassowary, *Casuarius casuarius*, suggests how climate change could ramp up the threat to tropical birds that already suffer from degraded, fractured habitat. This very large and flightless bird surely ranks high on any list of avian oddities. It stands up to two metres tall, on three-toed feet equipped with dagger-shaped inner toe claws. It has strong muscular legs, draping black body plumage and a naked neck of vivid blue (brighter still when aroused), complemented by long red wattles. Its blue head is crowned with a tall, soft and spongy helmet, or casque. When cornered it may kick out with both feet but usually flees, head lowered, into the rainforest at speeds reaching 40 kilometres per hour. Territorial and solitary, this ratite depends on dense tropical rainforest habitat that provides fleshy fruit throughout the year and permanent sources of freshwater for daily drinking and bathing (cassowaries can swim).

The southern cassowary is found in New Guinea, and in northern Australia as the *johnsonii* subspecies. A population in the Wet Tropics of Queensland is considered endangered, with fewer than 1200 adults remaining, but it also occurs further north in Australia's Cape York Peninsula, where it probably numbers fewer than 400 animals and is considered vulnerable.

Southern cassowaries are essential to the functioning of Australian rainforests because they eat fallen fruit whole and distribute the seeds across the jungle floor via their droppings. The female southern cassowary is larger and dominates the male, consorting with as many as two or three males in a breeding season. It falls to males to incubate the large, glossy, pale green eggs until they hatch after about 54 days. Males also care for the young over the three to six months they need to become independent.

Raising chicks and surviving has become more challenging since rainforest clearing severely fragmented their lowland habitat. Seventy-five per cent of former cassowary habitat has been removed, wiping out some local populations and threatening others. The majority of the remaining coastal cassowary habitat south of Cairns comprises a discontinuous band of vegetation on narrow coastal ranges. Moreover, extensive agricultural clearing and a major highway isolate this habitat from the main rainforest block of the Wet Tropics World Heritage Area to the west. This is the predicament facing a small population of cassowaries at Mission Beach, studied by Les Moore of Australia's James Cook University.

During the year 2000, Moore estimated that 110 cassowaries roamed the 130-square-kilometre Mission Beach study area, about two-thirds of them identified as adults or subadults. Because the adult cassowaries have a minimum home range of 4–6 square kilometres, about two-thirds of them crossed Mission Beach roads regularly, some of them three or four times per day. Consequently, vehicle collision was responsible for approximately 70 per cent of all known cassowary deaths, with up to four birds killed each year in this area. The rapidly increasing human population introduced another significant threat to cassowaries: the pet dog. Twenty-one per cent of known cassowary deaths are caused by dog attacks.

Then in March 2006, the severe tropical cyclone Larry struck this region. Gusts of up to 240 kilometres per hour severely damaged the forest canopy, snapping tree trunks, defoliating plants and knocking fruit and flowers to the ground. Foraging cassowaries were restricted to small paths through the debris and vines, and the fallen fruit was generally buried by debris and unavailable to the birds. The forest canopy and fruiting levels had still not recovered three years after the cyclone.[44]

Moore found that, in the first 12 months following the cyclone, known cassowary mortality in the Mission Beach area quadrupled over pre-cyclone levels, with 14 adults and subadults lost from this population in a single year. Almost all dependent chicks disappeared, presumed killed during the cyclone or soon after due to starvation. Sightings of cassowaries crossing Mission Beach roads decreased 75 per cent in the three years after the cyclone. Although changes in their behaviour may have been responsible, a more likely explanation is a significant decline in the cassowary population post-cyclone Larry.[45]

Moore concluded that this severe cyclone had a twofold effect on the small Mission Beach cassowary population. The primary effects were an increase in adult and subadult cassowary mortality, the death of all dependent chicks, and habitat destruction. The secondary effects included the immediate loss of food resources in the short to medium term, a significant reduction in their environment's carrying capacity, and an increase in malnutrition and disease in this weakened population. While it is possible that the total number of tropical cyclones may decrease in the Australian region, several models project an increase in the proportion of severe tropical cyclones. If this causes the quality of the remaining lowland cassowary habitat south of Cairns to decline further, it would lower an already reduced carrying capacity for cassowaries.

A small population can die out entirely by chance even when its members are healthy and its environment stable. However, the iconic Mission Beach cassowary population must also withstand habitat loss from burgeoning human development, excessive mortality from vehicle strikes and dog attacks, isolation from the other larger cassowary populations, and a possible increase in the proportion of severe cyclones. Cassowaries at Mission Beach appear to face an uncertain future. In February 2011, another severe cyclone, Yasi, devastated cassowary habitat in the Mission Beach area. Tropical birds elsewhere, especially those on coasts and islands, may also be vulnerable to the destructive effects of tropical cyclones. Even if they can cope with the effects of warming, their populations may succumb to extinction if intense cyclones destroy critical habitats, especially vegetation that is slow to regenerate.[4]

Recent research on hurricane-affected areas in the USA indicates that whereas some birds are relatively resilient to this disturbance (such as cavity nesters), others are not (for example, those that nest in forest canopies). It also suggests that the presence of intact forests nearby, but outside the hurricane path, become important alternate refuges for some species, such as canopy dwellers, that are adversely affected by these storms.[46]

Fragmentation problem heats up

The case of Mission Beach cassowaries demonstrates how habitat fragmentation creates problems for forest-dependent birds. Almost two-thirds of the world's bird species are found in forest habitats, mainly in the tropics where a high proportion of threatened bird species are concentrated. Moreover, many of these birds are fully dependent on forests. Yet in tropical and subtropical regions, forests are rapidly disappearing, most notably in Africa and South America. Extinction rates in the tropics are now at their most rapid, even as climate-change influences on all forests increase.[47]

After forests are cleared, remaining forest fragments cannot, in many cases, adequately host communities of birds and other species. Patch size is a critical factor. In the Brazilian Amazon, in places where deforestation has fragmented forests into patches of less than 100 hectares, only 15 years need pass before half the forest-dependent bird species in these patches are lost.[48] Habitat fragmentation increases the distance between isolated populations or subpopulations, reducing their opportunity to connect and exchange individuals and genes. 'Rescue effects' may occur if individuals are able to disperse from densely populated areas to low-density patches, reducing the chance of local extinctions. Yet where habitat fragmentation increases the isolation of patches, the chance for rescue effects is reduced. In a similar way, fully depopulated but suitable forest fragments are also less likely to be recolonised if habitat is fragmented and isolated. Tropical forest understorey birds in fragments seem to disperse little, avoid forest edges, gaps and open habitats, and rarely use the deforested areas around these patches. Taken together, factors like these explain why fragmentation increases the likelihood that a local population will become extinct, and why tropical forest understorey birds are extremely sensitive to this type of disturbance.[49]

Climate change will exacerbate these stresses by driving shifts in birds' ranges. As already emphasised, shifting and contracting ranges could serve to further fragment birds' ranges in tropical forests, especially on mountainous terrain. Birds of tropical mountain forests may be unable to venture across farmland, and other hot, bright and open landscapes, to disperse from one mountain zone to another.

Range shifts driven by climate change could also create problems where forests end in natural barriers or otherwise hostile habitats, effectively blocking forest birds' escape routes. In Central Africa, the tropical rainforest range of violet-tailed sunbirds terminates where savannah begins (chapter 3). Similarly, stay-at-home species like Mexican jays are unlikely to cross large expanses of very different habitats like desert lowlands.

Forests, stressed and diminished, may not keep up

Apart from these destructive synergies with forest fragmentation, how will climate change affect trees, the plants that structure the habitats and underpin the ecology of the majority of the world's birds?

Because tree distributions are strongly influenced by climate, changes in temperature, rainfall and evapotranspiration could affect them in important ways. These effects are still not well understood. Despite some reports that tropical forests are becoming more productive, individual tropical lowland trees in Costa Rica, have been shown to grow more slowly when the mean annual temperature is higher.[50] Studies of forests there, and in Panama and Malaysia, suggest that tropical tree growth rate is already slowing. Water balance may be even more important for tropical forests than warming, but uncertainties about future rainfall changes under global warming make it difficult to predict how these will modify forests. On tropical mountains, forests may dry out and be replaced by lower montane or non-montane plants. Climate modelling suggests that, as soil moisture declines, Amazon forests will become increasingly dry and die back.[51]

In mountains, trees may generally be unable to track shifting climate zones. In Amazonia, one study of 69 flowering plants (angiosperms) suggests that because 43 per cent of these species would be unable to track the radical distribution shifts that may be required, they would no longer be viable by 2095 under climate change.[52] Boreal forests will be under threat from intensified insect infestations, and increased fire frequency will be a general problem for these and other types of forests. In fact, modelling indicates that tropical, mountain and boreal forest habitats could die back significantly towards the end of this century due to climate change. Increased storm frequency will also affect forests.

The negative effects of fragmentation and isolation, already discussed for birds' ranges, also hold for trees. Even vast forests like the Amazon are well known to be fragmented. Although many plant species kept pace by making rapid responses during past eras of climatic change, today's human-altered landscapes pose a great obstacle to their capacity to successfully migrate. This could diminish or eliminate many of the means plants might use to respond to the rapid global warming now underway. The combined effects of these new climate-change stresses, imposed on the planet's already dwindling and fragmented tropical forests, is expected to create extensive conservation challenges.[53]

Beyond their ecological role, tropical forests have a 'climate-making' role. Forests in the Amazon basin make its western zone considerably moister than it would be otherwise, because they recycle moisture entering this ecosystem from the tropical Atlantic. If a significant portion of these forests were cleared or lost due to climate change, regional drying could trigger further forest loss.[53] Forest trees and soils also sequester roughly 2.2 times as much carbon as is now found in the atmosphere, and this highlights another reason for concern about forest degradation. Whether it results from climate-change effects or deforestation, the release of this stored carbon could further fuel global warming (chapter 7).

Novel climates and the threat to tropical lowlands

No community of species, now living in even hotter places, is available to replace tropical lowland species that shift upslope with climate change ...

Robert Colwell et al., 2008

We have explored the global warming threat of climates that disappear off tropical mountaintops, but what about tropical lowlands? The case of manakins, the Pipridae, suggests what may be in store. This family of small, fruit-eating birds is found in lowland rainforests and other tropical forests of Latin America. Research on 49 manakin and allied species revealed that those of flatland Amazon basin and cerrado habitats would be hardest hit, losing 80 per cent of their habitable area if they cannot disperse; 20 per cent of cerrado manikins could become extinct from this biome under climates projected for the mid-21st century.[54]

Novel climates are expected to concentrate in the tropics and subtropics, and the greatest discrepancies between present and future novel climates are expected to occur in Amazonian and Indonesian rainforests. These areas will become warmer than any climate is currently, and may also experience changes to their precipitation patterns.[55]

To keep up with climate change, plants and animals of some extensive lowland tropical biomes would need to disperse at some of the highest expected rates. This includes the species living in mangroves, flooded grasslands and deserts.[56] In the flat expanses of the Sahara Desert, for example, populations would need to disperse far greater distances to track climate change compared to those that are able to realise upslope shifts in mountainous areas.

Even if tropical lowland species are able to disperse to higher elevations or latitudes, what would take their place? Some species may already be approaching the upper limits of their tolerance for heat. Yet there are no communities currently adapted to life in hotter zones to replace those of tropical lowlands. A study on 1902 species of epiphytes, understorey plants, moths and ants in Costa Rica revealed that 53 per cent of these species, those found at the lowest elevations, could be lost from these areas due to possible range shifts and lowland extinctions driven by 3.2°C of warming.[16]

This estimate could prove overly pessimistic should these species be able to find cooler or wetter refuges at their current elevation. On the other hand, it could be optimistic if drying and more frequent fires worsen the brunt of climate change. In tropical lowlands, plants tolerant to heat or drought and adapted to fire could take over, fostering no-analogue communities and ecological surprises (chapter 3). Taken together, these observations explain why some argue that tropical lowland species will be threatened by climate-change-induced range shifts in the near term.[16]

Unknowns and challenges

Despite commanding greater attention in recent years, the threat of climate change to life in the tropics, where biodiversity is highest, is still relatively unexplored. This shortfall is starkly reflected in the IPCC's coverage of 28 586 data series that assess changes in land-based species with global warming; a mere 39 of these series come from regions outside Europe and North America. Lack of knowledge about tropical species frustrates efforts to conserve the world's birds, and even impedes progress in ornithology, ecology and conservation biology. Without more long-term studies of tropical birds, the current focus on temperate species will continue to bias our outlook on climate-change effects.

High on the list of important knowledge gaps is the lack of information on potential range shifts of tropical birds. Their upslope dispersal is likely to be underway in many tropical regions, yet very few attempts have been made to measure this. Also scarce are the baseline data needed to make such measurements, including precise information about the elevational limits of birds' ranges. These kinds of data are especially critical to determine the risk to tropical species now found within narrow bands of elevation. The mapped ranges of many range-restricted, threatened and specialised species are overestimates in many cases, and this could lead to their climate-change extinction risk being underestimated (chapter 3).

In the forests that underpin the lives of so many tropical birds, potential changes to precipitation may be even more important than warming, but these are difficult to predict. The typically complex interactions among species of tropical ecosystems are also poorly understood, making it very challenging to gauge outcomes for biodiverse habitats like tropical mountain cloud forests. A lack of detail on how tropical forests responded to climatic change in the past – even major forests such as the Amazon – adds to these challenges. Even less understood is how climate change may affect tropical coastal habitats, such as mangroves and wetlands. As for islands, despite their historic legacy of extinctions and high proportions of endemic and threatened birds, very few attempts have been made to assess the vulnerability of their wildlife to climate change.

Conclusion

There may persist a view that the tropics will be spared the severe effects of climate change, but growing evidence suggests otherwise. The world's tropical zones host the highest levels of biodiversity, but they are also experiencing the highest rates of deforestation and extinction, even as climate-change effects on them mount. The arrival of novel climates may reshuffle communities and produce ecological surprises in Earth's most species-rich zones.

Some tropical species have characteristics likely to increase their vulnerability to climate change, including a possibly greater sensitivity to warming and a tendency to have small ranges, a particular issue for the relatively large numbers of narrow-range tropical endemics. Elevational, rather than latitudinal, shifts appear to be the main response of tropical bird distributions to climate warming so far, and upslope shifts are also expected to predominate in the future. But it is increasingly clear that complex effects are likely. Birds, in their ranges, are likely to respond not only to altered temperature and precipitation, but also to changes in competition and the productivity of their environments, along with other biotic and abiotic factors.

Species-rich mountains are increasingly important refuges for endemics retreating from wide-ranging human influences. Already facing human encroachment from lowlands, mountain biodiversity will face a double jeopardy where climate warming imperils highland populations. Climate warming could also effectively place bird species on an escalator to extinction, where their habitat with suitable climate fragments, contracts and even vanishes off ridgelines, plateaus and mountain peaks. When elevational limits to their ranges are factored in, estimates of the climate-change extinction threat to birds increase greatly. Suitable habitat may be available in other highland areas, but upland bird populations might be disinclined to cross barriers of dissimilar habitat or simply be unable to disperse the distance required. Tropical mountain cloud forests – unique, rare and threatened – are the most vulnerable of all tropical forests to climate change. Loss of moisture input from clouds is expected to consign many of these biodiverse ecosystems to extinction, with major implications for their endemic populations.

Endemic-rich islands also have high proportions of threatened species. Like mountain birds, many island birds face large dispersal barriers, and could lack the capacity to traverse oceans or seas to track climate change. Islands also face a range of other climate threats including sea-level rise, more frequent and intense extreme weather, and heightened risk of exotic species invasions.

Almost two-thirds of the world's birds are found in forests, mainly tropical forests where high proportions of threatened species are concentrated. Forest fragmentation is expected to reduce the means by which plants kept up with past periods of rapid climatic change. By imposing new stresses on already degraded tropical forests, climate change will combine with habitat loss to create a major conservation challenge.

Chapter 7

SHIFTING GROUND ON CONSERVATION

Assessing birds' capacity to adapt to climate change

In a changed Everglades, more alteration looms

Rising sea levels are erasing familiar boundaries. In fact, conservationists may find themselves fighting for lands that will soon be under water.

Conservation Magazine, 2009

The evolving story of the Everglades in Florida, USA illustrates the difficult choices conservationists may face as global warming drives change and breeds uncertainty. In former times, Lake Okeechobee overflowed its banks during the annual wet season, feeding a vast, shallow sheet of fresh water that ambled slowly seawards for about 160 kilometres. In some areas the wetlands it created were almost as broad as the Florida peninsula itself. Lying at the confluence of temperate and subtropical realms, they still host explosive bird diversity. Pink-bodied roseate spoonbills, *Platalea ajaja*, snowy egrets, *Egretta thula*, and rare and endangered wood storks, *Mycteria americana*, are among the more than 350 species counted in the Everglades. This is, in fact, North America's most significant breeding ground for wading birds.

'They were changeless. They are changed,' wrote Marjory Stoneman Douglas, who dedicated her life to trying preserve the Everglades. Change began with flood control efforts in 1882, and over the next century this timeless 'river of grass' was reduced by half, its marshlands drained for agriculture and development. Although John James Audubon had once described flocks of waders so great they could 'actually block out the light from the sun for some time', bird abundance has plummeted by 90 per cent.

Now US government agencies are working to reverse this ecological tragedy by restoring freshwater flows. Mangrove forests, cypress swamps and other watery ecosystems will be rebuilt, and canals and levees removed. The expected cost is around US$12 billion over more than 30 years – the largest ecological restoration in history. Yet because much of Everglades National Park lies less than two metres above sea level, some are asking, 'Is it cost-effective to spend billions of dollars "restoring" the Everglades, when they may soon disappear beneath the sea?'[1] With one metre of sea-level rise, almost all Florida Keys and southern Everglades ecosystems would be severely reduced. Money may be better spent, they say, on strategies that assist species to retreat landwards and upslope. Others assert that restoring the wetlands is the best way to tackle climate change, and that strengthening freshwater flows would help to oppose salty ocean water influx into the ecosystem. The wide uncertainty about how much sea levels will rise makes restoration all the more important; this was the conclusion of an independent 2008 review.

Coastal wetlands are increasingly squeezed between the devil and the deep blue sea – between rising seas and encroaching human development. Those seeking to preserve wetlands face fraught choices, as do those aiming to conserve other vulnerable ecosystems. In the USA, for example, even though 59 per cent of species' recovery plans made between 2005 and 2008 addressed global warming as an extinction threat, government agencies have not responded with any national strategy, leaving a lack of guidance. Nonetheless, one widely accepted point is the need to help ecosystems adapt. A level of climate change is inevitable even if greenhouse gas emissions were to cease immediately. If this impact is not addressed, efforts to conserve birds will fall short. This reality demands a new era of conservation strategies to help smooth the way for inevitable change.

Researchers and conservation managers will be indispensable to this effort, but the public can also help. As an inclusive field, ornithology has always placed high importance on the participation of amateurs. In fact, non-professionals have permitted ornithology to contribute to ecology and conservation biology to an extent unmatched by the study of other animal groups. From reporting birds seen in backyards to joining a work party to restore bird habitat, the ways to help birds adapt to climate change are many.

With their climate tolerances pushed, can birds adapt?

But first, how might birds cope with climate change without the help of further conservation efforts? As already emphasised (chapter 3), the palaeontological record shows that range shifts were the predominant response of terrestrial species during past eras of rapid climatic shifts, and genetic adaptation was generally slow-paced and played a minor role. In future, to what extent could birds adapt to the rapid climate change now underway, unassisted by conservation efforts? The answer will depend on the resilience of their ecosystems and on the intrinsic capacity of each species to adapt.

Ecosystems vary in their capacity to resist long-lasting change caused by disturbances. Resilience is boosted by biological diversity, refugia and connectivity (we will come to this shortly). On the other hand, ecosystem resilience is drawn down where human activity erodes biodiversity and fragments habitats.

As in the past, birds may cope with global warming by dispersing to track suitable climatic and ecological conditions. Or they may adapt via changes in behaviour or physiology, or through evolutionary (genetic) change. Over the short term the former types of changes are expected to be most important. These adaptive responses, many already described, may include flexible behaviours like breeding earlier to track food supplies or modifying foraging strategies. Birds may also acclimate, retreat to small refugia, or change the type of habitat or microhabitat they use, for example, by seeking out shady, cool spots in the landscape. Adaptive behaviour may be as simple as avoiding activity during the heat of the day (most birds already do this, and the need to avoid longer periods of heat may curtail the time they can forage.)

The mechanisms some species have evolved to cope with unpredictable climates could also foster adaptation to climate change.[2] These traits may include morphological changes (some birds can shrink their guts, for example), energy-saving mechanisms like torpor, hibernation and energy storage (such as fattening or hoarding food), and the fine-tuning of breeding efforts to suit environmental conditions (as seen in opportunistic breeders like some zebra finches, or African birds that follow rains and breed just after the rain front passes). Hypothetically, species that possess these traits could have a selective advantage as climates become increasingly unstable. Nonetheless, the extent to which flexible behavioural and physiological responses like these can help birds cope with climate change is still unknown.

Turning to genetic responses, global warming is expected to put almost all of terrestrial life under intense selection pressure, and could dominate evolution this century and beyond.[3] In fact, birds and other organisms may already be adapting to climate change through inherited traits. This appears to be the most plausible explanation for the radically altered migration programming of some blackcaps, *Sylvia atricapilla*. A subpopulation of blackcaps breeding in central Europe has increasingly travelled to Britain to overwinter, instead of making a longer trip to Iberia. Interestingly, this British-wintering subpopulation is genetically distinct. It is programmed to migrate in this new direction, a change that constitutes an evolutionary shift.[4] Staying in Britain, where winters have become milder and shorter, saves these birds energy and time, and allows them to arrive earlier at breeding grounds to capture the best territories or mates.

Genetic change in migratory activity may occur surprisingly quickly, experiments suggest. When strong selection pressure for lower migratory activity in blackcaps is simulated in a completely migratory population, the first non-migratory individuals are found after only two generations under these artificial conditions.[5] Shorter migrations, some theorise, are the first and most significant way for such birds to evolve in response to global warming. This strategy could be a successful one for birds with genetically programmed migration behaviour, and that migrate short to medium distances (averaging 1000 km), as do many songbirds. But shortened trip length is unlikely to help birds migrating over ocean or desert barriers; if they stop short, they could find themselves in hostile environments.

Other possible demonstrations of birds' genetic responses to warming are thin on the ground. One avenue of inquiry centres on birds' conformity to Bergmann's rule. This well-known biogeographical tenet holds that, among warm-blooded animals, races from warm regions are smaller than the races from cold regions. It begs the question: will bird populations adapt to warming through reductions in their average body mass? Climate change was named the most likely cause for declining body size in some birds over the past century in Australia, and in recent decades in Europe and North America. In the USA, one study looked at measurements of both body mass and wing chord length (the distance between a bird's 'wrist' and tip of the longest primary feather) for almost half a million birds from 102 species over the 1961–2007 period. Many birds (mostly songbirds) displayed steady reductions; the higher the regional temperature during the previous year, the smaller the body and wing size.[6] Efforts continue to establish whether changes like these are indeed a response to climate change.[7]

Regardless, demonstrating a genetic response to climate change in wild birds is difficult. It requires measuring their fitness in the wild, and data on both parents and offspring. Whether or not climate change has already caused evolutionary change in birds is a debate likely to continue. This scarcity of valid evidence of evolution in concert with warming extends to genetic changes that would allow species to better tolerate heat.[8,9]

Yet even their ability to evolve in response to climate change is no guarantee a bird population will persist.[9] By the century's end, the global climate will probably be warmer than many of today's species experienced over the course of their evolution. Moreover, in many regions the rate of warming is also likely to be faster than today's biota have experienced. Considering the relatively minor role played by genetic evolution in past eras of rapid climatic shifts, there is scant evidence to suggest that many species can evolve sufficiently to retain their present-day ranges in the face of the current rapid pace of climate change.

Identifying at-risk birds

Conservationists must ask, 'which species are most vulnerable to climate change, and why?' Answers may be elusive. Information on specific climate-change threats to individual bird species and their ecosystems is lacking. Progress is being made as new indices and criteria are developed, like the IUCN's work to identify birds susceptible to climate change (chapter 5). A 'potentially threatened by climate change' classification should be considered for the Red List.[10] As climate-change impacts intensify, they could threaten many birds not yet considered at risk, like the upland endemics of Queensland's Wet Tropics (chapter 6), and to exacerbate the risk to threatened species. Tallies of climate-change susceptible birds will probably lengthen the list of species targeted for conservation.

Managing climate-change stressors in bird habitats

Tackling combined threats on Turkey's plateau

New conservation efforts will be needed to manage the climate-change threat to bird species. But as the case of Lake Kuyucuk in north-east Turkey shows, strategies already used to conserve birds may also help. An Important Bird Area and eastern Turkey's only Ramsar wetland, Lake Kuyucuk lies on a high, undulating plateau. It hosts at least 220 bird species, including globally endangered white-headed ducks, *Oxyura leucocephala*, whose males have striking, pale blue beaks. The lake also provides a vital stopover and refuelling site for migrants. Though overgrazing by livestock is the main threat to these birds, climate change may already be having considerable effects. Climate-change scenarios predict more rain for the region and faster spring snowmelt, which may explain recent events including torrential, unseasonal rains and floods.

Although Lake Kuyucuk is a protected wildlife reserve, local people graze their livestock at its shores. Reeds and other plants that provide good bird habitat have been eaten away. Wedged between thousands of cattle on a treeless steppe, sheepdogs, foxes and a fluctuating shoreline, bird nests are at risk from the slightest change in water levels. This includes crucial nesting and foraging habitat for thousands of ruddy shelduck, *Tadorna ferruginea*, rarely seen in Europe.

Despite its problems, the lake is an ideal candidate for wetland restoration because, unusually in Turkey, it has low levels of chemical pollution (although this may be changing with increasing fertiliser use in the region). In 2009, the KuzeyDoğa Society, a research and conservation organisation founded by Çağan Şekercioğlu, turned one of the lake's problems into a major asset. A thirty-year-old dirt road, about two metres above water level, bisected the lake at its north end, upsetting its natural water regime. With the help of local villagers, conservation scientists and the local government, they removed 50 metres of dirt from each end of the road to create an artificial island. Planting almost 100 birches, willows and other steppe wetland trees further improved the new island, providing vital breeding habitat for hundreds of birds.

(**Right**) Survival of king penguins at Possession Island in the Crozet Archipelago declined about 9 per cent in association with 0.26°C of sea surface warming. The warmer the surface waters, the fewer the fish near Crozet. Image: © Jean Patrice Robin - CNRS/DEPE

Figure 3 Numbers of additional world landbird species projected to be committed to extinction by 2100 under different climate warming and habitat loss scenarios and no conservation action. For each estimate of warming (based on IPCC 2007 projections), four habitat loss scenarios are included (based on four Millennium Assessment habitat-change scenarios; see colour key). The effects of three possible shifts in the lower elevational limit of bird species' ranges are also shown; the coloured bars show the results of an intermediate amount of elevational shift, and the superimposed dark grey bars span the effects of the best-case (none of lowland (< 500 m) species move upslope) and worst-case (all species move upslope) scenarios of climate warming. Source: Şekercioğlu C.H. et al. (2008) Climate change, elevational range shifts, and bird extinctions. Conservation Biology 22(1):140–150.

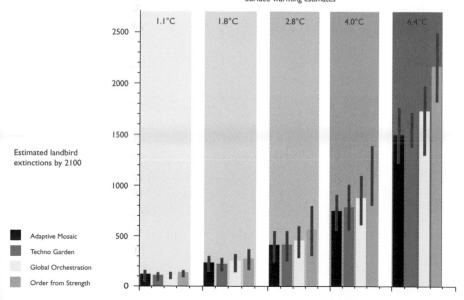

(**Above**) A Galápagos of the mainland: Gran Sabana in Venezuela is part of Pantepui, a legendary realm of table-top sky islands, separated by lowland savannah or forest. Climate change could drive very high local extinctions among native plant species that many Pantepui birds depend upon. Image: Çağan Şekercioğlu

(**Below**) Avian architect. The endemic golden bowerbird of Queensland's Wet Tropics builds towers up to three metres high to impress females and outshine competitors. The area with the climate of this bowerbird's cool upland habitat could contract almost 98 per cent with 3°C of climate warming. Image: © Thomas Rayner

(**Above left**) In Australia, large, flightless southern cassowaries are threatened by loss and fragmentation of their rainforest habitat. They are also vulnerable to severe cyclones, which could become more intense with climate change. Image: Çağan Şekercioğlu

(**Above right**) At the Monteverde cloud forest in Costa Rica, keel-billed toucans (normally intolerant of cloud forests) have extended their range upslope into the domain of cloud forest birds like the resplendent quetzal (shown here), in step with a drying trend. Rare, unique and biodiverse, many tropical mountain cloud forests could be consigned to extinction with climate change. Image: Çağan Şekercioğlu

(Above) A rainforest gorge near Monteverde Reserve, Costa Rica. Image: Çağan Şekercioğlu

(Inset) A keel-billed toucan. Image: Çağan Şekercioğlu

(**Below**) Recent changes to blackcaps' migratory routes provide some of the strongest signs of evolution in response to climate change. Image: Çağan Şekercioğlu

(**Bottom**) The Florida Everglades National Park, a hotspot for bird diversity, mostly lies less than two metres above sea level. Expected sea level rise with global warming complicates major efforts to restore this 'river of grass'. Image: Çağan Şekercioğlu

(**Top**) A green heron, *Butorides virescens*, hunting in the Florida Everglades. One metre of sea level rise would severely reduce almost all Florida Keys and southern Everglades ecosystems. Image: Çağan Şekercioğlu

(**Above**) Shade coffee plantations like this one, Finca El Jaguar in Nicaragua, may resemble native forest closely enough that their bird diversity is almost as high. Already important alternatives to sun coffee monoculture, shade plantations and other efforts to make human-altered habitat more bird-friendly could help wildlife disperse across the landscape to track climate change. Image: Çağan Şekercioğlu

(**Top**) Fire smoulders in eastern Papua New Guinea's Ramu Valley, beyond grassland favoured by the Papuan harrier. In 2007, fire destroyed some of the first Papuan harrier nests recorded by researchers. Tropical forest fires are increasingly frequent and severe, a trend expected to continue in many regions this century. Image: Rob Simmons

(**Above**) At Turkey's Lake Kuyucuk, the conservation group KuzeyDoğa Society, begun by Çağan Şekercioğlu, turned a disused roadway into an island. It will provide safe new habitat for nesting birds that were otherwise sandwiched between changing lake levels and grazing cattle on a treeless steppe. Image: Çağan Şekercioğlu

(**Above**) Corn field on deforested land in Sulawesi, Indonesia. At the tropics, both bird diversity and numbers of subsistence farmers are highest. Highly vulnerable to climate change, these farmers have limited coping capacity and may come under pressure to cultivate and degrade more marginal land and forests, driving further biodiversity loss.
Image: Çağan Şekercioğlu

(**Below**) Gouldian finches feeding on seeds of native spinifex grass in Australia. Historically, fire regimes promoted diverse native grasses that provide food for these finches across the year. Invasive gamba grass, however, chokes out native grasses. This exotic grass both promotes and is promoted by fire in a process that can transform ecosystems. With climate change invasive species are expected to become more common and spread more widely.
Image: Steve Murphy/Australian Wildlife Conservancy

The case of Lake Kuyucuk demonstrates how climate change could be superimposed on conservation challenges including the evil quartet: habitat destruction, introduced species, overexploitation and chains of extinction (chapter 5). Combined, these threats create synergies that severely ramp up the risk to birds and compromise efforts to conserve them. On the other hand, reducing non-climate threats can enhance the resilience of species and ecosystems and lessen their chances of succumbing to these 'threat cocktails'. Moreover, as efforts at Lake Kuyucuk suggest, it is possible to tackle climate-change stresses with strategies already used to conserve birds.

Reducing stresses to vulnerable habitats including wetlands, mountains, islands and coasts will be important to sustain ecosystem health. In many protected areas, work is already done to reduce non-climate stressors – efforts that may need bolstering with climate change. Outside protected areas, where habitat destruction is now the top biodiversity threat, degraded landscapes would need to be protected and repaired to increase their resilience to climate change.

Dynamic approaches for landscapes in flux

Managing for climate change is like learning to hit a moving target – it means that more nimble and innovative responses are required . . .

Lee Hannah & Rod Salm, 2005

At Albemarle and Pamlico Sounds, conservationists who have glimpsed the future are preparing for the inevitable, but staying flexible. In North Carolina a 320-kilometre coastal string of natural barrier islands, the Outer Banks, forms a massive closed lagoon. Even modest sea-level rise (18 centimetres) would degrade this healthiest and second-largest of the USA's estuaries, while a 60-centimetre rise would submerge much of the seaward portion of Albemarle Peninsula, most of which is under conservation.[11] In fact, the shielding Outer Banks are already eroding from combined sea-level rise and large storms, and natural wetland communities that cannot tolerate salty or brackish waters are in retreat.

The Alligator River Climate Change Adaptation Project marks the beginning of efforts to restore this area's ecosystems and test vital strategies to cope with sea-level rise. Anticipating the breaching of the Outer Banks, this project is building up oyster reefs along shorelines to duplicate the islands' barrier function. Onshore, given the expected landward retreat of natural communities, plans are afoot to place additional land under protection. From the ocean to mudflats and peat lands, all the way upslope to forest, seagrass, marsh grass, shrubs and trees are being planted or restored. Planting bald cypress, trees tolerant to inundation, on land currently above water will make soils more stable and ease the transition to a submerged ecosystem. But a critical part of the whole scheme is built-in flexibility. Given wide uncertainties about sea-level rise, monitoring will be used to guide efforts to acquire land and prepare habitats at appropriate times.

Vulnerable coastal wetlands underscore some critical conservation challenges posed by climate change. The most effective way to prevent extinctions is to manage species within their current ranges, where their needs will most likely be met. Yet bird populations that are now in protected areas may find these lands inundated by sea-level rise; or they may be driven by climate warming to disperse to habitats degraded by human activity. These prospects necessitate new strategies that recognise the dynamic nature of landscapes under climate change. Protected areas may need to grow, and the habitat quality of unprotected areas that connect them will need to improve.

Coping with uncertainty, compounded

Estimating the future range shifts of birds will be important, to indicate where new lands should be protected and pinpoint interconnecting areas that would optimise the chances for wildlife to disperse. Yet these estimates are only available for some species and regions, the picture for European-breeding birds being most comprehensive.

Another significant challenge is the uncertainty surrounding how much global temperature, sea level and precipitation patterns may change. This uncertainty is compounded when climate predictions are plugged into ecological models to predict range shifts and other wildlife responses. Still harder – perhaps impossible – to predict are new threats arising where birds become mismatched or their communities reshuffled, due to each species' unique response to climate change (chapters 1 and 2).

These uncertainties only increase when we consider points further into the future. Focusing on the near and medium-term (20–50 years) can help minimise this uncertainty, but still leave enough time to plan expanded protected areas. Looking to the long-term future, allowing for the wide range of possible outcomes will require options to be kept open. In the meantime, there is a vital role for monitoring and assessment, to gauge whether conservation efforts successfully sustain or increase bird populations in the face of climate change. Through this 'adaptive management' approach, measures can be adjusted over time when necessary.[10,11]

Still vital, but protected areas will need fortifying

Parks, private conservation grounds and other refuges are the primary approach to protecting endangered species, and the most effective part of today's conservation strategies. But will protected areas based on the 'still shots' of today's species distributions remain effective if climate change shakes up their ecological communities and forces out the species they were created to conserve? 'Yes' is the definitive answer.

Insights from a network of Important Bird Areas in Africa suggest why. Lying south of the Sahara, this network covers a total of seven per cent of the continent and harbours 875 priority birds: species globally threatened, restricted in their ranges or biome types, or congregating in large numbers. From 2025 to 2085, species turnover is expected to ramp up with climate change, and large range shifts are in store in some cases. Yet by 2085, 74–80 per cent of all birds[12] and 88–92 per cent of priority species are expected to retain suitable habitat in at least one Important Bird Area where they are now found. Just seven to eight per cent of priority species would completely lose suitable climate space from the entire network.[13] These insights highlight this network's importance – but make it sobering to consider that only 40 per cent of its 863 sites now have legal protection.

Protected areas now cover about 12.5 per cent of the planet's terrestrial surface. Beyond their boundaries, about 83 per cent of the world's lands have been directly affected by humans in some way. With undisturbed habitat outside reserves shrinking and habitat under protection increasing overall, most remaining natural lands may be restricted to protected areas by the time climate-change influence becomes pronounced.

Indeed, protected areas are expected to be pivotal under climate change. The lands least disturbed by human activity, they will give wildlife the best chance to respond naturally to range shifts and other changes driven by climate change. If stresses within protected areas are managed well, this may delay the loss of populations and provide a source of individuals to colonise new areas of suitable climate. Protected areas are also prime colonisation sites for species to shift into. They could underpin the portions of birds' ranges not expected to shift or anchor areas where a series of overlapping shifts converge.[14]

Under climate change, reserves will need to expand to adequately protect all intended species. Modelling suggests that the total reserve area in tropical Mexico already needs to expand by 42 per cent just to meet the current goals to protect 179 bird and mammal species. Yet under moderate climate change, by 2050 this would need to be augmented by a further 12 per cent (of the original 104 000-square-kilometre total protected area).[15] The more cost-effective way to expand, it turns out, would be to add the new reserve lands in a single step.[16]

Clearly, climate change adds impetus to an already existing need to expand protected areas and meet today's conservation goals. This includes more marine parks and presently unoccupied sites that could host seabird colonies in the future, to protect this bird group with a particularly high proportion of species already threatened on a global scale (chapter 4). Yet the costs and resources attached to augmenting conservation areas will probably compel managers to prioritise the most vulnerable parks, and within them endemic species most sensitive to climate change.

A rather straightforward way to protect bird habitat, if the means and politics permit, is to purchase it. In Australia's Central Desert the future looks drier still and water access will become critical to desert life's ability to adapt. Realising this, the Australian Wildlife Conservancy, in partnership with the Nature Conservancy, purchased 667 000 hectares of water-rich land in Kalamurina, where three rivers and three deserts converge – and more than 160 bird species are found. Importantly, this 2007 purchase connects two larger government land reserves, providing a more than seven-million-hectare continuous swathe of protected land.

Past and future havens from change

Over the course of evolutionary time, certain landscape features have buffered species from climatic changes that rendered large portions of their original ranges hostile. Though they may have been lost from the broader landscape, some plants and animals are able to persist in refugia, where habitats buffered from disturbance meet their ecological needs. This may explain why refugia are often richer in endemics than their surrounds. Refugia are expected to be important for conservation because, just as they have buffered life in the past, they could be critical for doing so under climate change.

Refugia could be important destinations for climate-sensitive species that, for example, retreat from a valley to a cooler location on a mountain slope, or retract to a moist and shaded gorge. These landscape features could increase the chance that species will persist, relocate and re-establish themselves, and that ecosystems will recover, giving organisms more opportunity and time to adapt and evolve.

Given the prospect of rapid climate change, refugia should be identified and made a priority for protection when reserves are planned. In the Wet Tropics of Queensland, for example, 45 per cent of endemic species were found to live in the coolest quarter of the rainforest.[17] By ascertaining what factors moderate the hottest temperatures, such as elevation, proximity to the coast and shading from dense foliage, important cool environments in the Wet Tropics region can now be flagged as targets to conserve and restore. In general, landscape connections between refugia and biodiversity-rich areas should be fostered. The natural capacity of refugia to provide resilience can even be enhanced, for example, by planting vegetation along river edges to help cool watercourses.

Beyond protected areas, smoothing the way

Events on the Ribble River demonstrate another conservation response to climate-change threats, one that increasingly looks to human-altered landscapes for solutions. Where the Ribble meets the sea, its girth swells to form the UK's most important river estuary for wintering birds, swans, geese and shorebirds being among the quarter of a million birds it harbours. The expectation of rising sea levels has prompted action to ensure there is habitat for these birds. In 2008, land that had been reclaimed for farming during the 1980s was returned to the sea by breaching a seawall. This transformed fields into 168 hectares of saltmarsh, saline lagoons and muddy creeks perfect for breeding waterfowl and waders.

The re-wilding of the Ribble signals the growing realisation that, with climate change, conservation efforts must extend beyond protected areas to lands now used for agriculture, forestry and other human activities.[18] This broader view sees protected areas as the fixed, truly natural elements in a broader landscape, or matrix, of human-altered land. Other vital parts of this total landscape picture are corridors or 'stepping stones' that link up the suitable ranges of birds and other wildlife.

From hostile to bird-friendly: habitat restoration

If this bigger, bolder approach is to work, lands outside protected areas must improve in terms of their quality, connectivity and permeability (the extent to which species can move freely across them). Returning human-altered landscapes to their most natural state possible will make them more hospitable to wildlife. And the more natural the landscape, the less the need to actively manage it to reduce climate-change stresses.

Efforts already underway, like bird-friendly coffee plantations, gain impetus under climate change. 'Sun' coffee monoculture plantations, with their single layer of coffee plants, make for poor bird habitat. Shade coffee plantations, with multiple layers of other trees and bushes, can provide nectar, insects and generally high-quality habitat for Neotropical migrants, like vulnerable cerulean warblers, *Dendroica cerulea*.[19] So closely may shade plantations resemble native forest, the bird diversity they harbour is almost as high – and significantly higher than sun coffee plantations. Importantly, these forest overstoreys can act as corridors for migratory species. Restoring landscapes like these will not only help wildlife on the move from climate change, it will also bolster forests' capacity to absorb carbon dioxide from the atmosphere.

Where lands are now used by people, conservation efforts will probably need to be managed in innovative and flexible ways, compared to the strict protection afforded many parks and reserves. Such flexible plans could include conservation 'concessions', whereby land is conserved in return for some form of payment or trust fund. Alternatively, land may be purchased, then leased to allow uses compatible with bird conservation, or used with the understanding that it might someday be activated as a conservation area.[18]

How much land will be needed would depend on birds' responses to climate change. If the present and expected future ranges of species overlap considerably, their movements, along with 'neighbourhood movers', may be captured within protected areas. 'Cross-country movers' will need to have their large range shifts considered under total landscape plans, along with species with ranges too large for any single protected area.[14] The needs of 'umbrella species', such as large, widely ranging carnivores, may underpin total landscape plans, because their protection would also secure that of other species in their ecological communities. These efforts would need to be guided by information on range shifts and birds' ability to disperse.

The complex planning of wider landscapes will be challenging. Stakeholders will be many, from farmers, local communities and governments to private companies and NGOs. These plans will need to be coordinated alongside other planning needs, such as forestry, agriculture or coastal development.

Some bird conservation groups already work with the public to make rural and urban landscapes less fragmented and more connected and permeable. In their boldest and most ambitious program to date, the Royal Society for the Protection of Birds recognises the importance of redoubling these conservation efforts in light of climate change. Its Futurescapes program seeks to both expand nature reserves *and* find ways to better meet the needs of wildlife alongside other human uses. Forty Futurescapes initiatives were underway in the UK by 2010, with plans to expand to 80 (www.rspb.org.uk/futurescapes). In south-central England, for example, a project to transform land now used as a conifer plantation back into heathland will provide habitat for Dartford warblers, *Sylvia undata*, as they disperse northwards to track climate change.

The RSPB, the Audubon Society and other bird conservation groups also advise rural property owners on how to improve landscapes by planting hedges (to provide corridors), creating healthy ponds, protecting stream banks to encourage vegetation, and removing invasive species. Numerous groups promote more bird-friendly urban areas as well; Birds Australia and the Australian Museum provide extensive, research-based advice on improving gardens as native bird habitat. Australian local governments even provide free native plants and on-site visits. In essence, a garden or rural property may ultimately be seen as an extension of the local ecoregion, and efforts that most reflect this will best help birds and other wildlife.

Making gardens and farms more bird-friendly may improve conditions for some species and facilitate their ability to expand across the landscape in a changing climate. However, they cannot replace the pristine habitats many birds depend upon, and are no substitute for the habitat preservation needs of any given region.

Connectivity: freedom to roam, a chance to adapt

The rare coastal California gnatcatcher generally only disperses short distances, flitting through adjoining, undisturbed sage scrub habitat (chapter 3). Its habit needs illustrate why connectivity is a key guiding concept behind the efforts to allow wildlife to disperse effectively. Connectivity is fostered by landscape interconnections that permit individuals to move between core protected areas and other natural lands. Restoring connectivity can reduce the negative effects of habitat fragmentation and habitat islands (chapter 6). Connectivity is already a valuable tool for conserving biodiversity but will become ever-more important under climate change.

Linking populations in this way improves their chances to exchange individuals and genes and sustain their genetic viability, generally increasing the odds they will persist or grow. It also allows populations to escape competition or other stresses. Connectivity enables important ecological functions, such as seed dispersal by rainforest birds. It can promote opportunities for species, as they interact across the broader landscape, to adapt and evolve. Without connectivity, other more costly, risky and problematic measures, such as assisted migration (see below), may ultimately be proposed to tackle climate change.

The scale of these interconnections can range from local corridors like vegetated streams or forest swathes through to broad corridors tens of kilometres wide and thousands of kilometres long. Designing seascapes for connectivity will also be important. Under its World Commission of Protected Areas, the IUCN is championing efforts by governments and NGOs for large-scale connectivity using mainly natural areas, especially the world's great mountain chains. Initiatives include North America's 3200 kilometre-long Yellowstone to Yukon (Y2Y) connectivity conservation corridor, and Ecuador's Condor Biosphere Reserve.[20] The latter encompasses high volcanoes and harbours more than 760 bird species, including the declining Andean condor, *Vultur gryphus*. Vast in scale and complex in execution, the bold vision driving these plans has captured wide support and could underpin many smaller-scale responses to climate change. 'It has the potential to be a major political force,' writes Graeme Worboys of the IUCN World Commission on Protected Areas.

Like other conservation efforts in an era of climate change, plans for connectivity must stay flexible as needs and targets evolve. However, after

2050, if species respond to mounting climate change with increasingly extensive range shifts, connectivity will become more difficult. Regardless, the dynamic plans needed to ensure connectivity are complex and time-consuming and depend on the judgement of planners.[14]

As alternatives to corridors, stepping stones are habitat patches large enough to allow species to breed successfully, expand across the landscape and track climate change. Patch size and closeness are critical for successful dispersal.

Move them or lose them? Assisted migration

Debate is needed about the guiding principles for a world in which conservation is no longer about saving existing ecosystems but about preserving biodiversity by facilitating change.

Tim Low, 2008

Some birds already appear unable to disperse or adapt quickly enough to keep up with climate change. If parts of the Earth warm by more than 4°C, some conservationists fear radical intervention may be needed to prevent extinctions. Assisted migration, once considered unthinkable, is one such extreme tactic. Also known as assisted colonisation and managed relocation, it essentially entails physically picking up potentially threatened species or populations and moving them to new, suitable areas.

Proponents of assisted migration (it has been used sparingly to date) argue it will be needed to overcome dispersal constraints that threaten extinction. Possible targets would be poor dispersers including flightless birds, weak flyers and species that rarely leave their home ranges.[10] Other candidates with dispersal constraints might be birds with fragmented habitats, habitat specialists, rare birds or birds that require unusual or difficult-to-locate conditions, or species dependent on climates that may simply vanish under global warming, such as those on tropical mountain tops.[21]

Some species, it is argued, may even require extensive assisted migration, to locations far beyond their original ranges. Assisted migration proponents assert that, armed with knowledge of species requirements, it may be carried out with reduced risks in some situations.[21] The IPCC also acknowledges that assisted migration may be needed, while conceding it is 'fraught with scientific uncertainties' and 'many surprises would be expected'.

Conservation history is replete with bird extinctions triggered by introduced species like rats, cats and reptiles. This ecological fallout is a cautionary tale about the enormous uncertainty and high stakes inherent in species introductions. Populations can mushroom, fuelling invasions that put other species or even entire ecosystems at risk, with potentially irreversible consequences. Even when moved within continents, newcomers can still have large effects. Although such invasions have been studied extensively, it is still difficult to know which species will become pests.[22]

Conversely, there is the possibility that costly efforts to relocate rare species could simply fail. Uncertainty about future climate conditions, or even what conditions an introduced species actually requires and tolerates, could contribute to failure.[22] Specialist species could languish if some unknown but important mutualism is missing. Other possible causes of 'transplant failure' are new or unexpected predators, competitors, diseases and even the chance an introduced species will hybridise with another in the new locale.

Extreme care and prior research on candidate species' distributions, dispersal ability and potential biotic interactions may help avert both invasions and failures. The extensive body of research on invasive species could guide these efforts, as could human society's long history of relocating birds, including their transport by European settlers. Once relocated, species would also need to be monitored.[10]

Yet shortfalls in time and money are likely to leave many important questions unanswered. 'We expect that future "assisted-migration biologists" will find themselves in a similar position to today's invasive species biologists: looking for useful generalizations in theory and struggling with unforeseen idiosyncrasies in practice,' write Jason McLachlan of the University of Notre Dame and colleagues, 'To an uncomfortable extent this war will have to be fought with "the army we have, not the army we want."'

These inherent risks explain why assisted migration remains highly controversial, often cited as a policy of last resort. Moreover, 'Maverick, unsupervised translocation efforts run the risk of undermining current conservation work,' caution McLachlan and his colleagues. Although scientists are already deliberating the potential risk-management strategies needed to guide assisted migration, the wider society also needs to join the discussion on whether its high-stakes actions are balanced by the climate-change extinction threat.[23]

Grass loving, but overwhelmed by gamba

Assisted migration aside, species invasions are a threat expected to intensify with climate change, with very real consequences for birds, as suggested by the case of the endangered Gouldian finch, *Erythrura gouldiae*. The survival of this vividly coloured finch of northern Australia pivots on grasses and fire. It breeds early in the dry season when fires, by burning underbrush, promote its ability to forage for grass seeds on the ground. Fires also facilitate, in subsequent years, a richer growth of the grasses these endangered endemics rely on during the wet season. Overall, a mosaic of burning across the landscape fosters a mix of grasses, making more food available over longer periods.

But some grass can be too much, even for this grass-seed specialist. Gamba grass, *Andropogon gayanus*, a gigantic African species, grows more than four metres tall. Introduced to Australia for cattle pastures, it has been nominated the greatest invasive species threat to Australia's biodiversity under climate change.[24] Gamba grass threatens the Gouldian finch and the near-threatened partridge pigeon, *Geophaps smithii*, another Australian endemic.

Australia's bushfire risk is ramping up with warming, but gamba grass fires are up to eight times as intense as native bushfires. Gamba grass fuels dangerous infernos that scorch treetops, and it can carry two fires in a single dry season. Normally fire-tolerant native species such as eucalypts die after repeated gamba-grass fires, eventually replaced by treeless plains. Moreover, because gamba grass both promotes fire and is promoted by fire, it fosters a positive feedback cycle that could accelerate with the increased fire risk expected under climate change, further reinforced by the release of stored carbon from trees as they burn. Its potential to completely transform an ecosystem makes gamba grass an extreme threat.

When fire transforms these landscapes, Gouldian finches lose their nesting sites in tree hollows. Fire may kill them in their nests or, once vegetation is lost, expose them to introduced predators such as cats and foxes. Gamba grass also chokes out other grasses, leaving this single species that can provide birds with food over only a short interval each year.

Wild, weedy and unwanted

People need to be shown, not just images of melting glaciers, but vistas of weed forests and urchin barrens.

Tim Low, 2008

The gamba grass threat is now attracting attention in Australia. But as a climate-change problem, invasive species have generally fallen below the radar, even though invader-driven extinctions and ecosystem damage could increase. Climate change and invasive species may feed off one another, but are often treated as separate issues.[25] 'Biologists have focused attention on native species likely to go extinct under climate change, but not on what will replace them,' says Tim Low, an Australian environmentalist and author of *Feral Future*, a book about invasive species.

Species can become invasive when given good opportunities to establish in new locations. They may also be good dispersers, tolerant of environmental conditions where they arrive and successful at obtaining the resources they need to survive and reproduce at their new locations. Many are also fast-growing.[25] This set of traits is expected to often help invasive species succeed where climate change improves their prospects.

Those hitching a ride with ships could benefit where shorter periods of sea ice allow for longer shipping seasons. The easing of cold conditions will also make new areas suitable for invaders.[26] Invasive species tend to spread more rapidly in disturbed and stressed ecosystems. So if climate change brings higher numbers of intense cyclones, and more droughts and fires, these would be expected to increase disturbance and accelerate their spread.[24] Extended droughts punctuated by very wet years, for example, facilitate weed expansion because other vegetation is weakened. With climate change, invasive species are expected to become more common and spread more widely and, where they do, their influences on bird populations can be expected to increase.

The densities of some invasive species populations already present in habitats may change with global warming. The numbers of 'sleeper' weeds (we will come to these shortly) or feral animals may increase, especially if their presence erodes populations of native species. 'Transformer' species like gamba grass, with their positive feedbacks of invasion and disturbance, are of highest concern under climate change because they can radically alter ecosystems.[24]

Loosening an invader's chokehold on a puffinry

Although some strategies now used to tackle invasives may become less effective with climate change, it will be ever more important to manage these species. One of the UK's larger colonies of Atlantic puffins, *Fratercula arctica*, on Craigleith Island in Scotland's Firth of Forth, illustrates why. It has faced an invasion of tree mallow, *Lavatera arborea*, a frost-sensitive herby biennial. Native to south-west and western coastal UK, this plant was probably introduced to the Firth of Forth region centuries ago for its medicinal value, and spread to Craigleith in the 1950s. Formerly kept in check by cold winters, it overran the Craigleith puffinry during the 1990s, and by 2006 blanketed 85 per cent of the island. Though milder winters are a plausible reason for its expansion, disappearance of the island's rabbits, grazers of tree mallow, due to disease may have played a role.

Despite increasing in prior decades, Craigleith's puffin populations declined between 1999 and 2003, even though numbers were still increasing on the nearby Isle of May over this period. (Seabirds in this area now appear to be declining due to food supply problems linked to ocean warming; chapter 4.) Growing as tall as three metres, tree mallow forms dense stands. Simply put, wherever tree mallow covered Craigleith, puffins tended to be absent. Puffins abandon burrows in these areas at substantial cost because they take considerable energy to dig.

In 2007, efforts got underway to tackle tree mallow on both Craigleith and the nearby island of Fidra. Dubbed 'SOS Puffin', this project was set up under the auspices of the Scottish Seabird Centre but is entirely led and run by volunteers. By May 2009, their work parties had tackled about 95 per cent of the original tree mallow cover on Craigleith. Counts indicate a six per cent increase in burrows apparently occupied by the puffins from 2009 to 2010 on Craigleith, and a 44 per cent increase on Fidra.[27]

An ounce of prevention is worth a pound of cure, and prevention is increasingly the watchword, given the wide uncertainties about the invasive species problems that climate change could unleash. Early eradication efforts can control and remove invasive species like sleeper weeds. These naturalised exotic plants can lurk under the radar in small areas, apparently benign, but are able to transform rapidly into full-blown pests when fire patterns, temperatures and other climate conditions change.[28] Proactive steps to make the broader landscape more resilient to disturbances would also foster resistance to invasions – a double benefit.

In these efforts it will be important to distinguish invasive species introduced recently by humans to negative effect from native species undergoing range shifts forced by climate change. Native species expanding their ranges in response to climate change should not be considered invasive.[26]

Monitoring and research to guide conservation

Laying down the baselines

The vast majority of change will take place unheralded, and will be detected only if carefully planned and effective monitoring systems are in place.

Lee Hannah & Rod Salm, 2005

The need for more research and monitoring, a persistent theme of this book, applies equally to the conservation challenges of climate change. In China, for example, bird diversity is rich, but avian research on climate change is lagging and relevant long-term records are extremely rare – if they exist at all.[29] A dearth of information on birds' ranges, numbers and ecology – including their climate sensitivity – hobbles these preservation efforts, especially in the tropics and subtropics.

The British Trust for Ornithology's Out of Africa appeal is one effort that aims to help fill this gap. Many of the African long-distance migratory birds that breed in Britain are in decline, but scanty information about their overwintering ecology hinders efforts to conserve them. In 2009, the Trust began to monitor birds in Ghana and Burkina Faso by ringing migrants in diverse habitats, from semi-desert to lush tropical rainforest. Taking the long view, the Trust and its partners are also collaborating with local conservationists and building capacity among African ornithologists.

Wide uncertainty about the future effects of climate change makes it difficult to anticipate many of its effects. Monitoring can address this problem as a critical part of a feedback loop to gauge the effectiveness of conservation efforts, inform flexible plans and guide nimble responses. If wetland bird populations decline to a critical level as precipitation patterns change, for example, monitoring could reveal the need to reduce water allocated for irrigation. In marine environments climate change has been the impetus for a monitoring renaissance[30] – a much-needed one at that, since many monitoring efforts begun in Europe after World War II ceased during the 1980s.

Long-term monitoring will be important in parks and reserves. Yet it will be even more vital in vast unprotected lands, where it is now rare, but would steer efforts to manage human-dominated landscapes.[18] Key wildlife responses to monitor may include population, distribution, and density changes. As to which species to monitor, obvious candidates include those already targeted by conservation, plus climate-change-susceptible species. Monitoring non-target and non-sensitive species would also be helpful since climate change may bring unanticipated results. Harmful invasives will probably need to be monitored over wider areas than in the past.

Feet on the ground, eyes on the sky

The ever-growing ranks of willing human observers can answer the need for better data on birds' responses to climate change, and make possible tasks otherwise too unwieldy.[31,32] In fact, volunteer ornithology networks have already enabled research that provides some of the best examples of climate-change effects on ecosystems. This contribution could build on the important role, extending back more than a century, which amateur birdwatchers have played in ornithology and conservation science.[32]

Citizen science networks can complement remote sensing and ecological studies. They can also continue to help answer important questions, such as how birds' phenology and distributions respond to climate change. These initiatives benefit from the internet, and the ubiquity of home computers and hand-held devices. The ongoing revolution in data collection and sharing increasingly allows observations by amateurs to be compiled and integrated by scientists.[33]

Imaging and other innovations are also revolutionising how data is collected. The watchful eyes and handwritten notes of naturalists are being replaced by remote digital cameras, sensors and computers. Imaging hardware placed in nest boxes can automatically detect birds' presence and count eggs. Remote cameras can capture images of plants, and new software can even identify and count individual flowers, slashing labour-intensive field work. Ever-more affordable and accessible, these technologies will further boost phenology networks.[33]

Amateur monitoring networks are fairly well established in Europe, North America, Australia and South Africa. They are scarcer in other parts of Africa, Asia and South America – most of the tropics. In the United Kingdom, the public's love affair with birds has fostered many networks. The Breeding Bird Survey, run by the British Trust for Ornithology and partner organisations, has contributed to dozens of scientific publications (www.bto.org/bbs). And the UK Phenology Network program Nature's Calendar (www.naturescalendar.org.uk) is the world's biggest phenology scheme, with a database of almost two million recorded dates, which builds on observations like those of Marsham (chapter 1).

Some North American networks have an intriguing history. In traditional Christmas 'side hunts', American hunters formed sides and competed to kill as many birds and other animals as possible, regardless of their rarity or beauty. In 1900, an officer of the newly formed Audubon Society, Frank M. Chapman, proposed the infinitely more wildlife-friendly Christmas Bird Count as an alternative. Another effort, the North American Breeding Bird Survey, was begun in 1966 out of concern for pesticide effects (www.pwrc.usgs.gov/BBS).

Other North American programs tap the considerable potential of the World Wide Web. Since 1999, the Cornell Lab of Ornithology has mounted cameras near nests to record birds' behaviours as their breeding cycles play out. 'NestCam' participants can view and classify online archived images of breeding behaviour from their home computers, while traditionalists can still continue to monitor nests in their own communities through the laboratory's related NestWatch program.

eBird, a Cornell Lab of Ornithology program run in partnership with the Audubon Society, feeds one of the world's largest and fastest-growing biodiversity data sources. In January 2010 alone, participants using online checklists reported more than 1.5 million observations of birds' presence or absence across North America. Later that year, eBird also began receiving observations of birds from any world region (ebird.org). Helpfully, a new iPhone® application called BirdsEye, powered by eBird, allows bird-watchers to keep tabs on recent reports of about 800 North American bird species, essentially guiding them to birds. This is just one of many new, birdwatcher-friendly 'apps' with useful features to identify birds, including photos, bird song and notes.

In Africa, the University of Cape Town's Animal Demography Unit is an important force behind growing birdwatcher networks. Its programs include the Coordinated Waterbird Count, a twice-yearly census of more than 400 South African wetlands (cwac.adu.org.za), and Coordinated Avifaunal Roadcounts, whereby volunteers log sightings of large and conspicuous land birds such as cranes, storks and bustards (car.adu.org.za).

India's MigrantWatch is one step towards filling the wide knowledge gaps surrounding climate-change effects on birds in developing countries. Seizing on a surging interest in birding and bird photography, and run by the National Centre for Biological Sciences in Bangalore in association with the journal *Indian Birds*, MigrantWatch aims to reveal how global warming affects the timing of long-distance migrations (www.migrantwatch.in). A special MigrantWatch campaign focuses on the pied cuckoo, *Clamator jacobinus*, whose pied subspecies is one of the few birds that migrates from Africa to India to breed. Known as the 'rain bird', its arrival in central and northern India is thought to presage the much-anticipated monsoon that brings relief to hot, dry landscapes – possibly explaining why it is fabled by ancient Hindu poets to live on raindrops.

In Australia, the longest-running bird survey is the Nest Record Scheme, operated by Birds Australia since 1964. Birds Australia also runs the world's largest continent-wide bird survey, the Atlas of Australian Birds, with a database of more than six million records (www.birdata.com.au/about_atlas.vm).

Combing basements and attics: data mining

A pressing need for long-term records to help unravel climate-change effects has galvanised efforts to 'mine' past observations lying dormant and unused. Thanks to the internet and home computers, crowdsourcing[34] can breathe new life into old records. One example is a database containing most of what is known about North American birds' natural history from the late 1880s to World War II. Members of the public carefully recorded their observations on cards and sent them to the US government. Even US President Theodore Roosevelt, who was a published ornithologist, contributed a record from the White House grounds. After languishing in leaky attics and storage areas for decades, these irreproducible data on roughly 850 bird species are now in the safe hands of the Patuxent Wildlife Research Center of the US Geological Survey. There the North American Bird Phenology Program is working with hundreds of volunteers to scan and transcribe the six million records. This will provide an unprecedented quantity of baseline data on birds' distribution, migration timing and routes, to help shed light on how these change with global warming.

Other vast data collections include the more than 92 million observations gathered by March 2011 under the Avian Knowledge Network. Based at the Cornell Lab of Ornithology and drawing on university, government and non-governmental organisations, this international effort combines existing bird distribution databases from bird monitoring, bird banding and citizen science programs. It aims to both organise this information and provide access to it.

Conserving migratory birds

Birds, especially migratory birds, do not respect political borders, and their migratory flyways may span vast areas of the planet. They are adapted to arriving at the right place at the right time, but climate change is altering these places and times. Migratory animals' routes may change and migratory networks could even collapse, if key sites are lost due to habitat destruction or if range shifts put them out of reach.[35] Climate change adds urgency to national and international cooperative efforts to enhance the conservation of these globetrotters, especially migratory waterbirds. These efforts must be underpinned by better knowledge of migratory paths and stopover sites.

Bird ringing and banding

That this Swallow breeding in the far west of Europe should have reached so far to the south-east of Africa as Natal, seems to me extraordinary.

Harry F. Witherby, 1912

A network of bird-ringing stations in the developing world would be a cost-effective way to monitor climate-change effects, especially for migratory birds. Bird-banding (or ringing) schemes comprise a more hands-on and technical style of monitoring. Anyone can report a banded bird, but training is needed to safely trap, handle and fit lightweight, uniquely numbered bands or rings onto birds' legs. These programs allow individual birds to be identified, relaying information on their movements, behaviours and survival.

Under the British Trust for Ornithology's ringing scheme a Manx shearwater, *Puffinus puffinus*, was recaptured at its burrow in Wales an astonishing 51 years after it was first ringed. The earliest ringing studies solved some of migration's mysteries, including routes, destinations and even the mechanisms birds use to migrate.[36] Still seen as essential, ringing programs today collect data on species, age, sex, body size and condition, genetics, parasites and diseases, length of stay and feather isotopes. They enable radio-tracking and satellite-tracking studies of birds that provide detailed information on habitat use and migrations. And they inform studies on ecology, population levels, endangered species and environmental impacts.

Running for more than a century in several countries, these programs could illuminate long-term trends in migratory behaviour and distribution shifts in concert with climate change, and indeed some already do. Critically, they could help identify fuelling and stopover sites and habitats used by long-distance migrants in decline, like many trans-Saharan migrants breeding in Europe.[36] More than ever, their role in the protection of birds will require that ringing programs adopt a coordinated and collaborative international approach, to allow information from several (and potentially hundreds of) ringing sites to be collected and compared.

Though well established in Europe and North America, these programs are few and far between elsewhere, being especially scarce in Africa where many European birds winter. Running ringing stations is labour-intensive, yet requires no expensive equipment. They can be managed by just two to four people who may be trained volunteers. Open to the public, these stations could help train future environmental scientists, create local jobs and promote awareness among local people and decision makers about birds, climate change and other environmental issues.

International policy for birds without borders

Global warming has added impetus to international efforts to protect migratory birds, but policy specifically geared to help these species adapt to climate change is still in its infancy.[35] Under the United Nations, the three main globally focused biodiversity conventions to look to are the Ramsar Convention on Wetlands, the Convention on Biological Diversity, and the

Convention on the Conservation of Migratory Species of Wild Animals (CMS).[37] Other relevant global entities are UNESCO's Man and Biosphere Programme and its World Heritage Convention, and BirdLife's Global Important Bird Area Programme.

The CMS has called for efforts to improve the understanding of climate-change effects and to help wildlife adapt. It is impossible to monitor the effects of global warming on all migratory species, so 17 animal groups have been nominated as proxies, including four bird groups: trans-Saharan migrants, Arctic shorebirds, Antarctic penguins and fish-eating seabirds.[38] The CMS also recognises the need for urgent measures to help migratory species adapt in the face of inevitable climate-change effects. The Ramsar Convention's focus is wetland vulnerability to global warming – specifically how these habitats that critically underpin the connectivity, corridors and flyways of migratory birds can cope with climate change and sea-level rise through adaptive management.[37]

Transnational conservation efforts could be important for non-migratory birds also. A species protected in one nation's nature reserve, for example, might shift into an area used for farming in a neighbouring country. Proactive strategies will be needed to ensure birds' range shifts can be accommodated.

The fallout of humanity's responses to climate change

> Until we recognize that conserving biodiversity is in the interest of local and global communities, the very schemes put in place to prolong our welfare and prosperity may, perversely, curtail them.
>
> James S. Paterson et al., 2008

Humanity's multifold responses to global warming could profoundly affect birds and other wildlife. These may be the consequences of measures to stem emissions, and of people's efforts, planned or unplanned, to adapt or even benefit from the effects of climate change. This realisation has prompted a growing concern that biodiversity conservation will be seen as an acceptable casualty to society's response to climate change.[39]

Global warming is likely to expose new parts of the planet to development – for example, where the loss of Arctic sea ice opens up new areas to shipping activity and fossil-fuel extraction. Climate change and responses to it may prompt societies to alter land use in ways that affect birds and their habitats. Efforts to reduce emissions from fossil fuels including coal, oil and gas are changing how societies source energy. Importantly, renewable energy from wind farms and solar plants lack the serious environmental threats posed by fossil fuel generation. To varying degrees, large-scale hydroelectric plants, biofuels and even wind farms all have implications for bird conservation; large-scale solar power facilities may also modify habitats if sited in sensitive areas.[39] In fact, a truly 'green' approach to energy use must emphasise the important contribution of energy conservation, energy efficiency and low-emission technologies, to optimise the use of existing power sources.

Dams and efficiency

Large-scale hydroelectric power plants have long been known to exact a huge environmental toll on ecosystems. They provide renewable energy, but these plants need to be constructed with the long-term integrity of river ecosystems in mind. In Turkey, this is not happening under a massive dam-building spree that would see more than 2000 hydroelectric power plants built on every river and most streams in the next 12 years. In Ethiopia, there are also plans for large new dams to generate power. The Gilgel Gibe III dam, for example, will flood the Omo River valley, home to critical ecosystems and some of Africa's most traditional tribes. Yet even as dam building expands in Ethiopia, transmission limitations equipment breakdowns and other types of problems at existing hydroelectric power plants are limiting power production to only a fraction of some plants' capacities. In Ethiopia and elsewhere, wiser use of existing plants and the power they produce could avert the need for more hydroelectric projects, and so avoid further negative results on ecosystems.

A hotter world stokes hunger for land

Forty per cent of Earth's land surface is already used to grow crops and pasture domestic animals, so it is hardly surprising that agriculture already affects bird populations and distributions greatly. Even slight warming, along with more frequent droughts, floods, heat stress and other climate-change effects could reduce agricultural yields in seasonally dry and low-latitude regions, and are likely to increase the number of people at risk of hunger. If the Asian monsoon shifts to a much drier state, or if Himalayan glaciers dwindle to the extent that their water-storage capacity is lost, the quantity and timing of water supplies to the large and fertile North Indian River Plain (Indo-Gangetic Plain) would be affected.[40] This could force large numbers of people to migrate to locations with better conditions.

In the tropics, where biodiversity is greatest, the numbers of subsistence and smallholder farmers are highest. These people will be very exposed to climate-change effects, but their coping capacity will be limited. They may seek to adapt by cultivating marginal land with techniques that degrade it or increasingly exploiting wildlife and clearing forests, causing permanent damage. In this way, climate change could drive further loss of biodiversity – including unexplored biodiversity.

REDD: forest protection or pulp fiction?

Intact forests have incalculable value to efforts to stem climate change, being one of the few 'win-win-win' options available.[39] Each year, clearing of forests and peat lands releases roughly 12 per cent of global greenhouse gas emissions from human sources, slightly less than those from fossil fuels burned for transport (15 per cent). Tackling deforestation would help stem emissions; in fact matching forests' carbon-absorbing potential by other means would cost hundreds of billions of dollars each year.[41] As a second 'win', reducing deforestation and allowing degraded forests to recover would help protect habitat for birds and other wildlife, especially critical for biodiversity-rich tropical forests. Third, intact forests could assist human societies to adapt to climate change, because they help reduce flooding and erosion.

In 2005, Papua New Guinea, Costa Rica and a coalition of other rain-forest nations proposed that poorer countries be paid to actively protect their existing forests. The United Nations recognised the value of this idea and in 2008 began the Reducing Emissions from Deforestation and Forest Degradation in Developing Countries Programme, or REDD. A derivative of REDD, known as REDD+, is the current focus of negotiations. It encompasses not only reducing emissions from forest damage, but also sustainable management of forests and conservation initiatives that enhance carbon uptake in the forests of developing countries.

REDD 'readiness' projects were already taking shape on the ground even before this program was agreed by parties to the United Nations

Framework Convention on Climate Change in Cancun, Mexico, in December 2010. Yet this program's worthy goal of promoting forest protection faces large hurdles. The Cancun agreement provided a work plan and guidelines, but there is still no concrete framework for how REDD+ will operate. Even definitions for key terms like 'deforestation' and 'sustainable management of forests' remain unsettled, although there is much devil in this detail.

There is concern, for example, that this program would permit continued logging or reward the creation of plantations, which store 40–60 per cent less carbon than intact natural forests and host greatly reduced biodiversity. Given expected growth in human populations and biofuel demand, pressure to use uncultivated land will increase. Care must be taken that deforestation does not simply increase outside areas protected under REDD+ deals (referred to as 'leakage').[42] It is hoped that the Cancun agreement's emphasis on halting and reversing forest loss (as well as reducing emissions) would help address issues like these. Yet another issue is the questionable 'permanency' of forests as carbon sinks where, for example, warming leads to more disturbances like forest fires. Some environmentalists also have serious concerns that REDD+ would not benefit local forest-dependent communities, would further marginalise indigenous peoples, and could be misused by corrupt politicians or illegal logging companies.[43]

Biofuels: fuelling controversy

Plantations are forests in uniform ... Industrial forests are to natural forests what military music is to music, and what military justice is to justice.

Eduardo Galeano, 2009

A rapid expansion underway in the cultivation of crops to produce biofuels is driven in part by their promise to reduce greenhouse gas emissions. Yet this expansion could threaten bird populations and even drive extinctions, as events on New Britain suggest. Lying off New Guinea, the crescent-shaped island of New Britain is part of a biodiversity hotspot recognised as a global conservation priority. Its tropical forests are thought to contain many species still unknown to science; a 2009 scientific expedition to the island revealed at least four new frog and three new rodent species. Numerous others, like the Bismarck kingfisher, *Alcedo websteri*, are known only from small numbers of sightings.

This kingfisher is endemic to New Britain, New Ireland and smaller neighbouring islands that together form a high priority Endemic Bird Area. Its striking, iridescent blue–green back can be spotted as it fishes along sluggish, medium-sized rainforest streams. Clearing of forests, especially up to river edges, severely affects this lowland forest specialist. It ranges over a very narrow band of altitude, from sea level to 100 metres. Most of its habitat on neighbouring New Ireland was lost early last century to land clearing for coconut plantations, and history is now repeating itself on New Britain.

Most of New Britain's lowland forest is slated for industrial logging, and satellite images reveal that nearly a quarter of remaining forests below 100 metres disappeared between 1989 and 2000. Though it is unclear whether oil palm plantations drive or follow this logging, the clearance pattern suggests a demand for land suitable for palm oil's cultivation. Oil palms yield a versatile oil used to make biofuel, cooking oil and other products. They are grown over short grass in plantations that would not support any of New Britain's 37 restricted-range bird species.

This helps explain why forest destruction from 1989 to 2000 almost doubled New Britain's total number of threatened or near threatened birds, to 21 species.[44] Hardest hit of all, the Bismarck kingfisher lost roughly a fifth of its habitat over this period, and its population probably declined by more than 30 per cent. Even the few small protected areas on New Britain are being logged, their remaining forest patches effectively islands in a lowland sea of palm plantations. Fear that the Bismarck kingfisher will become extinct has prompted a proposal for an urgently needed network of reserves in remaining intact lowland forest.[44]

Scenarios like this explain why conservation groups, including the RSPB and BirdLife International, warn that commercial biofuel demand is likely to threaten birds and other wildlife and drive more extinctions. In southern Thailand, bird species richness plummeted by at least 60 per cent after lowland forests were converted into oil palm and rubber plantations, and insect- and fruit-eating birds suffered most. Species with restricted ranges and high conservation status tended to be replaced by those with wide ranges and low conservation status.[45]

The loss of lowland forest to these plantations is especially common in parts of South-East Asia and South America. Indonesia and Malaysia have some of the world's most biodiverse tropical forests, but recently deforested lands in these two countries host 80 per cent of the world's oil palm plantations, according to Birdlife International. Biofuel demand is also one of the driving forces behind soya bean and sugarcane plantations destroying habitat in the cerrado ecoregion, the world's most wildlife-rich savannah and home to 837 bird species. Mainly located in central Brazil, the cerrado was largely intact during the 1960s, but by 2002 about 57 per cent of its original area had been destroyed.

'Biofuels have the potential to deliver major environmental benefits or to cause significant environmental harm,' writes Dermot Roddy of the Sir Joseph Swan Institute for Energy Research in the UK.[46] In theory, biofuels[47] produced from crops like sugarcane, canola, soya bean and palm oil could reduce transport emissions and increase energy security. In an ideal world, the carbon dioxide released when biofuels are burned would equal that absorbed during their growth. But this equation becomes very lopsided when their full life-cycle emissions, from land clearing to biofuel transport, are included. Biofuels grown on degraded agricultural land or made from biomass waste *can* result in immediate greenhouse gas emission reductions compared to fossil-fuel use. However, clearing carbon-rich rainforests, savannahs, peat lands and grasslands for biofuel plantations releases 17 to 420 times as much carbon dioxide as the use of the resulting biofuel would avoid.[48]

The 'food versus fuel' debate is another important sticking point. Biofuel production can compete with food supply and may already be driving food prices higher,[49] and this debate is expected to continue, according to the UN Food and Agriculture Organization. Alarm bells are also ringing because some new crops being considered for biomass energy production, like giant cane, *Arundo donax*, have much in common with invasive plants.[25] Taken together, these various threats explain why the rapid expansion of this industry has fuelled controversy.

Emissions targets: how much is too much?

What is happening, and what is likely to happen, convinces me that the world must be really ambitious and very determined at moving toward a 350 target.

Rajendra K. Pachauri, 2009

How much more climate change can be tolerated if birds and other biodiversity are to be preserved? By century's end, climate change could be the world's most important direct driver of biodiversity loss. Unchecked, this looming catastrophe could see a significant fraction of Earth's species extinguished within 100 years, while many other species would have their ranges reduced and their extinction risk raised.[40]

Conservationists seek to constrain global warming to a level that would limit extinctions and other impacts, and buy species more time to adapt. Marine environments add impetus to the call for emission reductions, since human efforts to help species to adapt to climate change are unlikely to be as feasible in the world's oceans.[35] Yet agreeing where to draw the line on global warming is difficult, because regions around the world vary in their vulnerability to global warming. Different peoples and societies are unlikely to agree on how much 'collateral damage' is acceptable, so there is still no global consensus on what level of climate change is considered dangerous.

Nevertheless, support has grown for a '2°C guardrail' – ensuring global average temperature rise does not exceed 2°C pre-industrial levels (remember, 0.76°C of this increase has already taken place). This is the benchmark set by the European Union, for example. What level of emission reductions would this guardrail require? Staying within a 2.0–2.4°C increase would mean stabilising the total concentration of carbon dioxide in the atmosphere at 350–400 ppm by 2015 (as of April 2011 this concentration was 392.5). And this would necessitate annual carbon dioxide emission reductions of 50–85 per cent by mid-century.[40,50] The sooner emissions begin to decline, the better the chances of restraining atmospheric greenhouse gas concentrations to a safe level.

However, it becomes increasingly apparent that 2°C may be too much. Staying under the 2°C guardrail will not be sufficient to prevent climate-change risks to many unique and threatened ecosystems, such as endangered species, biodiversity hotspots, coral reefs and tropical glaciers.[40] Modelling has shown that even 1.8°C surface warming could lead to hundreds of bird extinctions, and that these extinctions would rise rapidly with further warming (chapter 5).

Moreover, some tipping points may be reached at lower temperatures than previously suspected. With 2°C of warming these are a moderate risk.[40] Tipping points are critical thresholds at which even small disturbances or changes can radically alter systems over periods as short as decades or less, with severe and possibly irreversible results for ecosystems and societies.

The loss of Arctic sea ice, melting of the Greenland ice sheet and dieback of boreal and Amazon forests are severe impacts, or tipping elements, thought possible once tipping points are reached. If summer Arctic sea-ice loss has not already passed a tipping point, as some believe, it may be very close and occur 'well within this century'.[51] Once it is reached, a positive feedback would take hold. The exposed darker ocean surfaces will absorb much more solar radiation than does light-coloured ice, further amplifying warming and accelerating ice melt. Although the levels of warming required for other tipping elements are poorly known, even a small risk of triggering them is thought to be dangerous. Revelations about tipping points and other threats have prompted calls to set the guardrail lower.[52]

Unknowns and challenges

Those who seek to conserve birds in the face of climate change confront significant unknowns. Wide uncertainty about some future effects compels wildlife managers to consider multiple climate-change scenarios. Yet these very uncertainties may increase government reluctance to fund big adaptation plans like managed wetland retreat. Uncertainty as to how far birds will shift their ranges under climate change will also complicate conservation efforts to augment protected areas.

A dearth of specific information about how climate change will threaten individual species and ecosystems is another obstacle. Whether birds will be able to disperse and adapt through behavioural or physiological change, or evolve, is also little understood. Some species that are unable to adapt may become candidates for assisted migration, an option also fraught with uncertainty and risk. When climate-change scenarios fail to account for invasive species, they are likely to underestimate this threat to wildlife. More research is needed on the dangerous synergies possible between climate change, introduced species, habitat destruction, pollution and hunting.

Humanity's response to climate change is creating its own set of conservation challenges. How much will climate-stressed rural peoples drive the degradation of forests and other habitats in their own quest to adapt? How will efforts to reduce fossil-fuel use through expanded biofuel production avoid bad results for biodiversity and emissions growth? The rapid conversion of forests into plantations now underway highlights the urgent need for new standards to help prevent these negative outcomes.

Conclusion

Climate change is ushering in a 'brave new world' of conservation, one that necessitates a shift away from static protected areas and instead seeks to smooth the path for inevitable change. The extent to which bird species can adapt on their own, in their current ranges, will depend partly on their intrinsic capacities to do so. It will also depend on the resilience of their ecosystems – resilience that may already be compromised by habitat destruction. In the short term, birds are expected to adapt mainly by flexible behaviours or physiological means. Circumstantial evidence suggests some birds may be evolving in response to climate change. Changes to migration are likely to be the first and most significant genetic adaptations.

Successful conservation efforts will hinge on better information about individual species' susceptibility to climate change, assessments that are likely to expand the list of birds at risk. Those who seek to manage short- and medium-term climate-change effects will need to use nimble and flexible approaches in the face of uncertainty. This calls for an adaptive management approach, informed by ongoing monitoring and assessment.

The most effective way to stave off extinctions is to manage species within their current ranges. As such, a key step is to reduce non-climate threats and enhance ecosystem resilience. Because climate change is expected to drive some species out of protected areas, these moving conservation targets require a more dynamic approach. Protected areas will continue to be crucial, and may be seen as fixed, truly natural elements in a broader landscape of human-altered land to be flexibly managed for wildlife protection.

Protected areas may need to expand, while the quality, connectivity and permeability of unprotected land will need to be enhanced. Wildlife corridors or stepping stones of habitat will be vital for dispersal, even for highly mobile animals like birds. Populations unable to disperse or survive in their current ranges may become candidates for last-ditch conservation measures like assisted migration. Those who seek to conserve coastal wetlands, wedged between expanding human development and rising seas, are likely to face extensive challenges. Areas with disappearing climates are another special concern. They correspond to biodiversity hotspots, but even assisted migration may not be enough to preserve their biodiversity. Vigilance and careful management will be needed to control invasive species, especially transformer species like gamba grass that feed off large disturbances like fire.

Vigilance will also be needed to ensure biodiversity conservation does not become a casualty of humanity's response to climate change. Bird conservation groups warn that rapid expansion of biofuel feedstock crops may already be causing some bird population declines and could drive future extinctions. The worthy goals of REDD – to protect forests, their biodiversity and their vast carbon stores – could also be stymied if this program is poorly defined or inadequately monitored and policed.

Over the long term, the success of conservation efforts will pivot on restraining climate change to a manageable level. Emission reductions are critical. Despite the intractability of defining dangerous climate change, limiting global warming to below 2°C has been seen as an acceptable guardrail. Increasingly though, research suggests 2°C may be too much to avoid damage to many unique and threatened ecosystems, and to rule out the possibility of triggering tipping elements.

NOTES

Introduction: the free advice of birds

1 Cunningham D.M. & Moors P.J. (1994) The decline of rockhopper penguins *Eudyptes chrysocome* at Campbell Island, Southern Ocean and the influence of rising sea temperatures. Emu 94:27–36.

2 Hilton G.M. et al. (2006) A stable isotopic investigation into the causes of decline in a sub-Antarctic predator, the rockhopper penguin *Eudyptes chrysocome*. Global Change Biology 12(4):611–625.

3 Berthold P. et al. (2004) Preface. In: Møller A., Fiedler W. & Berthold P. (Eds) Birds and Climate Change, p. vii. Advances in Ecological Research 35. Amsterdam, Netherlands: Elsevier Academic Press.

4 The cryosphere is an important frozen part of the world's climate system, encompassing ice sheets, glaciers, snow, sea ice, river and lake ice, and permafrost and seasonally frozen ground.

5 Pimm S. et al. (2006) Human impacts on the rates of recent, present, and future bird extinctions. Proceedings of the National Academy of Sciences 103:10941–10946.

6 BirdLife International (2008) State of the World's Birds: Indicators for Our Changing World. Cambridge, UK: BirdLife International.

7 Şekercioğlu C.H. et al. (2004) Ecosystem consequences of bird declines. Proceedings of the National Academy of Sciences 101(52):18042–18047.

8 Şekercioğlu C.H. (2006) Increasing awareness of avian ecological function. Trends in Ecology and Evolution 21(8):464–471.

9 Zalasiewicz J. et al. (2008) Are we now living in the Anthropocene? GSA Today 18(2):4–8.

10 Carbon dioxide is the most important of the greenhouse gases emitted by human activity. Others include methane, nitrous oxide and halocarbons.

11 Allison I. et al. (2009) The Copenhagen Diagnosis, 2009: Updating the World on the Latest Climate Science. Sydney, Australia: University of New South Wales Climate Change Research Centre.

12 This compares temperatures during the period 2001–2005 to the period 1850–1899.

13 Stainforth D.A. et al. (2005) Uncertainty in predictions of the climate response to rising levels of greenhouse gases. Nature 433:403–406.

I Phenology: seasonal timing and mismatch

1 A more formal definition is given by the US/ISB Phenology Committee: 'the study of the timing of recurring biological events, the causes of their timing with regard to

biotic and abiotic forces, and the interrelation among phases of the same or different species'.

2 Puppi G. (2007) Origin and development of phenology as a science. Italian Journal of Agrometeorology 24–29(3).

3 Sparks T.H. & Menzel A. (2002) Observed changes in seasons: an overview. International Journal of Climatology 22(14):1715–1725.

4 Peñuelas J. & Filella I. (2001) Responses to a warming world. Science 294(5543):793–795.

5 Dunn P. (2004) Breeding dates and reproductive performance. In: Møller A., Fiedler W. & Berthold P. (Eds) Birds and Climate Change, p. 69; Advances in Ecological Research 35. Amsterdam, Netherlands: Elsevier Academic Press.

6 Miller-Rushing A.J. & Primack R.B. (2008) Global warming and flowering times in Thoreau's Concord: a community perspective. Ecology 89:332–341.

7 Newton I. (2008) The Migration Ecology of Birds. Oxford, UK: Academic Press.

8 Gwinner E. (1996) Circannual clocks in avian reproduction and migration. Ibis 138(1): 47–63.

9 *Zeitgeber*, German for 'time giver', is a term originated by the late German chronobiologist Jürgen Aschoff in the 1950s.

10 Dawson A. (2008) Review. Control of the annual cycle in birds: endocrine constraints and plasticity in response to ecological variability. Philosophical Transactions of the Royal Society B: Biological Sciences 363(1497):1621–1633.

11 Visser M.E. et al. (2009) Temperature has a causal effect on avian timing of reproduction. Proceedings of the Royal Society B: Biological Sciences 276:2323–2331.

12 Zann R.A. (1996) The zebra finch: a synthesis of field and laboratory studies. Oxford, UK: Oxford University Press.

13 Cary C. (2009) The impacts of climate change on the annual cycles of birds. Philosophical Transactions of the Royal Society B: Biological Sciences 364: 3321–3330.

14 Williams S.E. & Middleton J. (2008) Climatic seasonality, resource bottlenecks, and abundance of rainforest birds: implications for global climate change. Diversity and Distributions 14:69–77.

15 Cresswell W. & McCleery R. (2003) How great tits maintain synchronization of their hatch date with food supply in response to long-term variability in temperature. Journal of Animal Ecology 72(2):356–366.

16 Visser M.E. (2008) Keeping up with a warming world; assessing the rate of adaptation to climate change. Proceedings of the Royal Society B: Biological Sciences 275(1635):649–659.

17 Root T.L. et al. (2003) Fingerprints of global warming on wild animals and plants. Nature 421(6918): 57–60.

18 Parmesan C. & Yohe G. (2003) A globally coherent fingerprint of climate change impacts across natural systems. Nature 421:37–42.

19 Menzel A. et al. (2006) European phenological response to climate change matches the warming pattern. Global Change Biology 12:1969–1976.

20 Dunn P.O. & Winkler D.W. (2010) Effects of climate change on timing of breeding and reproductive success in birds. In: Moller A.P., Fiedler W. & Berthold P. (Eds) Effects of Climate Change on Birds, p. 113. Oxford, UK: Oxford University Press.

21 This estimate is based on information from 52 species.

22 Crick H.Q.P. & Sparks T.H. (1999) Climate change related to egg-laying trends. Nature 399:423–424.
23 Both C. et al. (2004) Large-scale geographical variation confirms that climate change causes birds to lay earlier. Proceedings of the Royal Society B: Biological Sciences 271:1657–1662.
24 Barbraud C. & Weimerskirch H. (2006) Antarctic birds breed later in response to climate change. Proceedings of the National Academy of Sciences 103(16):6248–6251.
25 Both C.M. et al. (2009) Climate change and unequal phenological changes across four trophic levels: constraints or adaptations? Journal of Animal Ecology 78:73–83.
26 Naef-Daenzner B. & Keller L.F. (1999) The foraging performance of great and blue tits (*Parus major* and *P. caeruleus*) in relation to caterpillar development, and its consequences for nestling growth and fledgling weight. Journal of Animal Ecology 68:708–718.
27 Also referred to as trophic mismatch or phenological disjunction.
28 Visser M.E. et al. (2006) Shifts in caterpillar biomass phenology due to climate change and its impact on the breeding biology of an insectivorous bird. Oecologia 147:164–172.
29 Charmantier A. et al. (2008) Adaptive phenotypic plasticity in response to climate change in a wild bird population. Science 320:800–803.
30 Visser M.E. & Both C. (2005) Shifts in phenology due to global climate change: the need for a yardstick. Proceedings of the Royal Society B: Biological Sciences 272:2561–2569.
31 Gaston A.J. et al. (2002) Heat and mosquitoes cause breeding failures and adult mortality in an Arctic-nesting seabird. Ibis 144(2):185–191.
32 Schiegg K. et al. (2002) Inbreeding and experience affect response to climate change by endangered woodpeckers. Proceedings of the Royal Society B: Biological Sciences 269:1153–1159.
33 Wilson S. et al. (2007) Breeding experience and population density affect the ability of a songbird to respond to future climate variation. Proceedings of the Royal Society B: Biological Sciences 274(1625):2669–2675.
34 Jiguet F. et al. (2007) Climate envelope, life history traits and the resilience of birds facing global change. Global Change Biology 13(8):1672–1684.
35 Ludwig G.X. et al. (2006) Short- and long-term population dynamical consequences of asymmetric climate change in black grouse. Proceedings of the Royal Society B: Biological Sciences 273:2009–2016.
36 Waite T.A. & Strickland D. (2006) Climate change and the demographic demise of a hoarding bird living on the edge. Proceedings of the Royal Society B: Biological Sciences 273(1603):2809–2813.

2 Migratory birds face climate turbulence

1 Gill R.E. et al. (2009) Extreme endurance flights by landbirds crossing the Pacific Ocean: ecological corridor rather than barrier? Proceedings of the Royal Society B: Biological Sciences 276(1656):447–457.
2 Şekercioğlu C.H. (2007) Conservation ecology: area trumps mobility in fragment bird extinctions. Current Biology 17:R283-R286.

3 Sanderson F.J. et al. (2006) Long-term population declines in Afro-Palearctic migrant birds. Biological Conservation 131:93–105.

4 Nebel S. et al. (2008) Long-term trends of shorebird populations in eastern Australia and impacts of freshwater extraction. Biological Conservation 141: 971–980.

5 Robinson R.A. et al. (2009) Travelling through a warming world: climate change and migratory species. Endangered Species Research 7:87–99.

6 Robinson R.A. et al. (2005) Climate change and migratory species. BTO Research Report 414, Department for Environment, Food and Rural Affairs, UK.

7 Stutchbury B.J.M. et al. (2009) Tracking long-distance songbird migration by using geolocators. Science 323:896.

8 Also known as instinct or calendar migrants; obligate migrants perform migrations at around the same time and across similar distances each year, often across long distances.

9 Berthold P. (1996) Control of Bird Migration. London, UK: Chapman & Hall.

10 Newton I. (2008) The Migration Ecology of Birds. Oxford, UK: Academic Press.

11 Gwinner E. & Helm B. (2003) Circannual and circadian contributions to the timing of avian migration. In: Berthold P. et al. (Eds) Avian Migration, p. 81. Berlin, Germany: Springer-Verlag.

12 Buehler D.M. & Piersma T. (2008) Travelling on a budget: predictions and ecological evidence for bottlenecks in the annual cycle of long-distance migrants. Philosophical Transactions of the Royal Society B: Biological Sciences 363:247–266.

13 Drent R.H. et al. (2007) Migratory connectivity in Arctic geese: spring stopovers are the weak links in meeting targets for breeding. Journal of Ornithology 148:S501–S514.

14 Dawson A. (2008) Review. Control of the annual cycle in birds: endocrine constraints and plasticity in response to ecological variability. Philosophical Transactions of the Royal Society B: Biological Sciences 363(1497):1621–1633.

15 Lehikoinen E. & Sparks T. (2010) Changes in migration. In: Møller A.P., Fiedler W. & Berthold P. (Eds) Effects of Climate Change on Birds, p. 89. Oxford, UK: Oxford University Press.

16 Tryjanowski P. & Sparks T.H. (2008) The relationship between phenological traits and brood size of the White stork Ciconia ciconia in western Poland. Acta Oecologica 33:203–206.

17 Lehikoinen E. et al. (2004) Arrival and departure dates. In: Møller A., Fiedler W. & Berthold P. (Eds) Birds and Climate Change, p. 1. Advances in Ecological Research 35. L Amsterdam, Netherlands: Elsevier Academic Press.

18 Miller-Rushing A.J. et al. (2008) Bird migration times, climate change, and changing population sizes. Global Change Biology 14(9):1959–1972.

19 Jenni L. & Kery M. (2003) Timing of autumn bird migration under climate change: advances in long-distance migrants, delays in short-distance migrants. Proceedings of the Royal Society B: Biological Sciences 270:1467–1471.

20 Gordo O. (2007) Why are bird migration dates shifting? A review of weather and climate effects on avian migratory phenology. Climate Research 35:37–58.

21 Van Buskirk J. et al. (2009) Variable shifts in spring and autumn migration phenology in North American songbirds associated with climate change. Global Change Biology 15:760–771.

22 Møller A.P. et al. (2010) Climate change affects the duration of the reproductive season in birds. Journal of Animal Ecology 79(4):777–784.

23 Sinelschikova A. et al. (2007) The influence of wind conditions in Europe on the advance of the spring migration of the song thrush (*Turdus philomelos*) in the southeast Baltic region. International Journal of Biometeorology 51:431–440.

24 Liechti F. (2006) Birds: blowin' by the wind? Journal of Ornithology 147: 202–211.

25 Møller A.P. (2004) Protandry, sexual selection and climate change. Global Change Biology 10:2028–2035.

26 Coppack T. & Pulido F. (2009) Proximate control and adaptive potential of protandrous migration in birds. Integrative and Comparative Biology 49(5): 493–506.

27 Laaksonen T. et al. (2006) Climate change, migratory connectivity and changes in laying date and clutch size of the pied flycatcher. Oikos 114(2):277–290.

28 Timing of caterpillar peaks varies not only from year to year, but also from location to location.

29 Both C. et al. (2006) Climate change and population declines in a long-distance migratory bird. Nature 441:81–83.

30 Both C. & Visser M.E. (2005) The effect of climate change on the correlation between avian life-history traits. Global Change Biology 11(10):1606–1613.

31 Both C. et al. (2010) Avian population consequences of climate change are most severe for long-distance migrants in seasonal habitats. Proceedings of the Royal Society B: Biological Sciences 277:1259–1266.

32 Inouye D.W. et al. (2000) Climate change is affecting altitudinal migrants and hibernating species. Proceedings of the National Academy of Sciences 97: 1630–1633.

33 Niehaus A.C. & Ydenberg R.C. (2006) Ecological factors associated with the breeding and migratory phenology of high-latitude breeding western sandpipers. Polar Biology 30:11–17.

34 Şekercioğlu C.H. (2010) Partial migration in tropical birds: the frontier of movement ecology. Journal of Animal Ecology 79:933–936.

35 Hüppop O. & Hüppop K. (2003) North Atlantic Oscillation and timing of spring migration in birds. Proceedings of the Royal Society B: Biological Sciences 270:233–240.

36 Conklin J.R. et al. (2010) Breeding latitude drives individual schedules in a transhemispheric migrant bird. Nature Communications 1(6):67.

37 Saino N. & Ambrosin R. (2008) Climatic connectivity between Africa and Europe may serve as a basis for phenotypic adjustment of migration schedules of trans-Saharan migratory birds. Global Change Biology 14(2):250–263.

38 Meltofte H. et al. (2007) Effects of climate variation on the breeding ecology of Arctic shorebirds. Bioscience 59:1–48.

39 Both C. (2010) Flexibility of timing of avian migration to climate change masked by environmental constraints en route. Current Biology 20:243–248.

40 Newson S.E. et al. (2009) Indicators of the impact of climate change on migratory species. Endangered Species Research 7:101–113.

41 Boano G. et al. (2004) Nightingale *Luscinia megarhynchos* survival rates in relation to Sahel rainfall. Avocetta 28:77–85.

42 Doswald N. et al. (2009) Potential impacts of climatic change on the breeding and non-breeding ranges and migration distance of European *Sylvia* warblers. Journal of Biogeography 36:1194–1208.
43 Jonker R.M. et al. (2010) Predation danger can explain changes in timing of migration: the case of the barnacle goose. PLoS ONE 5(6):e11369.
44 Van der Jeugd H.P. et al. (2009) Keeping up with early springs: rapid range expansion in an avian herbivore incurs a mismatch between reproductive timing and food supply. Global Change Biology 15:1057–1071.

3 Range shifts and reshuffled communities

1 This scenario assumes concentrations of carbon dioxide in the atmosphere will double over pre-industrial levels by 2060.
2 Sorenson L.G. et al. (1998) Potential effect of global warming on waterfowl breeding in the Northern Great Plains. Climatic Change 40:343–369.
3 Johnson W.C. et al. (2010) Prairie wetland complexes as landscape functional units in a changing climate. BioScience 60(2):128–140.
4 Though conceptually similar, the term 'range' entails a greater focus on what factors determine the distribution of a species.
5 Jetz W. et al. (2008) Ecological correlates and conservation implications of overestimating species geographic ranges. Conservation Biology 22(1):110–119.
6 Şekercioğlu C.H. et al. (2008) Climate change, elevational range shifts, and bird extinctions. Conservation Biology 22(1):140–150.
7 Jiguet F. et al. (2006) Thermal range predicts bird population resilience to extreme high temperatures. Ecological Letters 9(12):1321–1330.
8 Simmons R. (2010) In litt., 20 July 2010.
9 Jankowski J. E. et al. (2010) Squeezed at the top: interspecific aggression may constrain elevational ranges in tropical birds. Ecology 91:1877–1884.
10 Böhning-Gaese K. & Lemoine N. (2004) Importance of climate change for the ranges, communities and conservation of birds. In: Møller A., Fiedler W. & Berthold P. (Eds) Birds and Climate Change, p. 211. Advances in Ecological Research 35. Amsterdam, Netherlands: Elsevier Academic Press.
11 Steig E.J. et al. (2009) Warming of the Antarctic ice-sheet surface since the 1957 International Geophysical Year. Nature 457:459–463.
12 Parmesan C. & Yohe G. (2003) A globally coherent fingerprint of climate change impacts across natural systems. Nature 421:37–42.
13 Root T.L. et al. (2003) Fingerprints of global warming on wild animals and plants. Nature 421(6918):57–60.
14 Hickling R. et al. (2006) The distributions of a wide range of taxonomic groups are expanding polewards. Global Change Biology 12:450–455.
15 Brommer J.E. & Møller A.P. (2010) Range margins, climate change, and ecology. In: Møller A.P. Fiedler W. & Berthold P. (Eds) Effects of Climate Change on Birds, p. 249. Oxford, UK: Oxford University Press.
16 Thomas C.D. et al. (2006) Range retractions and extinction in the face of climate warming. Trends in Ecology & Evolution 21:415–416.
17 Thomas C.D. & Lennon J.L. (1999) Birds extend their ranges northwards. Nature 399:213.

18 Brommer J.E. (2008) Extent of recent polewards range margin shifts in Finnish birds depends on their body mass and feeding ecology. Ornis Fennica 85:109–117.

19 Tryjanowski P. et al. (2005) Uphill shifts in the distribution of the white stork *Ciconia ciconia* in southern Poland: the importance of nest quality. Diversity and Distributions 11:219–223.

20 Popy S. et al. (2010) A weak upward elevational shift in the distributions of breeding birds in the Italian Alps. Journal of Biogeography 37(1):57–67.

21 La Sorte F.A. & Thompson F.R. III (2007) Poleward shifts in winter ranges of North American birds. Ecology 88(7):1803–1812.

22 Zuckerberg B. et al. (2009) Poleward shifts in breeding bird distributions in New York State. Global Change Biology 15(8):1866–1883.

23 Ma Z. et al. (2000) Effects of climate change on the distribution of cranes in China. Global Environmental Research 4:231–237.

24 Peh K.S.-H. (2007) Potential effects of climate change on elevational distributions of tropical birds in southeast Asia. The Condor 109:437–441.

25 Newton I. (2008) The Migration Ecology of Birds. Oxford, UK: Academic Press.

26 Visser M.E. et al. (2009) Climate change leads to decreasing bird migration distances. Global Change Biology 15:1859–1865.

27 Žalakevicius M. & Švažas S. (2005) Global climate change and its impact on wetlands and waterbird populations. Acta Zoologica Lituanica 14(3):211–217.

28 Although a detailed critique of climate-envelope models is beyond the scope of this book, interested readers may find the following article and its references to be a good starting point: Araújo M.B. et al. (2009) Reopening the climate envelope reveals macroscale associations with climate in European birds. Proceedings of the National Academy of Sciences 106(16):E45–E46.

29 Huntley B. et al. (2007) A Climatic Atlas of European Breeding Birds. Barcelona, Spain: Lynx Edicions.

30 Compared to the 1961–90 period.

31 Virkkala R. et al. (2008) Projected large-scale range reductions of northern-boreal land bird species due to climate change. Biological Conservation 141(5):1343–1353.

32 Erasmus B.F.N. et al. (2002) Vulnerability of South African animal taxa to climate change. Global Change Biology 8:679–693.

33 Huntley B. et al. (2006) Potential impacts of climate change upon geographical distributions of birds. Ibis 148:8–28.

34 Less than 50 000 square kilometres.

35 Simmons R.E. et al. (2004) Climate change and birds: perspectives and prospects from southern Africa. Ostrich 75(4):295–308.

36 Rodenhouse N.L. et al. (2008) Potential effects of climate change on birds of the Northeast. Mitigation & Adaptation Strategies for Global Change 13(5/6): 517–540.

37 Currie D.J. (2001) Projected effects of climate change on patterns of vertebrate and tree species richness in the conterminous United States. Ecosystems 4:216–225.

38 Under a doubling of atmospheric carbon dioxide from pre-industrial levels.

39 Price J.T. & Root T.L. (2005) Potential impacts of climate change on Neotropical migrants: management implications. General Technical Report: PSW-GTR-191, USDA Forest Service, USA.

40 Peterson A.T. et al. (2002) Future projections for Mexican faunas under global climate change scenarios. Nature 416:626–629.

41 Marini M.A. et al. (2009) Predicted climate-driven bird distribution changes and forecasted conservation conflicts in a Neotropical savanna. Conservation Biology 23:1558–1567.

42 McInnes L. et al. (2009) Where do species' geographic ranges stop and why? Landscape impermeability and the Afrotropical avifauna. Proceedings of the Royal Society B: Biological Sciences 276:3063–3070.

43 Galbraith H. et al. (2002) Global climate change and sea level rise: potential losses of intertidal habitat for shorebirds. Waterbirds 25(2):173–183.

44 Garnett S.T. & Brook B.W. (2007) Modelling to forestall extinction of Australian tropical birds. Journal of Ornithology 148(Suppl 2):S311–S320.

45 MacDonald G.M. (2010) Global warming and the Arctic: a new world beyond the reach of the Grinnellian niche? Journal of Experimental Biology 213:855–861.

46 Piersma T. & Lindström Å. (2004) Migrating shorebirds as integrative sentinels of global environmental change. Ibis 146:61–69.

47 Berry P.M. et al. (2001) Impacts on terrestrial environments. In: Harrison P.A., Berry P.M. & Dawson T.P. (Eds) Climate Change and Nature Conservation in Britain and Ireland: (the MONARCH Project), p. 43. Technical report 43150. Oxford, UK: UKCIP.

48 Jensen R.A. et al. (2008) Prediction of the distribution of Arctic-nesting pink-footed geese under a warmer climate scenario. Global Change Biology 14(1):1–10.

49 Devictor V. et al. (2008) Distribution of specialist and generalist species along spatial gradients of habitat disturbance and fragmentation. Oikos 117:507–514.

50 Travis J.M.J. (2003) Climate change and habitat destruction: a deadly anthropogenic cocktail. Proceedings of the Royal Society B: Biological Sciences 270:467–473.

51 Jetz W. et al. (2007) Projected impacts of climate and land-use change on the global diversity of birds. PLoS Biology 5(6):e157.

52 Overpeck J. et al. (2005) A 'paleoperspective' on climate variability and change. In: Lovejoy T.E. and Hannah. L. (Eds) Climate Change and Biodiversity, p. 91. New Haven & London: Yale University Press.

53 Loarie S.R. et al. (2009) The velocity of climate change. Nature 462:1052–1055.

54 Leemans R. & Eickhout B. (2004) Another reason for concern: Regional and global impacts on ecosystems for different levels of climate change. Global Environmental Change 14:219–228.

55 Devictor V. et al. (2008) Birds are tracking climate warming, but not fast enough. Proceedings of the Royal Society B: Biological Sciences 275(1652):2743–2748.

56 Hannah L. et al. (2005) Biodiversity and climate change in Context. In: Lovejoy T.E. & Hannah. L. (Eds) Climate Change and Biodiversity, p. 3. New Haven & London: Yale University Press.

57 Preston K.L. et al. (2008) Habitat shifts of endangered species under altered climate conditions: importance of biotic interactions. Global Change Biology 14(11):2501–2515.

58 Williams J.W. & Jackson S.T. (2007) Novel climates, no-analog plant communities, and ecological surprises. Frontiers in Ecology and the Environment 5:475–482.

59 Stralberg D. et al. (2009) Re-shuffling of species with climate disruption: a no-analog future for California birds? PLoS ONE 4(9):e6825.

4 Seabirds herald ocean changes

1 Boersma P.D. (1977) An ecological and behavioral study of the Galápagos penguin. The Living Bird 15:43–93.

2 Boersma P.D. (1978) Breeding patterns of Galápagos penguins as an indicator of oceanographic conditions. Science 200(4349):1481–1483.

3 Vargas F.H. et al. (2007) Modelling the effect of El Niño on the persistence of small populations: The Galápagos penguin as a case study. Biological Conservation 137(1):138–148.

4 Boersma P.D. (2008) Penguins as marine sentinels. BioScience 58(7):597–607.

5 Durant J.M. et al. (2007) Climate and the match or mismatch between predator requirements and resource availability. Climate Research 33(2):271–283.

6 Şekercioğlu C.H. et al. (2004) Ecosystem consequences of bird declines. Proceedings of the National Academy of Sciences 101(52):18042–18047.

7 Hoegh-Guldberg O. & Bruno J.F. (2010) The impact of climate change on the world's marine ecosystems. Science 328:1523–1528.

8 Rayner N.A. et al. (2006) Improved analyses of changes and uncertainties in sea surface temperature measured in situ since the mid-nineteenth century: the HadSST2 dataset. Journal of Climate 19:446–469.

9 The pattern of ocean warming is not uniform around the world, and estimates for it still lack data from certain regions, including much of the Southern Ocean.

10 Wang M. & Overland J.E. (2009) A sea ice free summer Arctic within 30 years? Geophysical Research Letters 36:L07502.

11 According to a higher (AZ) emissions scenario. See: Steinacher M. et al. (2009) Imminent ocean acidification in the Arctic projected with the NCAR global coupled carbon cycle-climate model. Biogeosciences 6:515–533.

12 Secretariat of the Convention on Biological Diversity (2009) Scientific Synthesis of the Impacts of Ocean Acidification on Marine Biodiversity. Technical Series No. 46. Montreal, Canada: Secretariat of the Convention on Biological Diversity.

13 Harley C.D.G. et al. (2006) The impacts of climate change in coastal marine systems. Ecology Letters 9:(2)228–241.

14 Ainley D.G. & Blight L.K. (2009) Ecological repercussions of historical fish extraction from the Southern Ocean. Fish and Fisheries 10:13–38.

15 Boyce D. et al. (2010). Global phytoplankton decline over the past century. Nature 466:591–596.

16 Richardson A.J. & Schoeman D.S. (2004) Climate impact on plankton ecosystems in the Northeast Atlantic. Science 305(5690):1609–1612.

17 Beaugrand G. et al. (2010) Rapid biogeographical plankton shifts in the North Atlantic Ocean. Global Change Biology 15(7):1790–1803.

18 Dulvy N.K. et al. (2008) Climate change and deepening of the North Sea fish assemblage: a biotic indicator of warming seas. Journal of Applied Ecology 45(4):1029–1039.

19 Irons D.B. et al. (2008) Fluctuations in circumpolar seabird populations linked to climate oscillations. Global Change Biology 14(7):1455–1463.

20 Edwards M. & Richardson A.J. (2004) Impact of climate change on marine pelagic phenology and trophic mismatch. Nature 430:881–884.

21 Beaugrand G. et al. (2008) Causes and projections of abrupt climate-driven ecosystem shifts in the North Atlantic. Ecology Letters 11(11):1157–1168.

22 Grémillet D. & Boulinier T. (2009) Spatial ecology and conservation of seabirds facing global climate change: a review. Marine Ecology Progress Series 391:121–137.

23 Atmospheric carbon dioxide concentrations of about 450 ppm, or temperature increase of more than 2°C above pre-industrial temperatures.

24 Richardson K. et al. (2009) Synthesis Report. Climate Change: Global Risks, Challenges & Decisions. Copenhagen, Denmark: University of Copenhagen.

25 Mallory M.L. (2010). In litt., 3 March 2010.

26 Gaston A.J. et al. (2005) Climate change, ice conditions and reproduction in an Arctic nesting marine bird: Brunnich's guillemot (*Uria lomvia L.*). Journal of Animal Ecology 74(5): 832–841.

27 Formed as continental glaciers or ice sheet flow down to the sea, ice shelves are thick platforms of ice floating on the ocean surface.

28 Ainley D.G. (2002) The Adélie penguin: Bellwether of Climate Change. New York, USA: Columbia University Press.

29 Ducklow H.W. et al. (2007) Marine pelagic ecosystems: the West Antarctic Peninsula. Philosophical Transactions of the Royal Society B: Biological Sciences 362:67–94.

30 McClintock J. et al. (2008) Ecological Responses to Climate Change on the Antarctic Peninsula. American Scientist 96:302–310.

31 Atkinson A. et al. (2004) Long-term decline in krill stock and increase in salps within the Southern Ocean. Nature 432:100–103.

32 Fraser W.R. & Hofmann E.E. (2003) A predator's perspective on causal links between climate change, physical forcing and ecosystem response. Marine Ecology Progress Series 265:1–15.

33 Montes-Hugo M. et al. (2009) Recent changes in phytoplankton communities associated with rapid regional climate change along the western Antarctic Peninsula. Science 323:1470–1473.

34 Above pre-industrial levels.

35 Ainley D. et al. (2010) Antarctic penguin response to habitat change as Earth's troposphere reaches 2°C above preindustrial levels. Ecological Monographs 80(1): 49–66.

36 Hedd A. et al. (2006) Effects of interdecadal climate variability on marine trophic interactions: rhinoceros auklets and their fish prey. Marine Ecology Progress Series 309:263–278.

37 Gjerdrum C. et al. (2003) Tufted puffin reproduction reveals ocean climate variability. Proceedings of the National Academy of Sciences 100(16):9377–9382.

38 April sea surface temperatures greater than 7.5°C.

39 Bertram D.F. et al. (2009) Seabird nestling diets reflect latitudinal temperature-dependent variation in availability of key zooplankton prey populations. Marine Ecology Progress Series 393:199–210.

40 Richardson A. J. (2008) In hot water: zooplankton and climate change. ICES Journal of Marine Science 65:279–295.

41 Wolf S.G. et al. (2009) Range-wide reproductive consequences of ocean climate variability for the seabird Cassin's auklet. Ecology 90(3):742–753.

42 Sydeman W.J. et al. (2006) Planktivorous auklet *Ptychoramphus aleuticus* responses to ocean climate, 2005: Unusual atmospheric blocking? Geophysical Research Letters 33:L22S09.
43 Arnott S.A. & Ruxton G.D. (2002) Sandeel recruitment in the North Sea: demographic, climatic and trophic effects. Marine Ecology Progress Series 238:199–210.
44 Wanless S. et al. (2010). Birds over troubled waters: effects of climate change on North Sea seabirds. British Ornithologists' Union Annual Conference Proceedings – Climate Change and Birds, University of Leicester, April 6–8.
45 Smithers B.V. et al. (2003) Elevated sea-surface temperature, reduced provisioning and reproductive failure of wedge-tailed shearwaters (*Puffinus pacificus*) in the southern Great Barrier Reef, Australia. Marine and Freshwater Research 54(8): 973–977.
46 Erwin C.A. & Congdon B.C. (2007) Demographic and reproductive impacts on seabirds? In: Olsen P. (Ed) The State of Australia's Birds 2007: Birds in a Changing Climate. Melbourne, Australia: Birds Australia.
47 Congdon B.C. et al. (2007) Vulnerability of seabirds on the Great Barrier Reef to climate change In: Johnson J. & Marshall P. (Eds) Climate Change and the Great Barrier Reef, p. 427. Townsville, Australia: Great Barrier Reef Marine Park Authority.
48 Devney C.A. et al. (2009) Sensitivity of tropical seabirds to El Niño precursors. Ecology 90(5):1175–1183.
49 Peck D.R. et al. (2004) Sea surface temperature constrains wedge-tailed shearwater foraging success within breeding seasons. Marine Ecology Progress Series 281:259–266.
50 Erwin C.A. & Congdon B.C. (2007) Day-to-day variation in sea-surface temperature negatively impacts sooty tern (*Sterna fuscata*) foraging success on the Great Barrier Reef, Australia. Marine Ecology Progress Series 331:255–266.
51 Devney C.A. et al. (2010) Plasticity of noddy parents and offspring to sea-surface temperature anomalies. PLoS ONE 5(7):e11891.
52 Hulsman K. & Devney C. (2010) Potential impacts of changing SSTs and sea level rise on seabirds breeding on the Great Barrier Reef. In: Kirkwood J. & O'Connor J. (Eds) The State of Australia's Birds 2010. Melbourne, Australia: Birds Australia.
53 Dunlop J.N. (2007) Climate change signals in the population dynamics and range expansions of seabirds breeding off South-Western Australia. In Olsen P. (Ed) The State of Australia's Birds 2007: Birds in a Changing Climate. Melbourne, Australia: Birds Australia.

5 Climate change, abundance and extinction

1 Shaffer S.A. et al. (2006) Migratory shearwaters integrate oceanic resources across the Pacific Ocean in an endless summer. Proceedings of the National Academy of Sciences 103(34):12799–12802.
2 Veit R. et al. (1997) Apex marine predator declines ninety percent in association with changing oceanic climate. Global Change Biology 3(1):23–28.
3 Gregory R.D. et al. (2009) An indicator of the impact of climatic change on European bird populations. PLoS ONE 4(3):e4678.
4 McKechnie A. & Wolf B.O. (2010) Climate change increases the likelihood of catastrophic avian mortality events during extreme heat waves. Biology Letters 6(2):253–256.

5　Jiguet F. et al. (2010) Population trends of European common birds are predicted by characteristics of their climatic niche. Global Change Biology 16:497–505.

6　Halupka L. et al. (2008) Climate change affects breeding of reed warblers *Acrocephalus scirpaceus*. Journal of Avian Biology 39(1):95–100.

7　Husby A. et al. (2009) Decline in the frequency and benefits of multiple brooding in great tits as a consequence of a changing environment. Proceedings of the Royal Society B: Biological Sciences 276:1845–1854.

8　Oswald S.A. et al. (2008) Heat stress in a high-latitude seabird: effects of temperature and food supply on bathing and nest attendance of great skuas *Catharacta skua*. Journal of Avian Biology 39(2):163–169.

9　Ashbrook K. et al. (2008) Hitting the buffers: conspecific aggression undermines benefits of colonial breeding under adverse conditions. Biology Letters 4:630–633.

10　Sanz J.J. et al. (2003) Climate change and fitness components of a migratory bird breeding in the Mediterranean region. Global Change Biology 9(3):461–472.

11　Thomas D.W. et al. (2001) Energetic and fitness costs of mismatching resource supply and demand in seasonally breeding birds. Science 291 (5513):2598–2600.

12　Assessed as being of the highest conservation concern.

13　Møller A.P. et al. (2010) Rapid change in host use of the common cuckoo *Cuculus canorus* linked to climate change. Proceedings of the Royal Society B: Biological Sciences 15 September 2010; doi: 10.1098/rspb.2010.1592.

14　Pearce-Higgins J.W. et al. (2010) Impacts of climate on prey abundance account for fluctuations in a population of a northern wader at the southern edge of its range. Global Change Biology 16(1):12–23.

15　Sæther B.-E. et al. (2004) Climate influences on avian population dynamics. In: Møller A., Fiedler W. & Berthold P. (Eds) Birds and Climate Change, p. 185. Advances in Ecological Research 35. Amsterdam, Netherlands: Elsevier Academic Press.

16　Bolger D.T. et al. (2005) Avian reproductive failure in response to an extreme climatic event. Oecologia 142:398–406.

17　van Vliet A. & Leemans R. (2006) Rapid species' responses to changes in climate require stringent climate protection targets. In: Schellnhuber H.J., Cramer W., Nakićenović N. et al. (Eds) Avoiding Dangerous Climate Change, p. 135. Cambridge, UK: Cambridge University Press.

18　Albright T.P. et al. (2009) Effects of drought on avian community structure. Global Change Biology 16:2158–2170.

19　Knutson T.R. et al. (2010) Tropical cyclones and climate change. Nature Geoscience 3:157–163.

20　Butler R.W. (2000) Stormy seas for some North American songbirds: are declines related to severe storms during migration? Auk 117:518–522.

21　Frederiksen M. et al. (2008) The demographic impact of extreme events: stochastic weather drives survival and population dynamics in a long-lived seabird. Journal of Animal Ecology 77:1020–1029.

22　Schmutz J.A. (2008) Stochastic variation in avian survival rates: Life-history predictions, population consequences, and the potential responses to human perturbations and climate change. In: Thomson D.L., Cooch E.G. & Conroy M.J. (Eds) Modeling Demographic Processes in Marked Populations, p. 441. Springer Series: Environmental and Ecological Statistics 3.

23 Martin T.E. (2007) Climate correlates of 20 years of trophic changes in a high-elevation riparian system. Ecology 88(2):367–380.

24 Ims R.A. et al. (2008) Collapsing population cycles. Trends in Ecology and Evolution. 23(2):79–86.

25 Kausrud K.L. et al. (2008) Linking climate change to lemming cycles. Nature 456(7218):93–97.

26 Gilg O. et al. (2009) Climate change and cyclic predator-prey population dynamics in the high Arctic. Global Change Biology 15(11):2634–2652.

27 Arctic Climate Impact Assessment (2004) Impacts of Warming; Arctic climate Impact Assessment. Cambridge, UK: Cambridge University Press.

28 Şekercioğlu C.H. (2006) Increasing awareness of avian ecological function. Trends in Ecology & Evolution 21:464–471.

29 Şekercioğlu C.H. (2006) Ecological significance of bird populations. In: del Hoyo J., Elliott A. & Christie D.A. (Eds) Handbook of the Birds of the World, volume 11, p. 15. Barcelona and Cambridge: Lynx Press and BirdLife International.

30 Sætre G.P. et al. (1999) Can environmental fluctuation prevent competitive exclusion in sympatric flycatchers? Proceedings of the Royal Society of London B: Biological Sciences 266:1247–1251.

31 Ahola M.P. et al. (2007) Climate change can alter competitive relationships between resident and migratory birds. Journal of Animal Ecology 76(6):1045–1052.

32 Fretwell P.T. & Trathan P.N. (2009) Penguins from space: Faecal stains reveal the location of emperor penguin colonies. Global Ecology and Biogeography: 18:543–552.

33 Barbraud C. & Weimerskirch H. (2001) Emperor penguins and climate change. Nature 411:183–186.

34 Massom R.A et al. (2009) Fast ice distribution in Adélie Land, East Antarctica: interannual variability and implications for emperor penguins Aptenodytes forsteri. Marine Ecology Progress Series 374:243–257.

35 Jenouvrier S. et al. (2009) Limitation of population recovery: a stochastic approach to the case of the emperor penguin. Oikos 118(9):1292–1298.

36 Jenouvrier S. et al. (2009) Demographic models and IPCC climate projections predict the decline of an emperor penguin population. Proceedings of the National Academy of Sciences 106:1844–1847.

37 Ainley D. et al. (2010) Antarctic penguin response to habitat change as Earth's troposphere reaches 2°C above preindustrial levels. Ecological Monographs 80(1): 49–66.

38 Pounds A.J. et al. (1999) Biological response to climate change on a tropical mountain. Nature 398:611–615.

39 Pounds A.J. et al. (2006) Widespread amphibian extinctions from epidemic disease driven by global warming. Nature 439:161–167.

40 Thomas C.D. et al. (2004) Extinction risk from climate change. Nature 427: 145–148.

41 Myers N. et al. (2000) Biodiversity hotspots for conservation priorities. Nature 403:853–858.

42 Malcolm J.R. et al. (2006) Global warming and extinctions of endemic species from biodiversity hotspots. Conservation Biology 20(2):538–548.

43 Above pre-industrial levels.

44 Foden W. et al. (2009) Species susceptibility to climate change impacts. In: Vié J.-C., Hilton-Taylor C. & Stuart S.N. (Eds) Wildlife in a Changing World – An Analysis of the 2008 IUCN Red List of Threatened Species. Gland, Switzerland: IUCN.

45 Şekercioğlu C.H. et al. (2008) Climate change, elevational range shifts, and bird extinctions. Conservation Biology 22(1):140–150.

46 Defined as those with 90 per cent or more of their breeding range inside Europe.

47 Ohlemuller R. et al. (2008) The coincidence of climatic and species rarity: high risk to small-range species from climate change. Biology Letters 4(5):568–572.

48 Shoo L.P. et al. (2005) Potential decoupling of trends in distribution area and population size of species with climate change. Global Change Biology 11:1469–1476.

49 Li J. et al. (2009) How do species respond to climate change along an elevation gradient? A case study of the grey-headed robin (Heteromyias albispecularis). Global Change Biology 15:255–267.

50 Zöckler C. & Lysenko I. (2000) Water birds on the edge: first circumpolar assessment of climate change impact on Arctic breeding water birds. WCMC Biodiversity Series No. 11. Cambridge, UK: World Conservation Monitoring Centre.

51 Simmons R.E. et al. (2004) Climate change and birds: perspectives and prospects from southern Africa. Ostrich 75(4):295–308.

52 Şekercioğlu C.H. et al. (2004) Ecosystem consequences of bird declines. Proceedings of the National Academy of Sciences 101(52):18042–18047.

53 La Sorte F.A. et al. (2009) Disparities between observed and predicted impacts of climate change on winter bird assemblages. Proceedings of the Royal Society B: Biological Sciences 276:3167–3174.

54 Brook B.W. et al. (2008) Synergies among extinction drivers under global change. Trends in Ecology & Evolution 23:453–460.

55 Also known as extinction cascades, these occur when primary extinctions of key species in an ecosystem trigger secondary extinctions.

56 Pounds J.A. & Puschendorf R. (2004) Clouded futures. Nature 427:107–109.

57 Şekercioğlu C.H. (2007) Conservation ecology: Area trumps mobility in fragment bird extinctions. Current Biology 17:R283–R286.

58 Rubolini D. et al. (2010) Migratory behaviour constrains the phenological response of birds to climate change. Climate Research 42:45–55.

59 Møller A.P. et al. (2008) Populations of migratory bird species that did not show a phenological response to climate change are declining. Proceedings of the National Academy of Sciences 105(42):16195–16200.

60 Le Bohec C. et al. (2008) King penguin population threatened by Southern Ocean warming. Proceedings of the National Academy of Sciences 105(7):2493–2497.

6 Tropical warming and habitat islands

1 Frith C.B. & Frith D.W. (2004) The Bowerbirds. Oxford, UK: Oxford University Press.

2 Hilbert D.W. et al. (2004) Golden bowerbird (Prionodura newtonia) habitat in past, present and future climates: predicted extinction of a vertebrate in tropical highlands due to global warming. Biological Conservation 116(3):367–377.

3 Stattersfield A.J. et al. (1998) Endemic Bird Areas of the World: Priorities for Biodiversity Conservation. Cambridge, UK: Birdlife International.

4 Şekercioğlu C.H. (2011) Climate change and tropical birds. In: Sodhi N.S., Şekercioğlu C.H., Barlow J. & Robinson S.K. (Eds) Conservation of Tropical Birds. Oxford, UK: Wiley-Blackwell.

5 Bush M.B. & Hooghiemstra H. (2005) Tropical biotic responses to climate change. In: Lovejoy T.E. and Hannah. L. (Eds) Climate Change and Biodiversity, p. 125. New Haven & London: Yale University Press.

6 Bonebrake T.C. & Mastrandrea M.D. (2010) Tolerance adaptation and precipitation changes complicate latitudinal patterns of climate change impacts. Proceedings of the National Academy of Sciences 107(28):12581–12586.

7 Defined as those with an estimated total global breeding range of less than 50 000 km^2 throughout historical time.

8 An island biodiversity hotspot between the Australian and Asian continental shelves.

9 Williams J.W. et al. (2007) Projected distributions of novel and disappearing climates by 2100 AD. Proceedings of the National Academy of Sciences 104:5738–5742.

10 Kier G. et al. (2009) A global assessment of endemism and species richness across island and mainland regions. Proceedings of the National Academy of Sciences 106(23):9322–9327.

11 This total of 153 extinctions includes 14 bird species categorised as 'critically endangered and possibly extinct', and one species classed as 'critically endangered and possibly extinct in the wild', according to BirdLife International.

12 Raxworthy C. et al. (2008) Extinction vulnerability of tropical montane endemism from warming and upslope displacement: a preliminary appraisal for the highest massif in Madagascar. Global Change Biology 14(8):1703–1720.

13 Shoo L. et al. (2005) Climate warming and the rainforest birds of the Australian wet tropics. Biological Conservation 25(3):335–343.

14 Williams S.E. et al. (2010) Elevational gradients in species abundance, assemblage structure and energy use of rainforest birds in the Australian Wet Tropics bioregion. Austral Ecology 35(6):650–664.

15 Tingley M.W. et al. (2009) Birds track their Grinnellian niche through a century of climate change. Proceedings of the National Academy of Sciences 106:19637–19643.

16 Colwell R.K. et al. (2008) Global warming, elevational range shifts, and lowland biotic attrition in the wet tropics. Science 322:258–261.

17 Even in the temperate zone (45°N or S), where the amount of temperature change for a given shift in latitude is higher than in the tropics, one must travel poleward for 1000 kilometres to experience a temperature decrease of about 6.9°C.

18 Şekercioğlu C.H. (2007) Global warming creates a stairway to heaven. Scitizen. Available at http://scitizen.com/climate-change/global-warming-creates-a-stairway-to-heaven_a-13-1283.html. Accessed 5 January 2011.

19 Şekercioğlu C.H. et al. (2008) Climate change, elevational range shifts, and bird extinctions. Conservation Biology 22(1):140–150.

20 Pimm S.L. (2008) Biodiversity: climate change or habitat loss – which will kill more species? Current Biology 18(3):R117–119.

21 Based on the IPCC A2 scenario. See: La Sorte F.A. & Jetz W. (2010) Projected range contractions of montane biodiversity under global warming. Proceedings of the Royal Society B: Biological Sciences 277:3401–3410.

22 Rull V. (2010) The Guayana Highlands: a natural laboratory for the biogeographical and evolutionary study of the neotropical flora. In: Sánchez-Villagra M.R., Aguilera

O.A. & Carlini A.A. (Eds) Urumaco and Venezuelan Palaeontology – the Fossil Record of the Northern Neotropics, p. 84. Indiana, USA: Indiana University Press.

23 Nogué S. et al. (2009) Modeling biodiversity loss by global warming on Pantepui, northern South America: projected upward migration and potential habitat loss. Climatic Change 94:77–85.

24 Williams S.E. & Middleton J. (2008) Climatic seasonality, resource bottlenecks, and abundance of rainforest birds: implications for global climate change. Diversity and Distributions 14:69–77.

25 Loope L.L. & Giambelluca T.W. (1998) Vulnerability of island tropical montane cloud forests to climate change, with special reference to East Maui, Hawaii. Climatic Change 39:503–517.

26 Foster P. (2001) The potential negative impacts of global climate change on tropical montane cloud forests. Earth-Science Reviews 55(1–2):73–106.

27 Pounds A.J. et al. (2005) Responses of natural communities to climate change in a highland tropical forest. In: Lovejoy T.E. and Hannah L. (Eds) Climate Change and Biodiversity, p. 70. New Haven & London: Yale University Press.

28 Pounds A.J. et al. (1999) Biological response to climate change on a tropical mountain. Nature 398:611–615.

29 Jankowski J.E. et al. (2010) Squeezed at the top: interspecific aggression may constrain elevational ranges in tropical birds. Ecology 91:1877–1884.

30 Wet Tropics Management Authority (2008) Climate Change in the Wet Tropics: Impacts and Responses. State of the Wet Tropics Report 2007–2008. Cairns, Australia: Wet Tropics Management Authority.

31 Bubb P. et al. (2004) Cloud Forest Agenda. Cambridge, UK: United Nations Environment Programme–World Conservation Monitoring Centre.

32 Simmons R.E. (2010) The nest, eggs and diet of the Papuan Harrier from Eastern New Guinea. Journal of Raptor Research 44(1):12–18.

33 Simmons R.E. & Legra L.A.T. (2009) Is the Papuan Harrier a globally threatened species? Ecology, climate change threats and first population estimates from Papua New Guinea. Bird Conservation International 19:1–13.

34 Drake B.G. et al. (2005) Synergistic effects. In: Lovejoy T.E. & Hannah. L. (Eds) Climate Change and Biodiversity, p. 296. New Haven & London: Yale University Press.

35 Cochrane M.A. (2003) Fire science for rainforests. Nature 421:913–919.

36 McCormack J.E. et al. (2008) Integrating paleoecology and genetics of bird populations in two sky island archipelagos. BMC Biology 6:28.

37 McCormack J.E. et al. (2009) Sky islands. In: Gillespie R.G. and Clague D. (Eds) Encyclopedia of Islands, pp. 839. Berkeley, USA: University of California Press.

38 Westcott D.A. & Kroon F.J. (2002) Geographic song variation and its consequences in the golden bowerbird. The Condor 104(4):750–760.

39 Pratt H.D. (2002) The Hawaiian Honeycreepers. Oxford, UK: Oxford University Press.

40 Atkinson C.T. & LaPointe D.A. (2009) Introduced avian diseases, climate change, and the future of Hawaiian honeycreepers. Journal of Avian Medicine and Surgery 23:53–63.

41 Benning T.L. et al. (2002) Interactions of climate change with biological invasions and land use in the Hawaiian Islands: Modeling the fate of endemic birds using

geographic information system. Proceedings of the National Academy of Sciences 99(22):14246–14249.

42 Freed L.A. et al. (2005) Increase in avian malaria at upper elevation in Hawai'i. Condor 107:753–764.

43 Fordham D.A. & Brook B.W. (2010) Why tropical island endemics are acutely susceptible to global change. Biodiversity Conservation 19:329–342.

44 Moore L.A. (2009) Mission Beach cassowary road research project. Final report October 2009. Study undertaken on behalf of Terrain NRM and James Cook University, Cairns Campus, north Queensland.

45 Moore L.A. (2010) Impact of severe cyclones on an endangered species: the Southern Cassowary *Casuarius casuarius johnsonii*, Mission Beach, north Queensland. In prep.

46 Rittenhouse C.D. et al. (2010) Avifauna response to hurricanes: regional changes in community similarity. Global Change Biology 16:905–917.

47 Bush M.B. & Flenley J.R. (2007) Preface. In: Bush M.B. & Flenley J.R. (Eds) Tropical Rainforest Responses to Climatic Change, p xi. Chichester, UK: Praxis.

48 Ferraz G. et al. (2003). Rates of species loss from Amazonian forest fragments. Proceedings of the National Academy of Sciences 100:14069–14073.

49 Şekercioğlu C.H. (2007) Conservation ecology: area trumps mobility in fragment bird extinctions. Current Biology 17:R283–R286.

50 Clark D.A. et al. (2003) Tropical rain forest tree growth and atmospheric carbon dynamics linked to interannual temperature variation during 1984–2000. Proceedings of the National Academy of Sciences 100(10):5852–5857.

51 Huntingford C. et al. (2008) Towards quantifying uncertainty in predictions of Amazon 'dieback'. Philosophical Transactions of the Royal Society B: Biological Sciences 363:1857–1864.

52 Miles L. et al. (2004) The impact of global climate change on tropical forest biodiversity in Amazonia. Global Ecology and Biogeography 6:553–565.

53 Hannah L. & Lovejoy T. (2007) Conservation. climate change, and tropical forests. In: Bush M.B. & Flenley J.R. (Eds) Tropical Rainforest Responses to Climatic Change, p. 367. Chichester, UK: Praxis.

54 Under a moderate climate-change scenario (that is, the average of A2 and B2 IPPC scenarios); see Anciaes M. & Peterson A.T. (2006) Climate change effects on Neotropical manakin diversity based on ecological niche modelling. Condor 108(4):778–791.

55 Williams J.W. & Jackson S.T. (2007) Novel climates, no-analog plant communities, and ecological surprises: past and future. Frontiers in Ecology and Evolution 5:475–482.

56 Loarie S.R. et al. (2009) The velocity of climate change. Nature 462:1052–1055.

7 Shifting ground on conservation

1 Noss R. et al. (2008) Between the devil and the deep blue sea: characteristics of terrestrial climate sensitive species. Presented at: Florida's Wildlife: On the Frontline of Climate Change Conference, Orlando, 1–3 October.

2 Canale C.I. & Henry P.-Y. (2010) Adaptive phenotypic plasticity and resilience of vertebrates to increasing climatic unpredictability. Climate Research 43:135–147.

3 Thomas C.D. (2005) Recent evolutionary effects of climate change. In: Lovejoy T.E. & Hannah L. (Eds.) Climate Change and Biodiversity, p. 75. Yale University Press, New Haven & London.

4 Berthold P. et al.(1992) Rapid microevolution of migratory behaviour in a wild bird species. Nature 360:668–670.

5 Pulido F. & Berthold P. (2010) Current selection for lower migratory activity will drive the evolution of residency in a migratory bird population. Proceedings of the National Academy of Sciences 107:7341–7346.

6 Van Buskirk J. et al. (2010) Declining body sizes in North American birds associated with climate change. Oikos 119(6):1047–1055.

7 Yom-Tov Y. & Geffen E. (2010) Recent spatial and temporal changes in body size of terrestrial vertebrates: probable causes and pitfalls. Biological Reviews 11: November 2010.

8 Gienapp P. et al. (2008) Climate change and evolution: disentangling environmental and genetic responses. Molecular Ecolology 17:167–178.

9 Bradshaw W.E. & Holzapfel C.M. (2006) Evolutionary response to rapid climate change. Science 312:1477–1478.

10 Miller-Rushing A.J. et al. (2010) Conservation consequences of climate change for birds. In: Møller A.P., Fiedler W. & Berthold P. (Eds) Effects of Climate Change on Birds, p. 295. Oxford, UK: Oxford University Press.

11 Lawler J.J. et al. (2009) Resource management in a changing and uncertain climate. Frontiers in Ecology and the Environment 8:35–43.

12 The wider sub-Saharan region harbours a total of 1679 breeding and bird species.

13 Hole D.G. et al. (2009) Projected impacts of climate change on a continent-wide protected area network. Ecology Letters 12(5):420–431.

14 Hannah L. & Hansen L. (2005) Designing landscapes and seascapes for change. In: Lovejoy T.E. & Hannah L. (Eds) Climate Change and Biodiversity, p. 329. New Haven, USA: Yale University Press.

15 This would provide protection for 160 of the 179 target species.

16 Hannah L. et al. (2007) Protected area needs in a changing climate. Frontiers in Ecology and the Environment 5:131–138.

17 Shoo L.P. et al. (2010) Targeted protection and restoration to conserve tropical biodiversity in a warming world. Global Change Biology 17(1):186–193.

18 Da Fonseca G.A.B. et al. (2005) Managing the matrix. In: Lovejoy T.E. and Hannah L. (Eds) Climate Change and Biodiversity, p. 346. New Haven, USA: Yale University Press.

19 Bakermans M.H. et al. (2009) Migratory songbird use of shade coffee in the Venezuelan Andes with implications for the conservation of the cerulean warbler. Biological Conservation 142(11):2476–2483.

20 Worboys G.L. (2008) Large scale connectivity conservation in mountains: a critical response to climate change. Presented at: International Workshop on Protected Area Management and Biodiversity Conservation, Taipei, 2–3 September.

21 Hoegh-Guldberg O. et al. (2008) Assisted colonization and rapid climate change. Science 321:345–346.

22 McLachlan J.S. et al. (2007) A framework for debate of assisted migration in an era of climate change. Conservation Biology 21:297–302.

23 Richardson D.M. et al. (2009) Multidimensional evaluation of managed relocation. Proceedings of the National Academy of Sciences 106:9721–9724.

24 Low T. (2008) Climate change and invasive species: a review of interactions. November 2006 Workshop Report to Australia. Department of the Environment, Water, Heritage and the Arts, Australia.

25 Pyke C.R. et al. (2008) Current practices and future opportunities for policy on climate change and invasive species. Conservation Biology 22(3):585–592.

26 Hellmann J.J. et al. (2008) Five potential consequences of climate change for invasive species. Conservation Biology 22:534–543.

27 Hunt J. (2010) In litt., 20 August 2010.

28 Wet Tropics Management Authority (2008) Climate change in the Wet Tropics: impacts and responses. Cairns, Australia: State of the Wet Tropics Report 2007–2008.

29 Shi J-B et al. (2006) A review of impacts of climate change on birds: implications of long-term studies. Zoological Research 27:637–646.

30 Richardson A.J. (2008) In hot water: zooplankton and climate change. ICES Journal of Marine Science, 65:279–295.

31 Şekercioğlu C.H. (2002) Impacts of birdwatching on human and avian communities. Environmental Conservation 29:282–289.

32 Greenwood J.J.D. (2007) Citizens, science and bird conservation. Journal of Ornithology 148: S77–S124.

33 Morisette J.T. et al. (2009) Tracking the rhythm of the seasons in the face of global change: phenological research in the 21st century. Frontiers in Ecology and the Environment 7(5):253–260.

34 Whereby tasks are outsourced to the wider community through an open call; today usually communicated and managed via the internet.

35 Robinson R.A. et al. (2009) Travelling through a warming world: climate change and migratory species. Endangered Species Research 7:87–99.

36 Bairlein F. & Schaub M. (2009) Ringing and the study of mechanisms of migration. Ringing & Migration 24:162–168.

37 Boere G.C. & Taylor D. (2004) Global and regional governmental policy and treaties as tools towards the mitigation of the effects of climate change on waterbirds. In: Rehfisch M.M., Feare C.F., Jones N.V. et al.. (Eds) Climate Change and Coastal Birds, p. 111. Ibis 146 (Suppl. 1).

38 Newson S.E. et al. (2009) Indicators of the impact of climate change on migratory species. Endangered Species Research 7:101–113.

39 Paterson J.S. et al. (2008) Mitigation, adaptation and the threat to biodiversity. Conservation Biology 22(5):1352–1355.

40 Richardson K. et al. (2009) Synthesis report. Climate Change: Global Risks, Challenges & Decisions. Copenhagen, Denmark: University of Copenhagen.

41 Canadell J.G. &. Raupach M.R. (2008) Managing forests for climate change mitigation. Science 320(5882):1456–1457.

42 Miles L. & Kapos V. (2008) Reducing Greenhouse Gas Emissions from Deforestation and Forest Degradation: global land-use implications. Science 320(5882):1454–1455.

43 Friends of the Earth International (2009) REDD myths: a critical review of proposed mechanisms to reduce emissions from deforestation and degradation in developing countries. FoEI Report.

44 Buchanan G.M. et al. (2008) Using remote sensing to inform conservation status assessment: estimates of recent deforestation rates on New Britain and the impacts upon endemic birds. Biological Conservation 141:56–56.

45 Aratrakorn S. et al. (2006) Changes in bird communities following conversion of lowland forest to oil palm and rubber plantations in southern Thailand. Bird Conservation International 16:1:71–82.

46 Roddy D. (2009) Biofuels: environmental friend or foe? Energy 162(EN3):121–130.

47 Biofuels, including bioethanol or biodiesel, are produced from biomass (organic matter from non-fossil sources). Liquid or gaseous fuels, they may be used in place of the fossil fuels including gasoline and diesel.

48 Fargione J. et al. (2008) Land clearing and the biofuel carbon debt. Science 319(5867):1235–1238.

49 Hoogeveen J. et al. (2009) Increased biofuel production in the coming decade: to what extent will it affect global freshwater resources? Irrigation and Drainage 58:S148–S160.

50 As a percentage of 2000 emissions levels.

51 Lenton T.M. et al. (2008) Tipping elements in the Earth's climate system. Proceedings of the National Academy of Sciences 105(6):1786–1793.

52 Meyer L.A. (2009) News in climate science and exploring boundaries: a policy brief on developments since the IPCC AR4 report in 2007. Report No. 500114013A. The Netherlands: Netherlands Environmental Assessment Agency.

INDEX